IMAGE COMICS, INC.

Robert Kirkman - chief operating officer
Erik Larsen - chief financial officer
Todd McFarlane - president
Marc Silvestri - chief executive officer
Jim Valentino - vice-president

Eric Stephenson - publisher
Todd Martinez - sales & licensing coordinator
Jennifer de Guzman - pr & marketing director
Branwyn Bigglestone - accounts manager
Emily Miller - administrative assistant
Jamie Parreno - marketing assistant
Sarah deLaine - events coordinator
Kevin Yuen - digital rights coordinator
Tyler Shainline - production manager
Drew Gill - art director
Jonathan Chan - design director
Monica Garcia - production artist
Vincent Kukua - production artist
Jana Cook - production artist
www.imagecomics.com

HEART. First printing. July 2012. ISBN: 978-1-60706-578-4

Published by Image Comics, Inc. Office of publication: 2134 Allston Way, 2nd Floor, Berkeley, CA 94704. Copyright © 2012 Blair Butler & Kevin Mellon. Originally published in single magazine form as HEART #1-4 by Image Comics. All rights reserved. HEART, its logos, and all character likenesses herein are trademarks of Blair Butler & Kevin Mellon, unless expressly indicated. Image Comics® and its logos are registered trademarks and copyright of Image Comics, Inc. All rights reserved. No part of this publication may be reproduced or transmitted, in any form or by any means (except for short excerpts for review purposes) without the express written permission of Blair Butler, Kevin Mellon, or Image Comics, Inc. All names, characters, events, and locales in this publication, except for satirical purposes, are entirely fictional, and any resemblance to actual persons (living or dead) or entities or events or places is coincidental or for satirical purposes. Printed in Korea.

Foreign licensing inquiries, write to:
foreignlicensing@imagecomics.com

heart

BY:
BLAIR BUTLER
AND
KEVIN MELLON

LETTERS AND DESIGN BY:
CRANK!

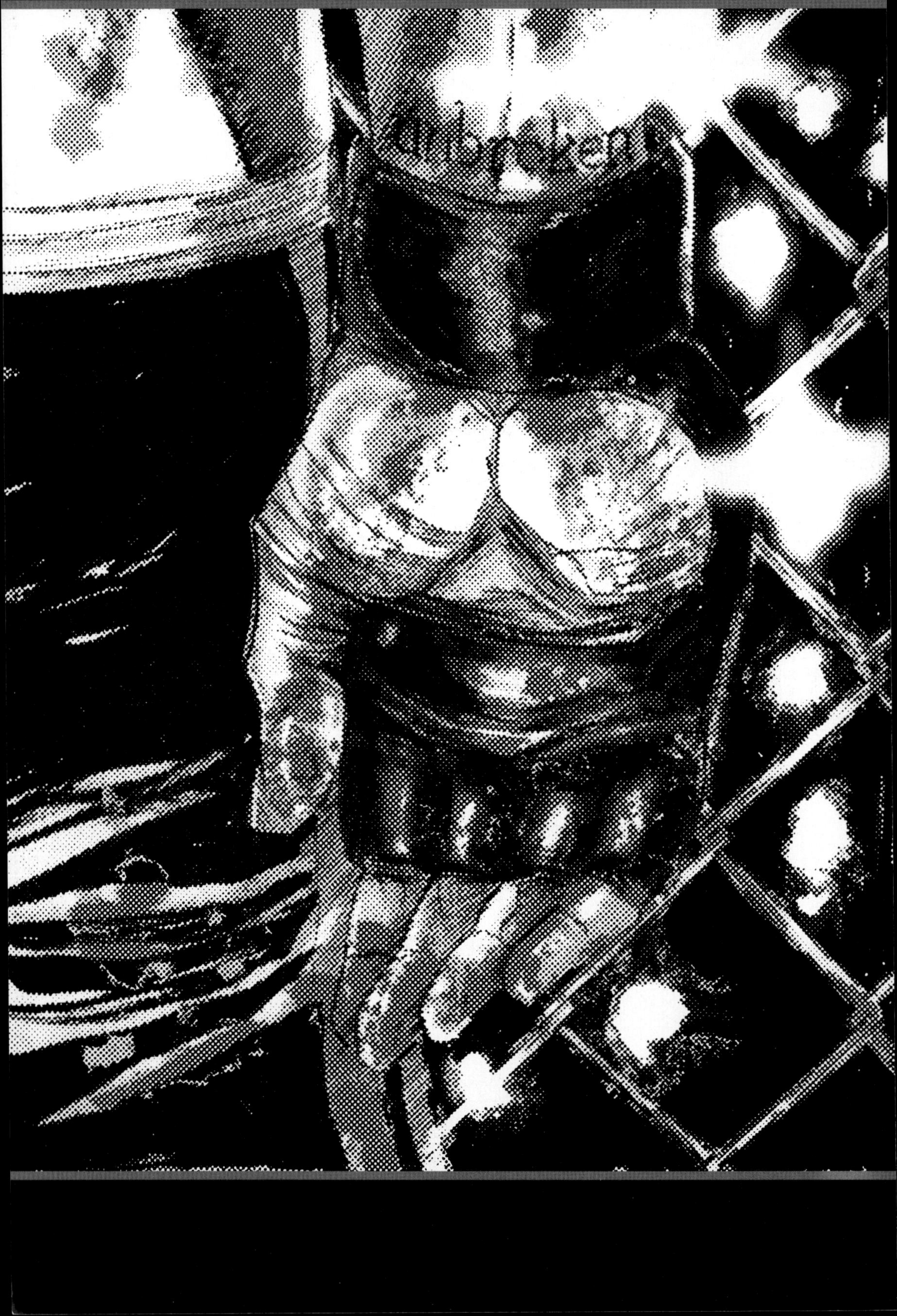

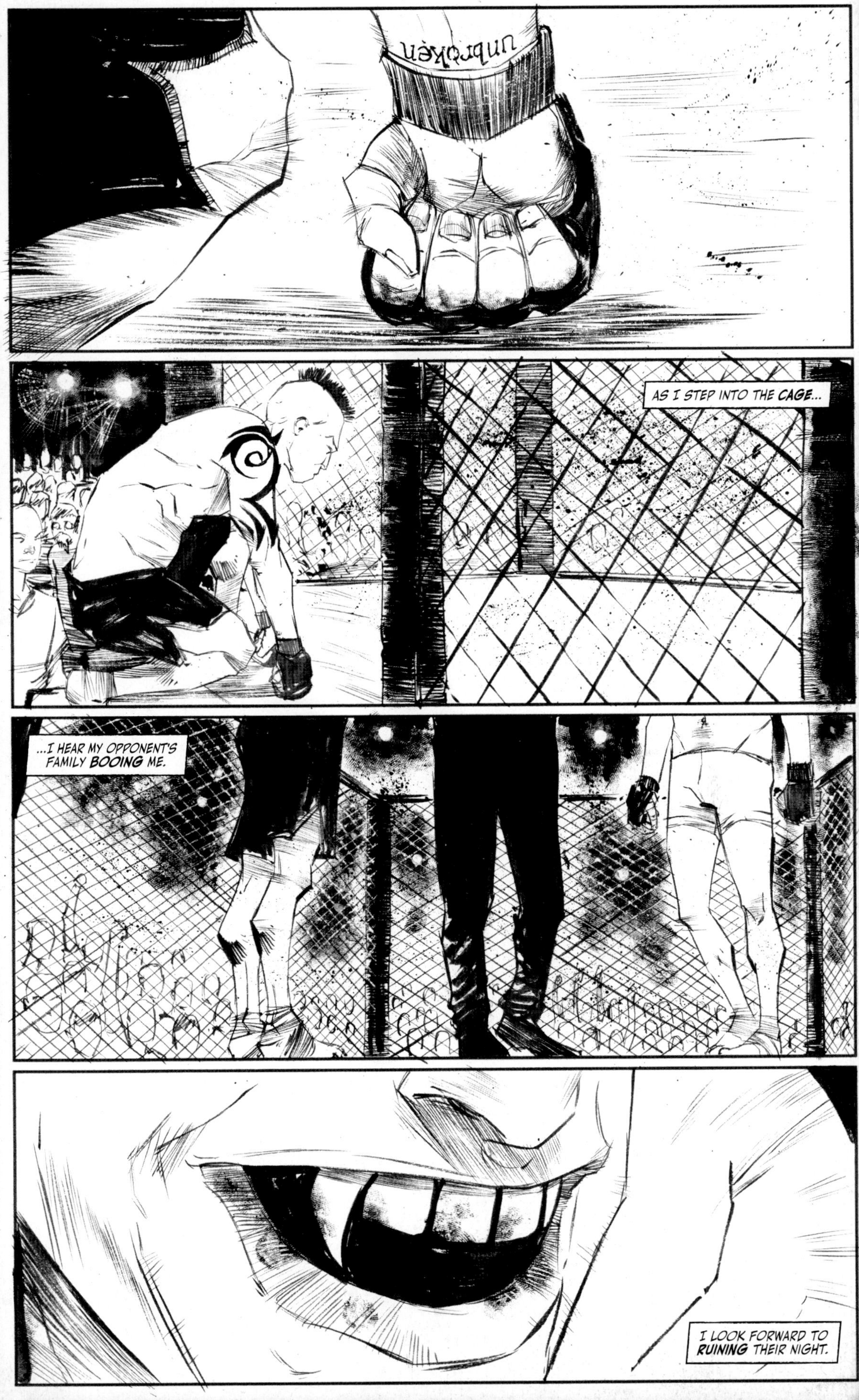
unbroken
AS I STEP INTO THE CAGE...
...I HEAR MY OPPONENT'S FAMILY BOOING ME.
I LOOK FORWARD TO RUINING THEIR NIGHT.

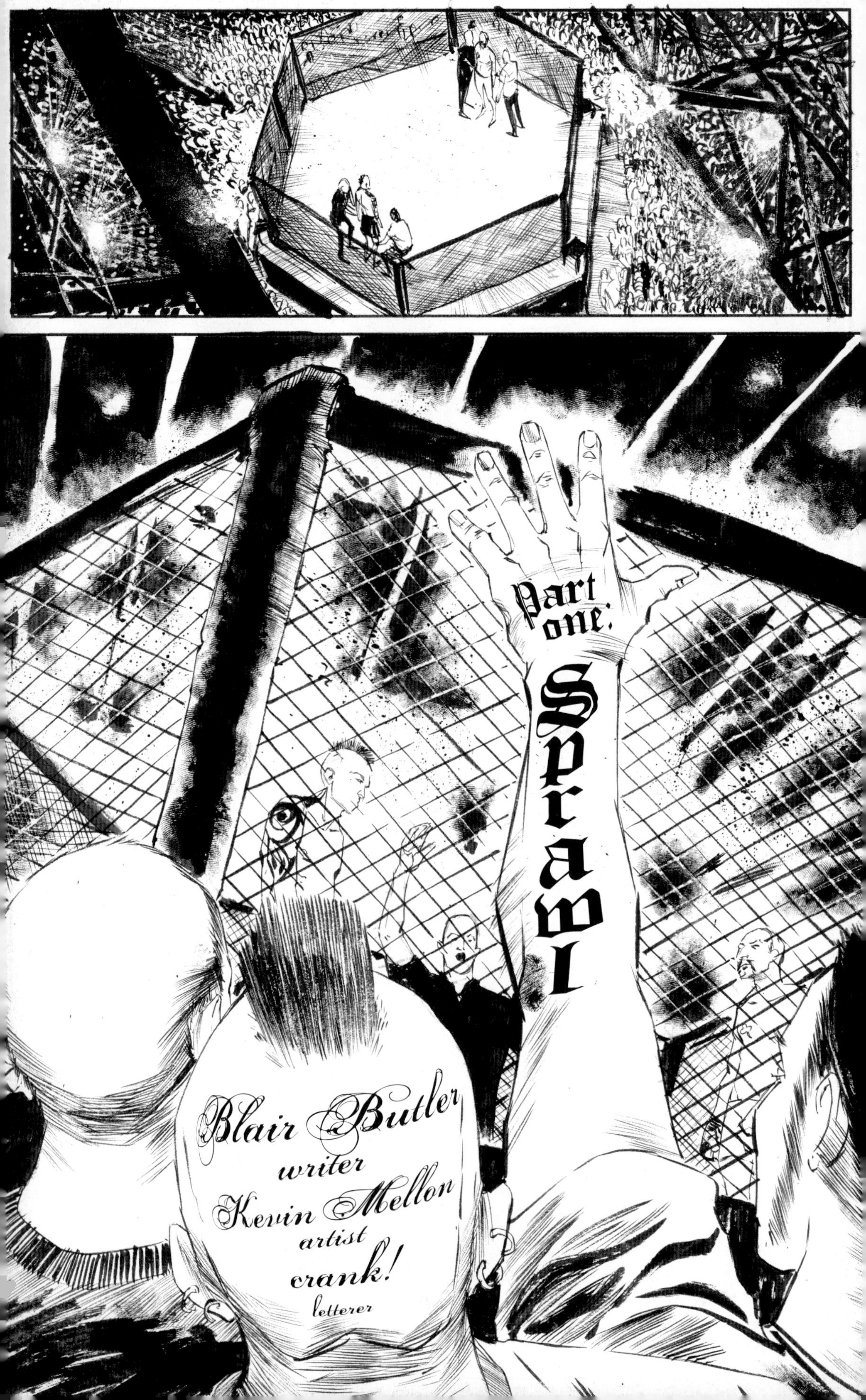

part one.
Sprawl
Blair Butler
writer
Kevin Mellon
artist
crank!
letterer

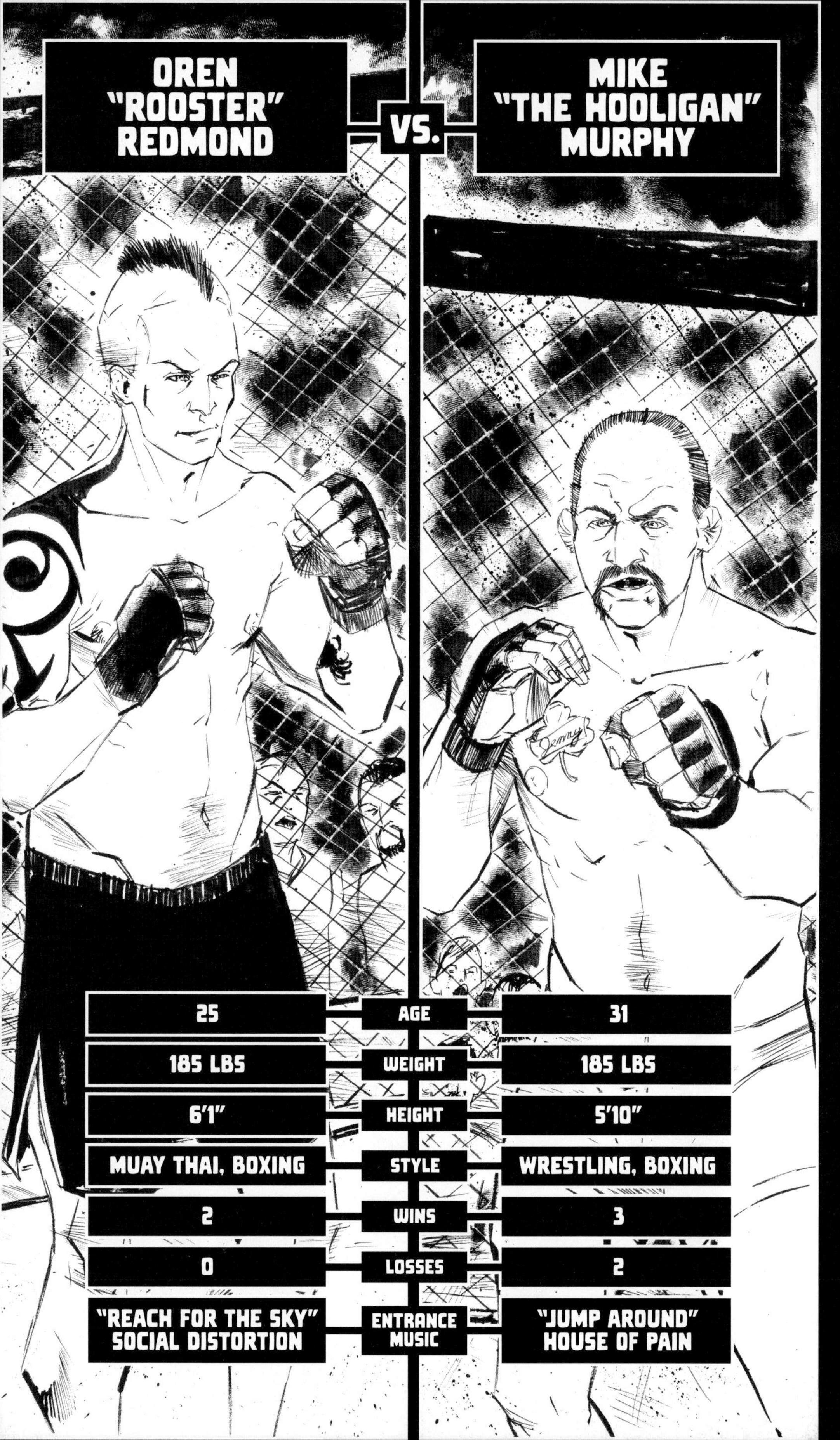
OREN "ROOSTER" REDMOND
VS.
MIKE "THE HOOLIGAN" MURPHY
25
AGE
31
185 LBS
WEIGHT
185 LBS
6'1"
HEIGHT
5'10"
MUAY THAI, BOXING
STYLE
WRESTLING, BOXING
2
WINS
3
0
LOSSES
2
"REACH FOR THE SKY" SOCIAL DISTORTION
ENTRANCE MUSIC
"JUMP AROUND" HOUSE OF PAIN

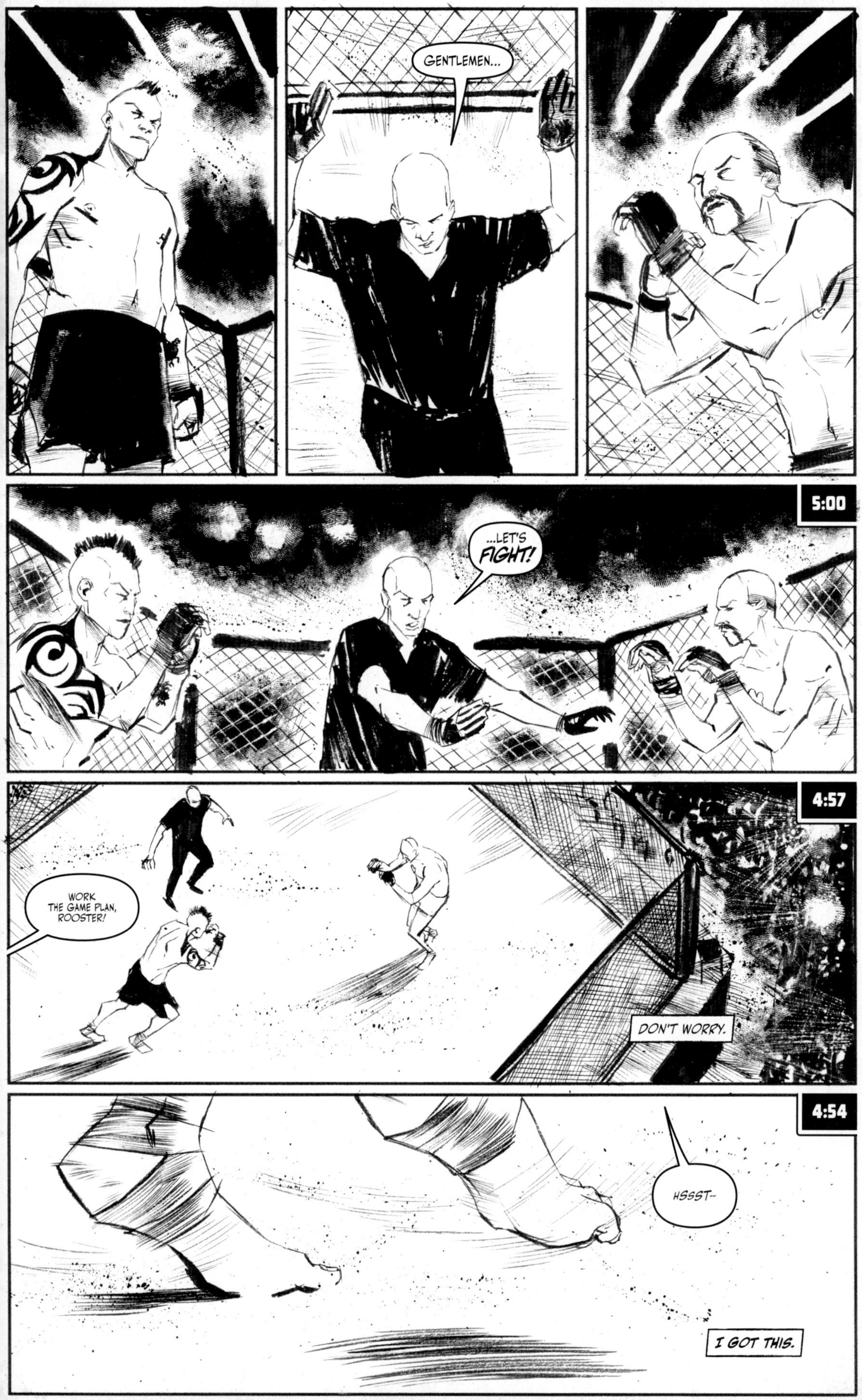
GENTLEMEN...
5:00
...LET'S FIGHT!
4:57
WORK THE GAME PLAN, ROOSTER!
DON'T WORRY.
4:54
HSSST--
I GOT THIS.

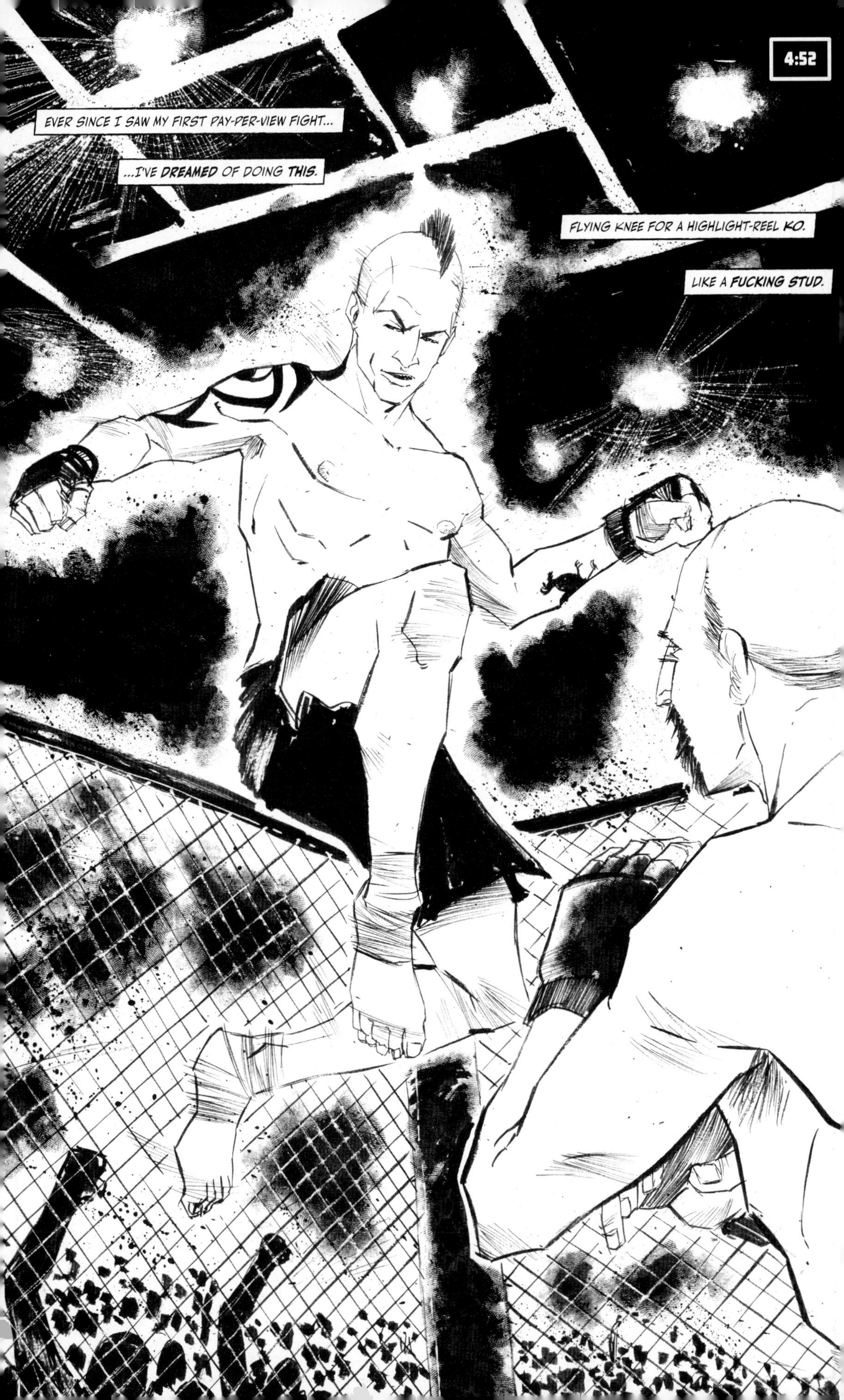
4:52
EVER SINCE I SAW MY FIRST PAY-PER-VIEW FIGHT...
...I'VE DREAMED OF DOING THIS.
FLYING KNEE FOR A HIGHLIGHT-REEL KO.
LIKE A FUCKING STUD.

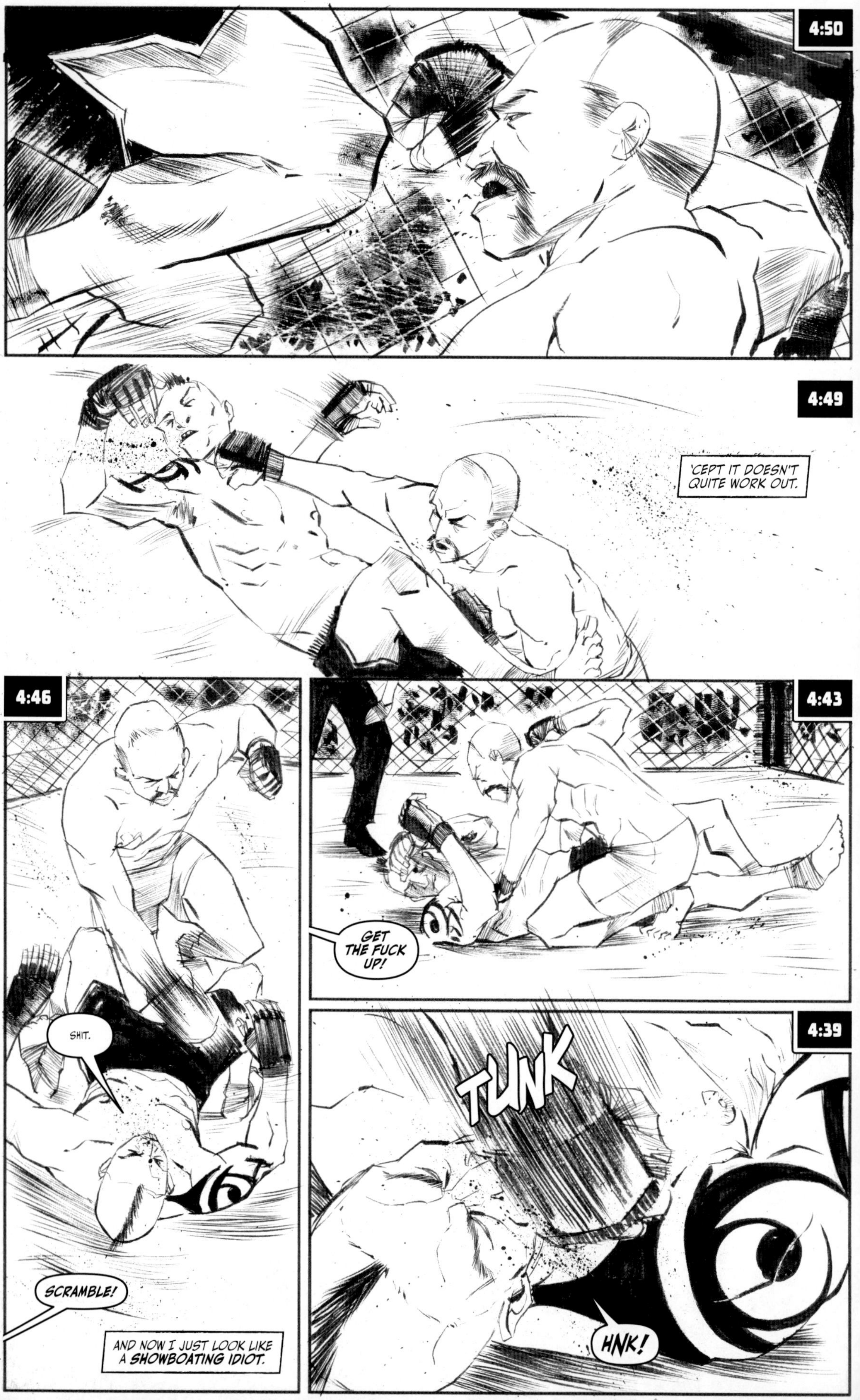
4:50
4:49
'CEPT IT DOESN'T QUITE WORK OUT.
4:46
SHIT.
SCRAMBLE!
AND NOW I JUST LOOK LIKE A SHOWBOATING IDIOT.
4:43
GET THE FUCK UP!
4:39
TUNK
HNK!

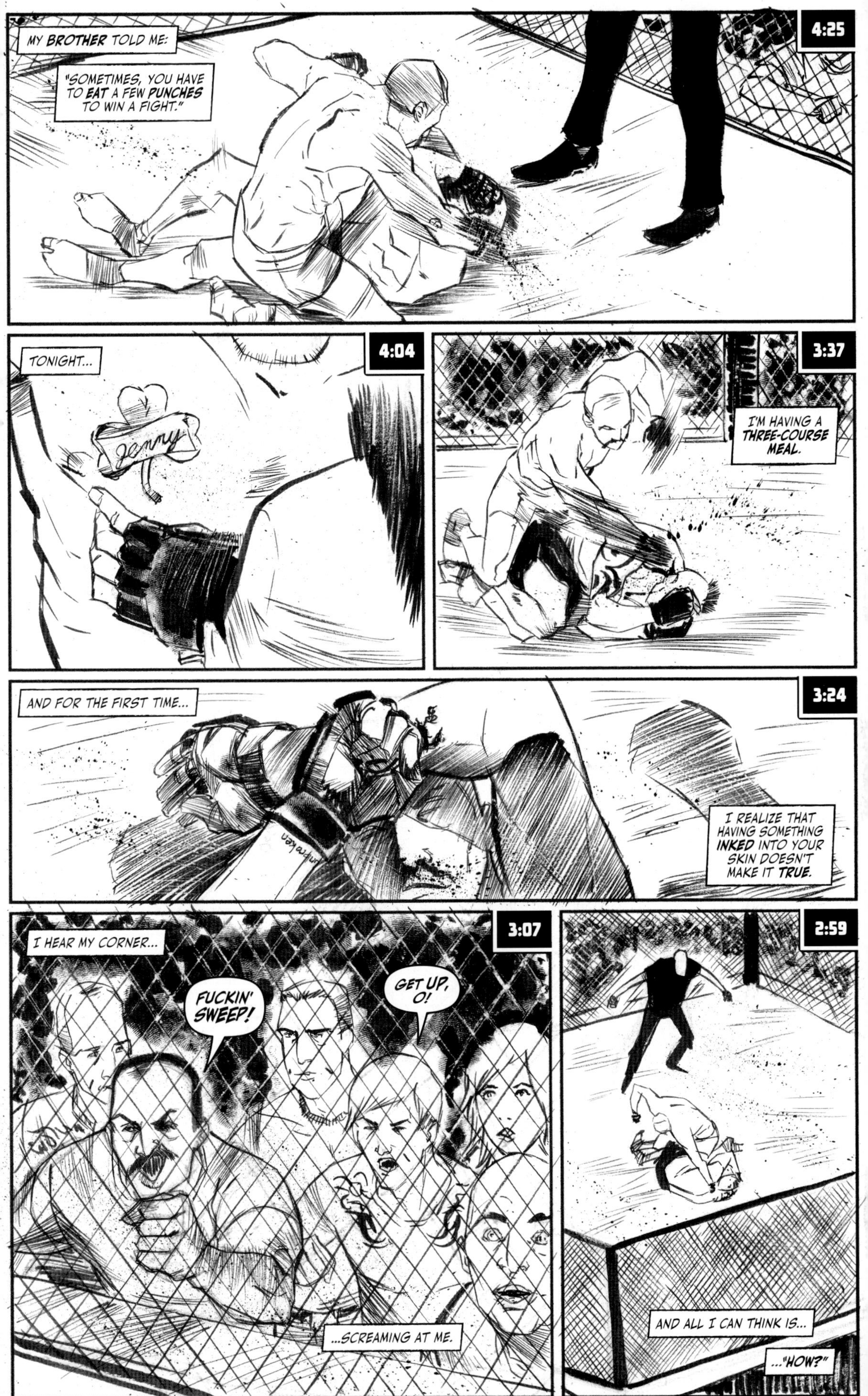
4:25
MY BROTHER TOLD ME:
"SOMETIMES, YOU HAVE TO EAT A FEW PUNCHES TO WIN A FIGHT."
4:04
TONIGHT...
Jenny
3:37
I'M HAVING A THREE-COURSE MEAL.
3:24
AND FOR THE FIRST TIME...
I REALIZE THAT HAVING SOMETHING INKED INTO YOUR SKIN DOESN'T MAKE IT TRUE.
3:07
I HEAR MY CORNER...
FUCKIN' SWEEP!
GET UP, O!
...SCREAMING AT ME.
2:59
AND ALL I CAN THINK IS...
..."HOW?"

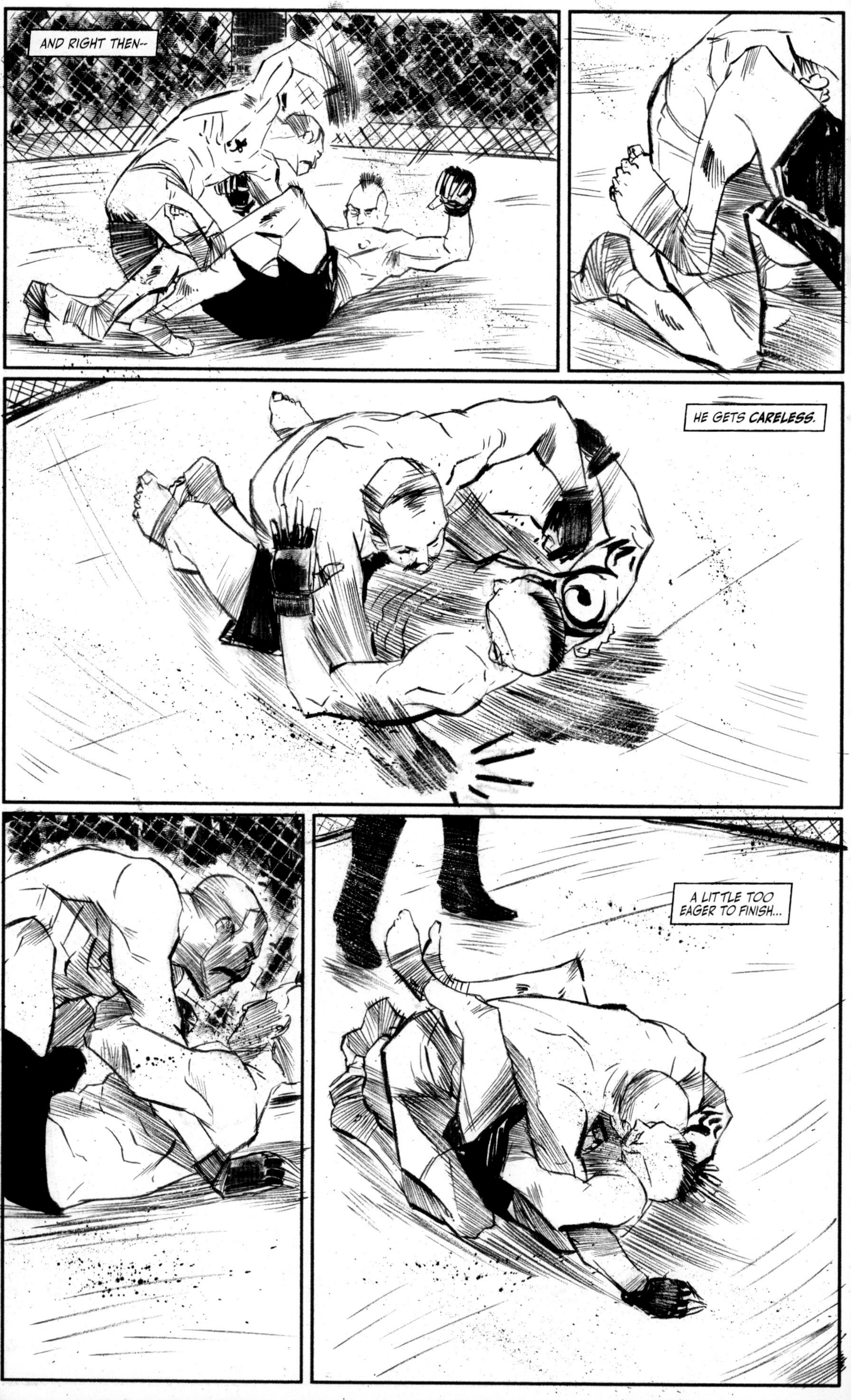
AND RIGHT THEN--
HE GETS **CARELESS.**
A LITTLE TOO EAGER TO FINISH...

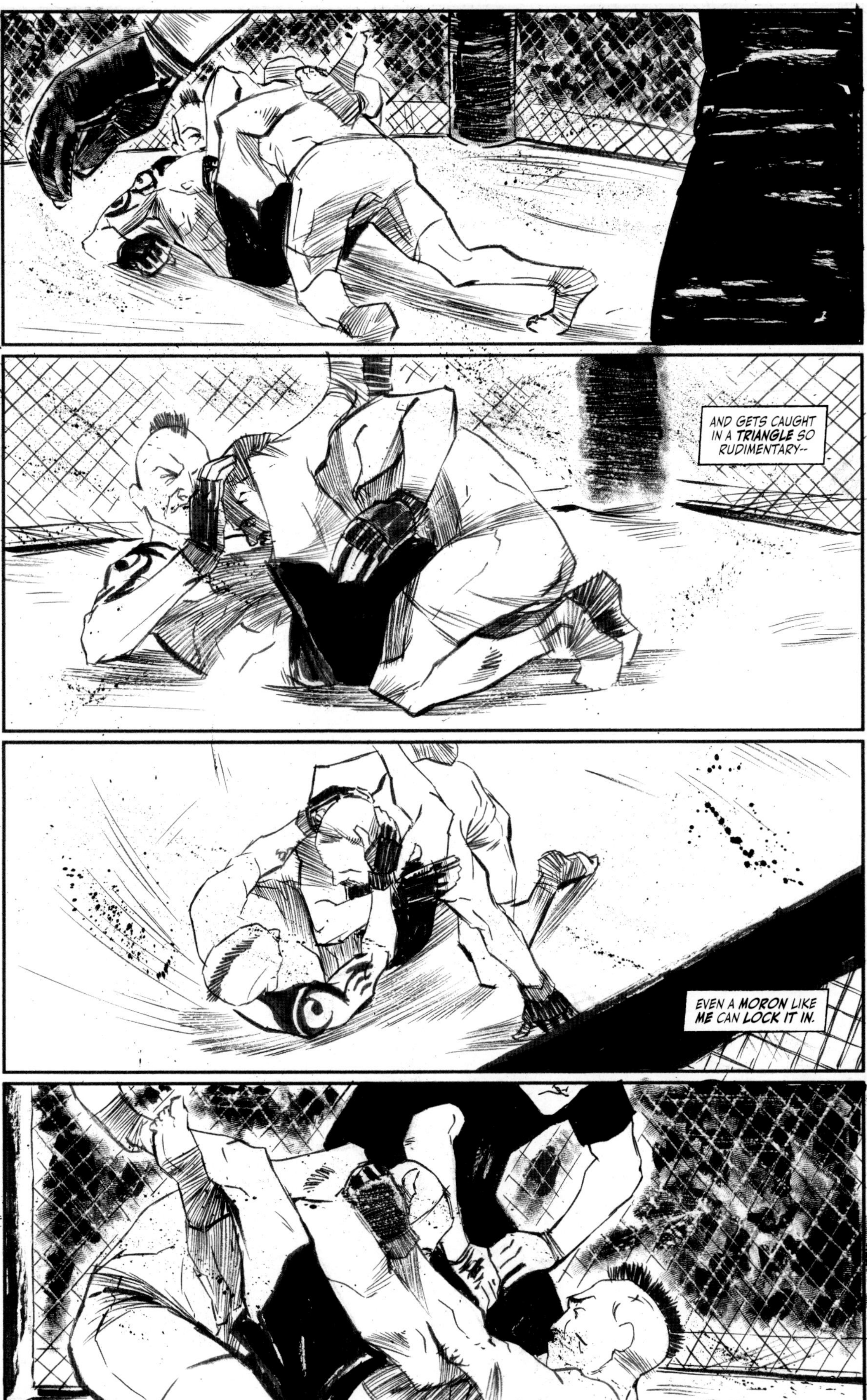
AND GETS CAUGHT IN A TRIANGLE SO RUDIMENTARY--
EVEN A MORON LIKE ME CAN LOCK IT IN.

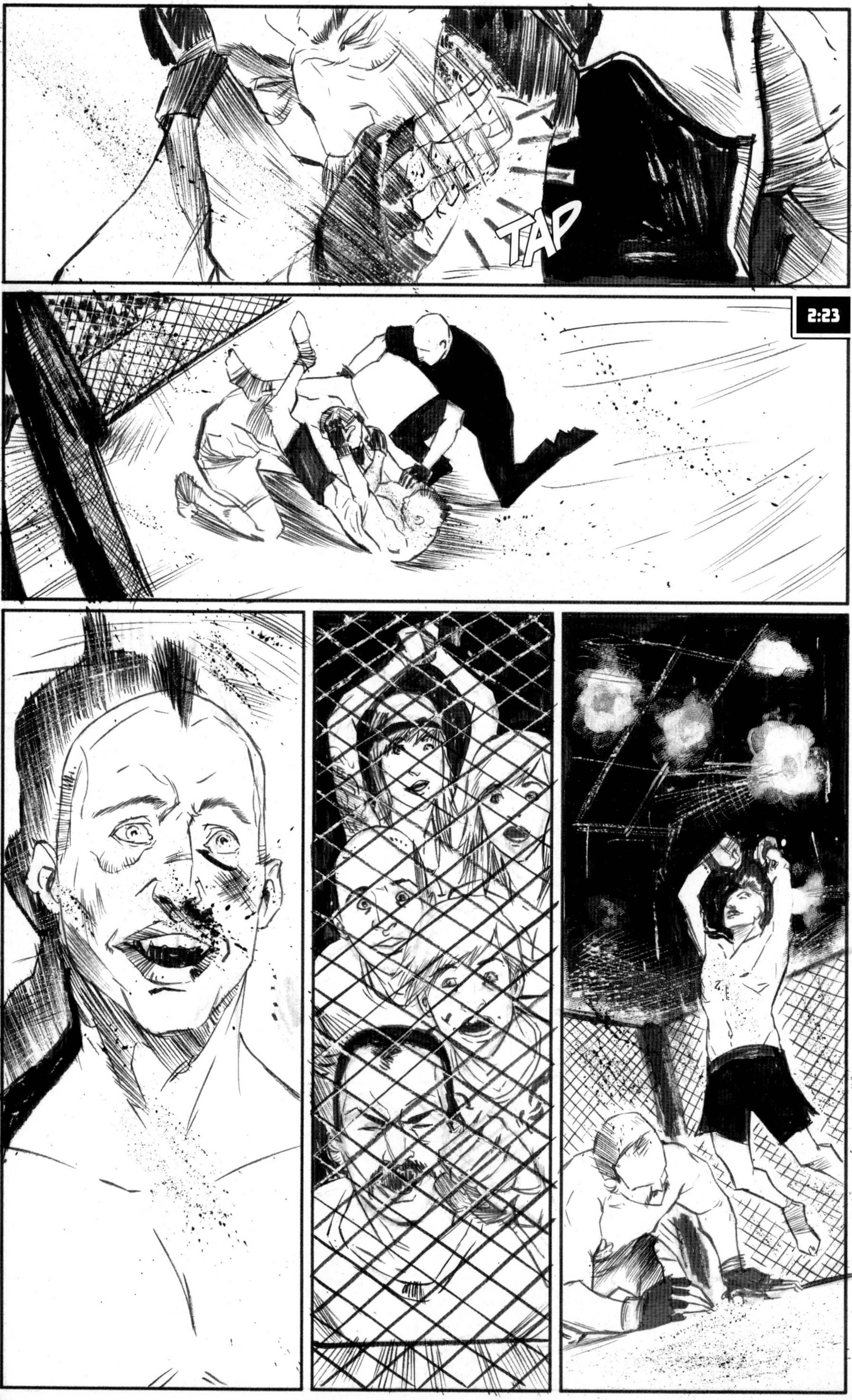
TAP
2:23

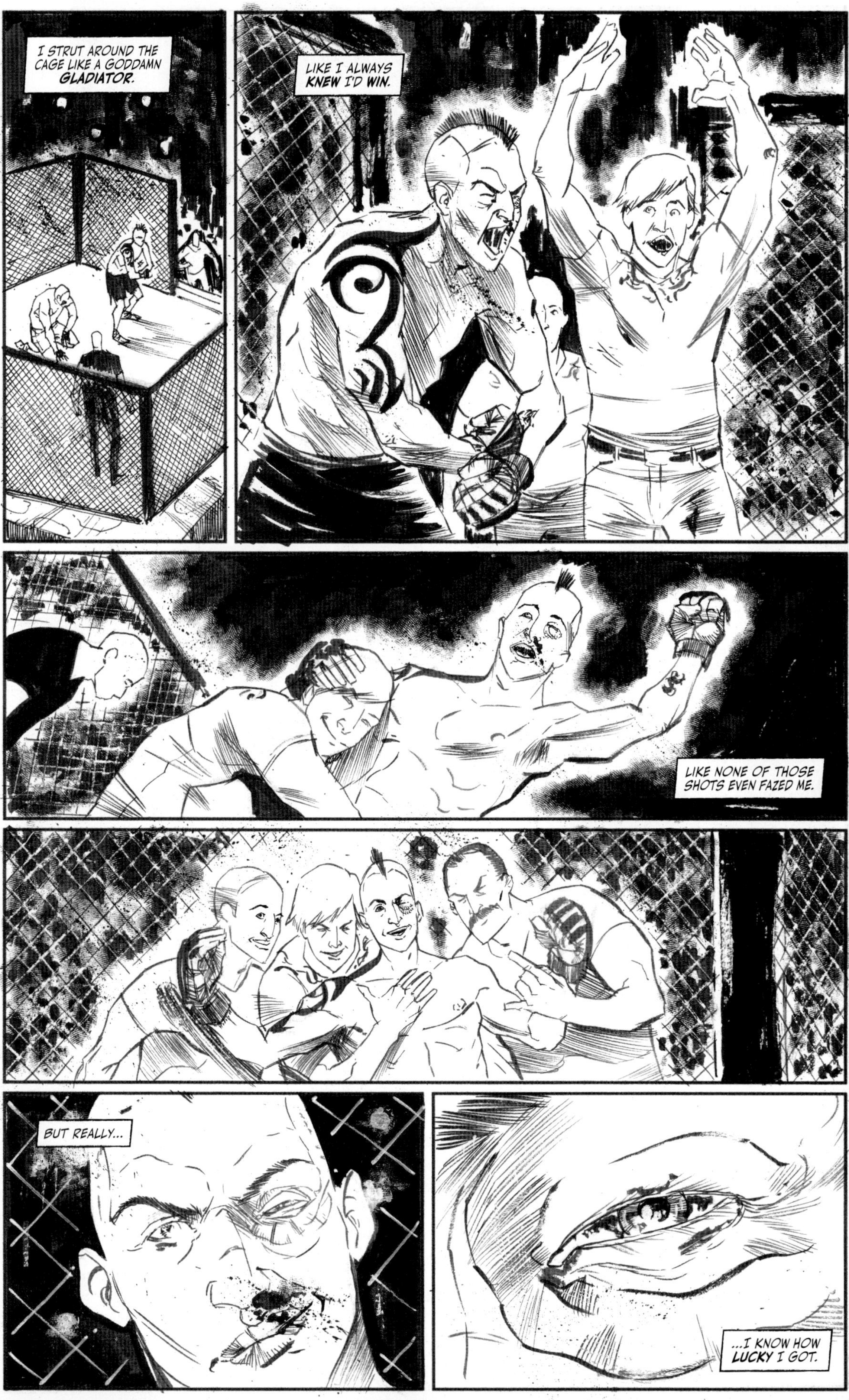
I STRUT AROUND THE CAGE LIKE A GODDAMN GLADIATOR.
LIKE I ALWAYS KNEW I'D WIN.
LIKE NONE OF THOSE SHOTS EVEN FAZED ME.
BUT REALLY...
...I KNOW HOW LUCKY I GOT.

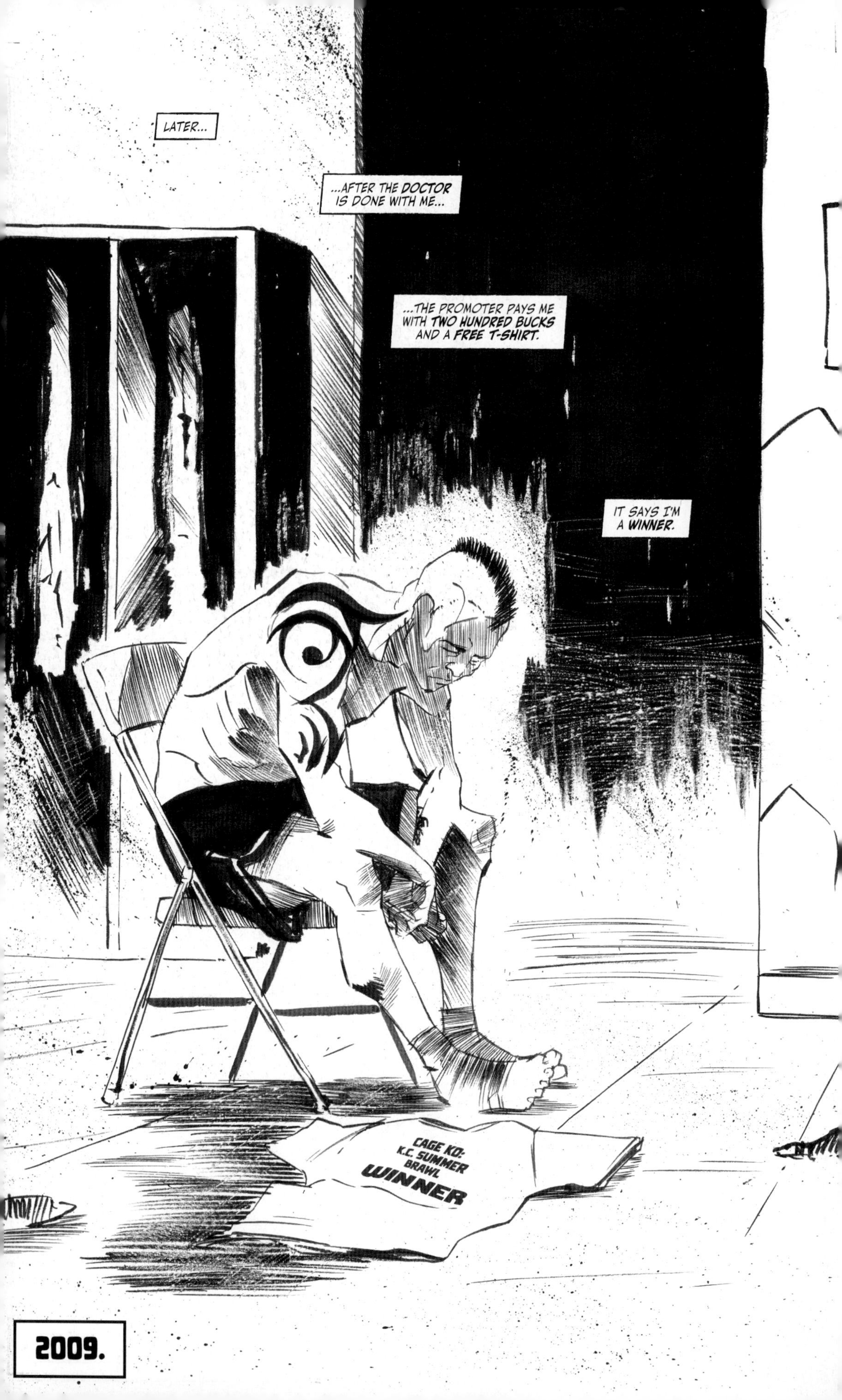
LATER...
...AFTER THE DOCTOR IS DONE WITH ME...
...THE PROMOTER PAYS ME WITH TWO HUNDRED BUCKS AND A FREE T-SHIRT.
IT SAYS I'M A WINNER.
CAGE KO: K.C. SUMMER BRAWL WINNER
2009.

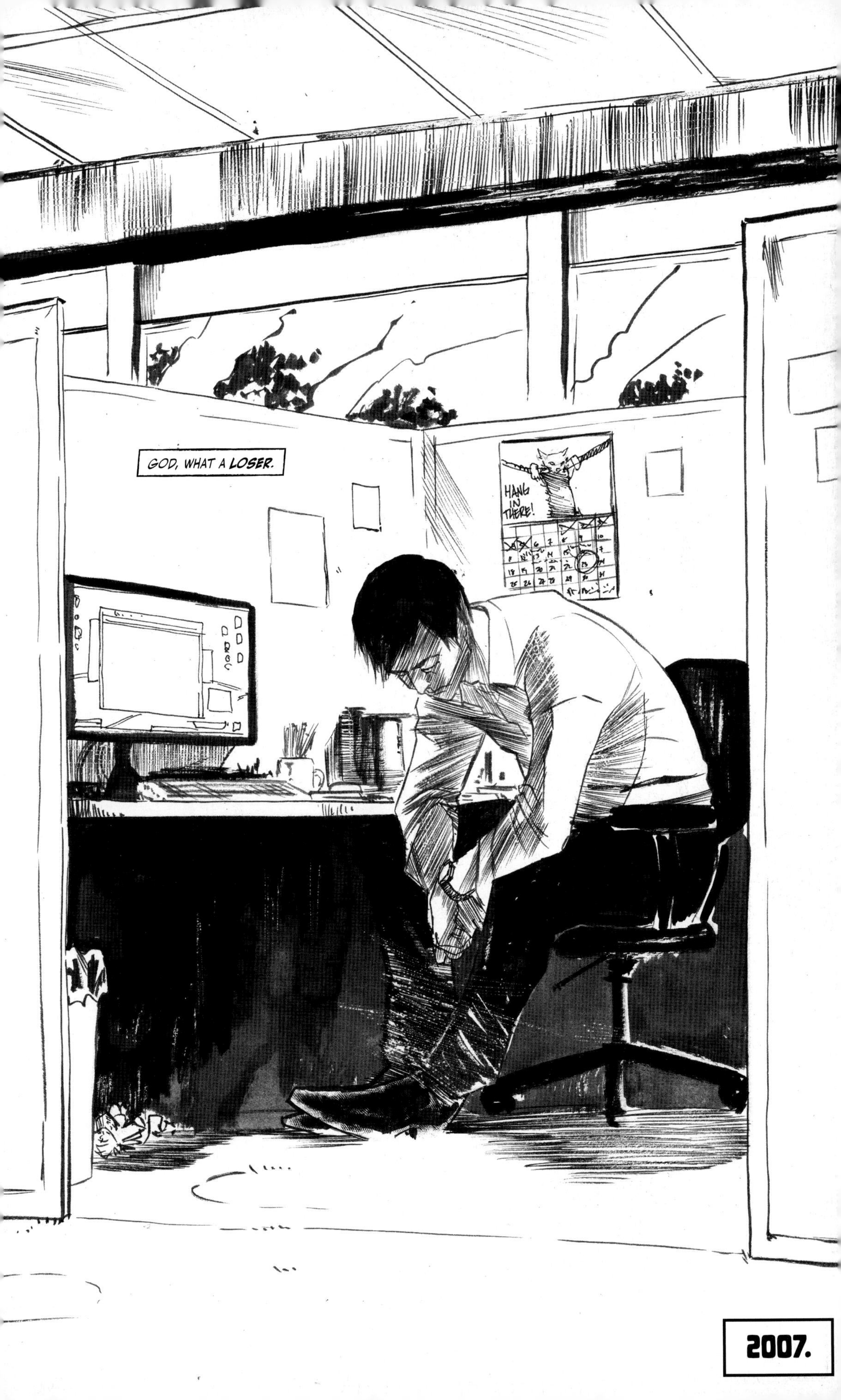
GOD, WHAT A LOSER.
HANG IN THERE!
2007.

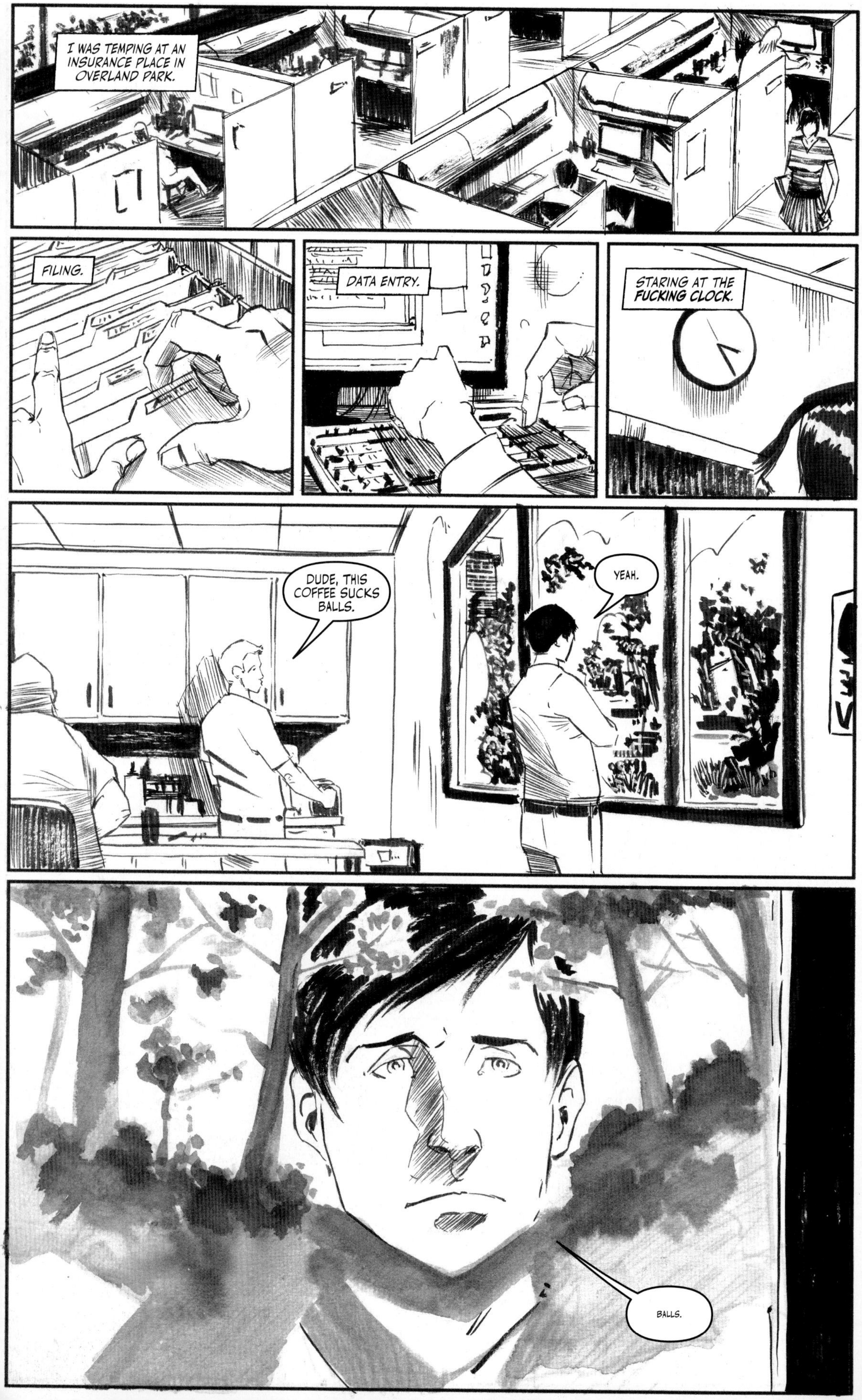
I WAS TEMPING AT AN INSURANCE PLACE IN OVERLAND PARK.
FILING.
DATA ENTRY.
STARING AT THE **FUCKING CLOCK.**
DUDE, THIS COFFEE SUCKS BALLS.
YEAH.
BALLS.

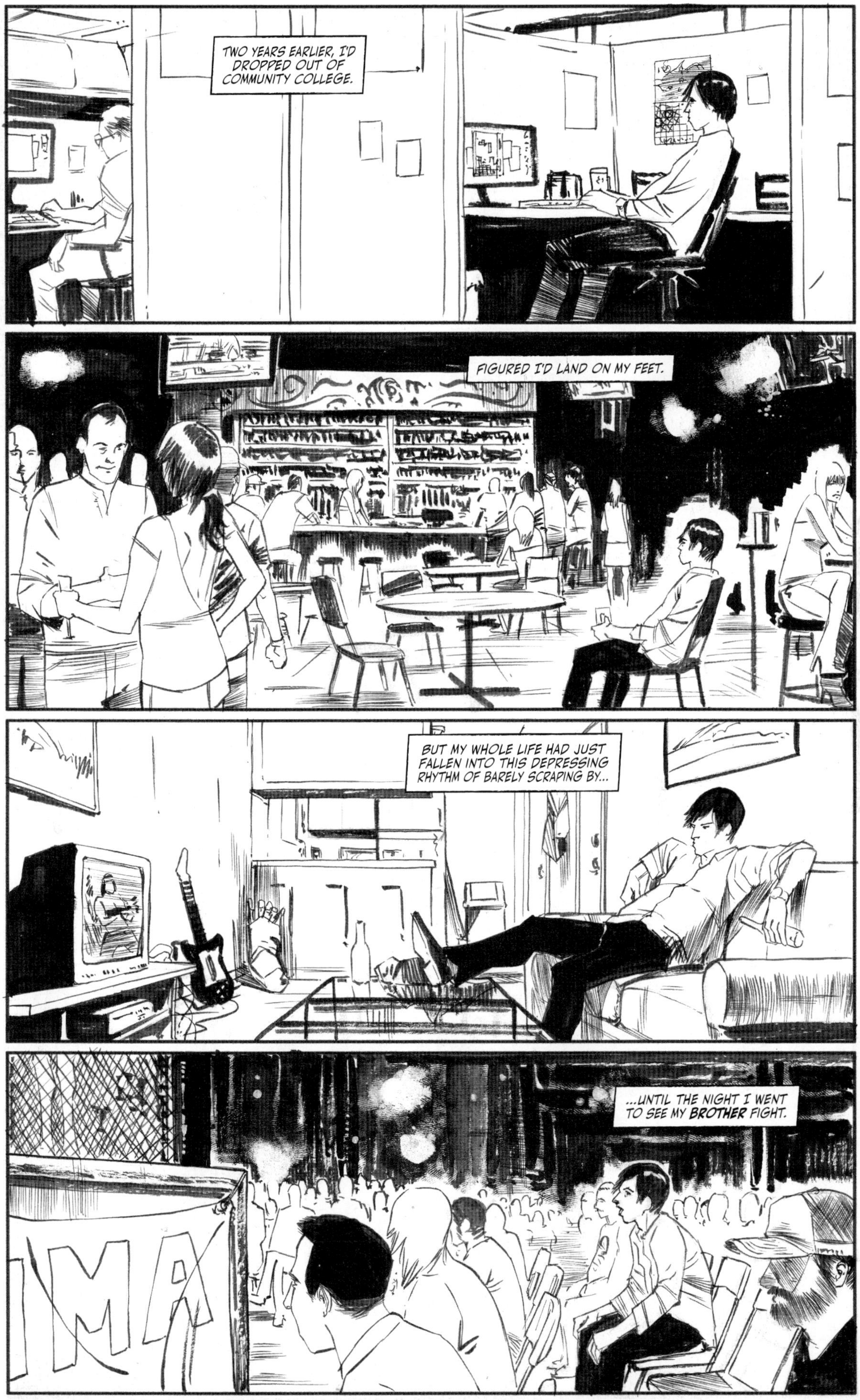
TWO YEARS EARLIER, I'D DROPPED OUT OF COMMUNITY COLLEGE.
FIGURED I'D LAND ON MY FEET.
BUT MY WHOLE LIFE HAD JUST FALLEN INTO THIS DEPRESSING RHYTHM OF BARELY SCRAPING BY...
...UNTIL THE NIGHT I WENT TO SEE MY BROTHER FIGHT.
MA

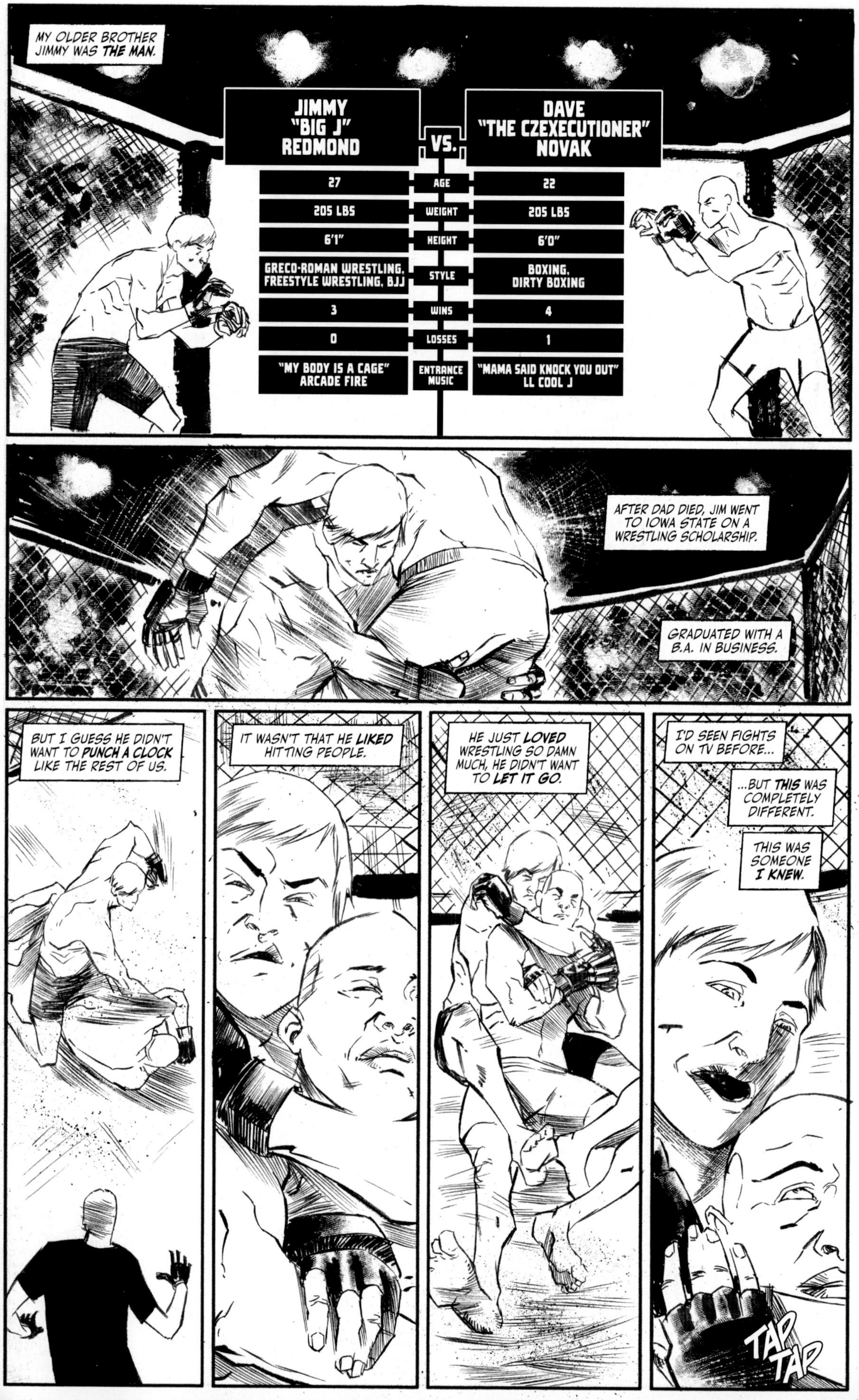
MY OLDER BROTHER JIMMY WAS THE MAN.
JIMMY "BIG J" REDMOND
VS.
DAVE "THE CZEXECUTIONER" NOVAK
27 AGE 22
205 LBS WEIGHT 205 LBS
6'1" HEIGHT 6'0"
GRECO-ROMAN WRESTLING, FREESTYLE WRESTLING, BJJ STYLE BOXING, DIRTY BOXING
3 WINS 4
0 LOSSES 1
"MY BODY IS A CAGE" ARCADE FIRE ENTRANCE MUSIC "MAMA SAID KNOCK YOU OUT" LL COOL J
AFTER DAD DIED, JIM WENT TO IOWA STATE ON A WRESTLING SCHOLARSHIP.
GRADUATED WITH A B.A. IN BUSINESS.
BUT I GUESS HE DIDN'T WANT TO PUNCH A CLOCK LIKE THE REST OF US.
IT WASN'T THAT HE LIKED HITTING PEOPLE.
HE JUST LOVED WRESTLING SO DAMN MUCH, HE DIDN'T WANT TO LET IT GO.
I'D SEEN FIGHTS ON TV BEFORE...
...BUT THIS WAS COMPLETELY DIFFERENT.
THIS WAS SOMEONE I KNEW.
TAP TAP

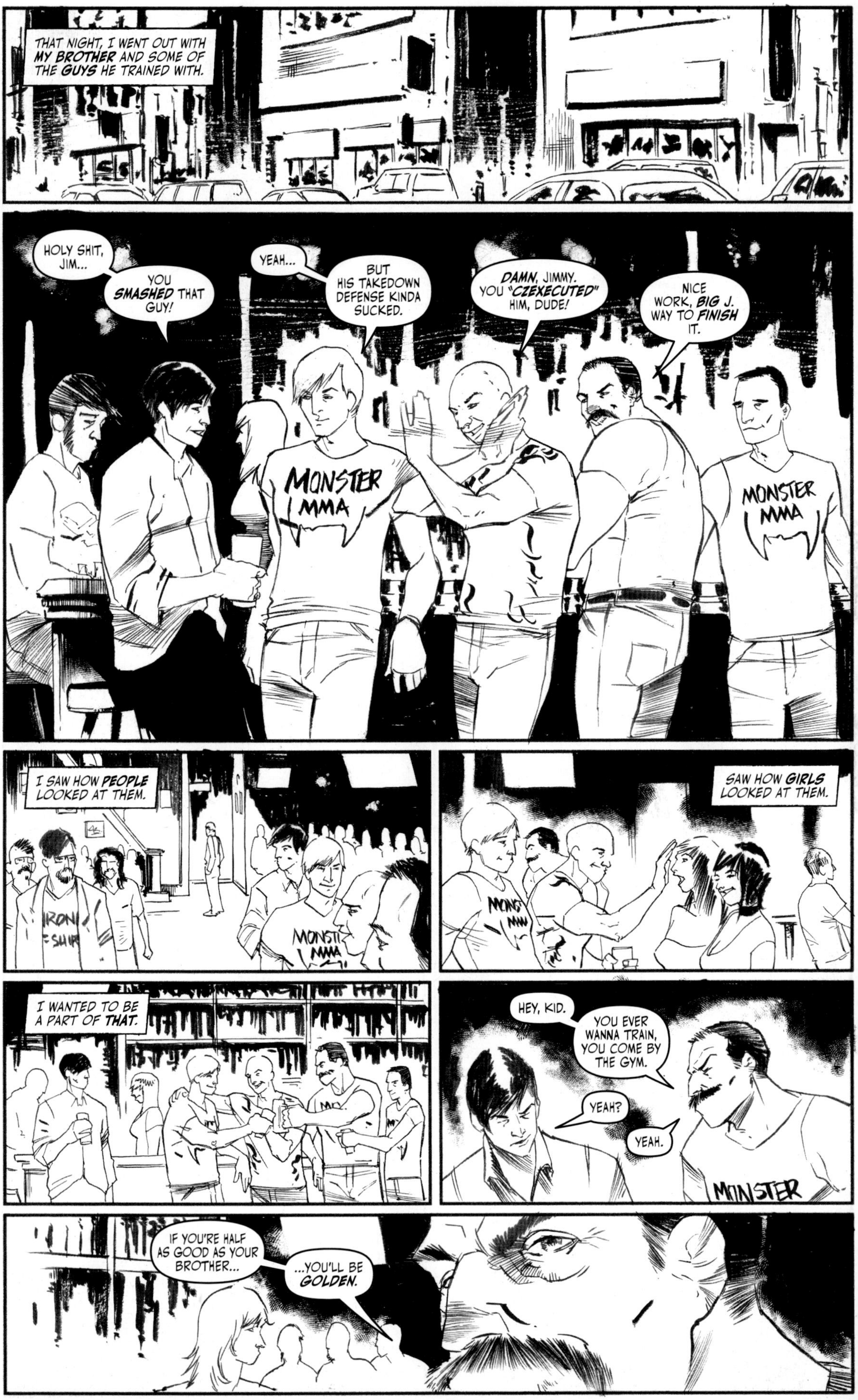
THAT NIGHT, I WENT OUT WITH MY BROTHER AND SOME OF THE GUYS HE TRAINED WITH.
HOLY SHIT, JIM...
YOU SMASHED THAT GUY!
YEAH...
BUT HIS TAKEDOWN DEFENSE KINDA SUCKED.
DAMN, JIMMY. YOU "CZEXECUTED" HIM, DUDE!
NICE WORK, BIG J. WAY TO FINISH IT.
MONSTER MMA
MONSTER MMA
I SAW HOW PEOPLE LOOKED AT THEM.
SAW HOW GIRLS LOOKED AT THEM.
I WANTED TO BE A PART OF THAT.
HEY, KID.
YOU EVER WANNA TRAIN, YOU COME BY THE GYM.
YEAH?
YEAH.
MONSTER
IF YOU'RE HALF AS GOOD AS YOUR BROTHER...
...YOU'LL BE GOLDEN.

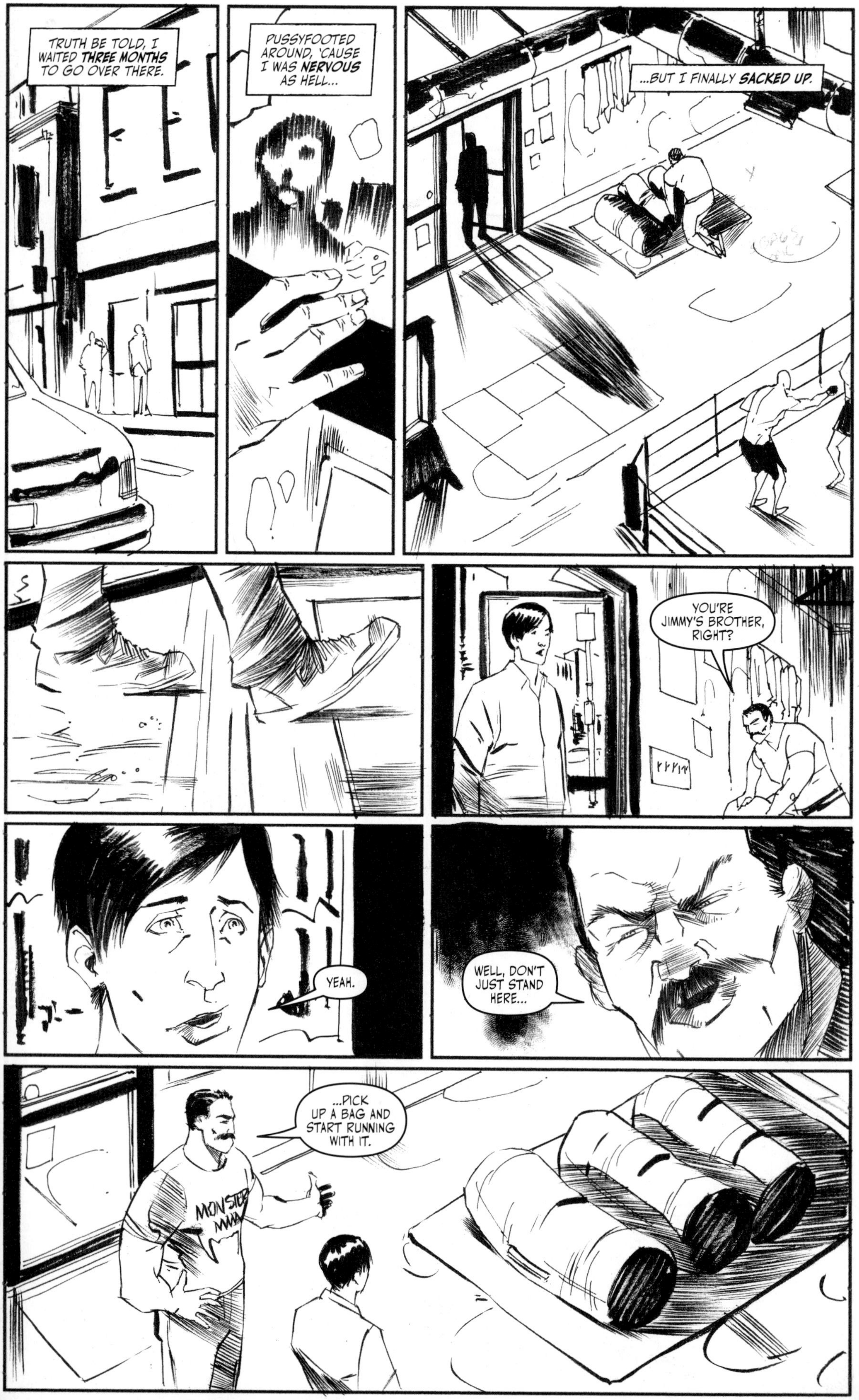
TRUTH BE TOLD, I WAITED THREE MONTHS TO GO OVER THERE.
PUSSYFOOTED AROUND, 'CAUSE I WAS NERVOUS AS HELL...
...BUT I FINALLY SACKED UP.
YOU'RE JIMMY'S BROTHER, RIGHT?
YEAH.
WELL, DON'T JUST STAND HERE...
...PICK UP A BAG AND START RUNNING WITH IT.
MONSTER MMA

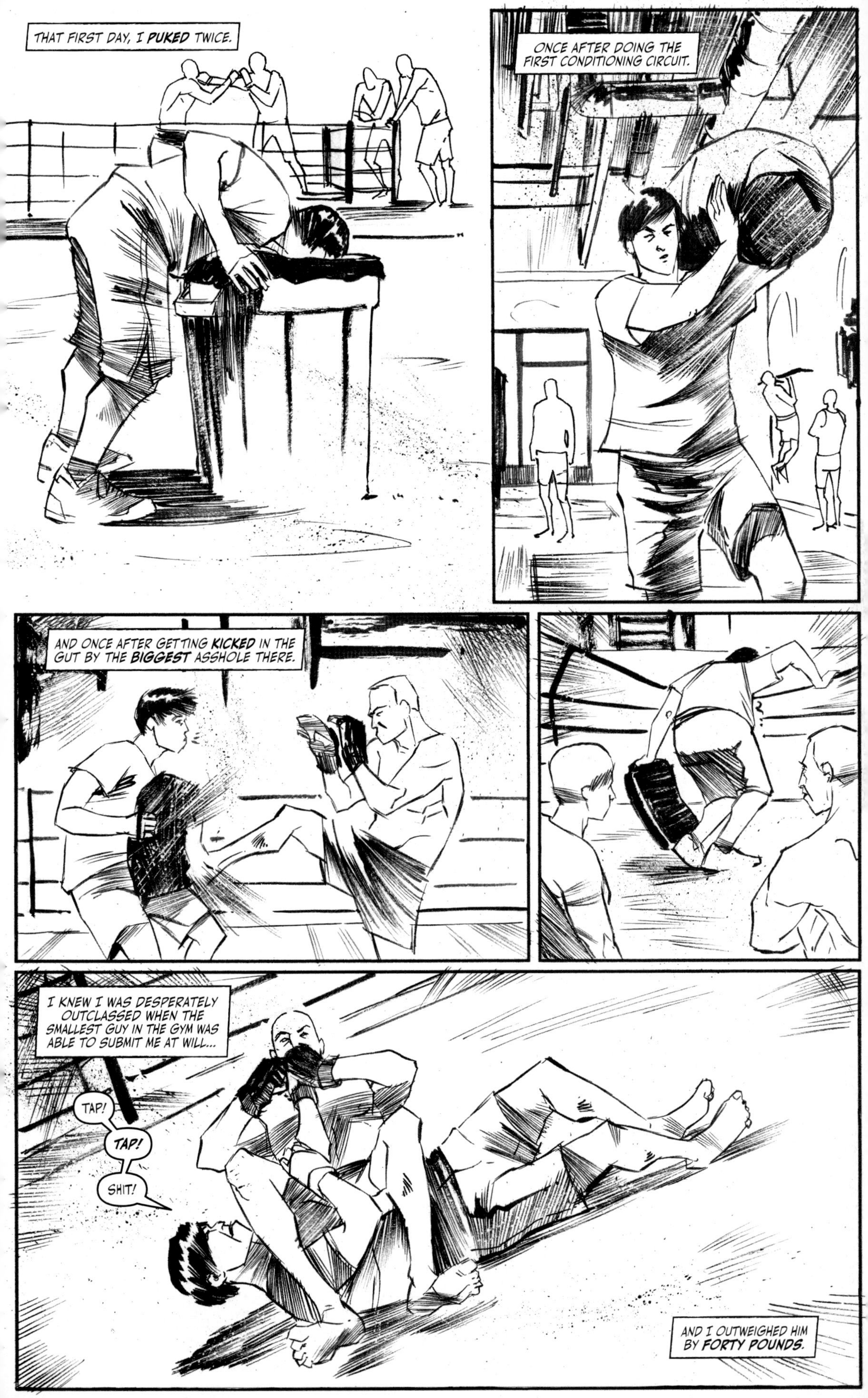
THAT FIRST DAY, I PUKED TWICE.
ONCE AFTER DOING THE FIRST CONDITIONING CIRCUIT.
AND ONCE AFTER GETTING KICKED IN THE GUT BY THE BIGGEST ASSHOLE THERE.
I KNEW I WAS DESPERATELY OUTCLASSED WHEN THE SMALLEST GUY IN THE GYM WAS ABLE TO SUBMIT ME AT WILL...
TAP!
TAP!
SHIT!
AND I OUTWEIGHED HIM BY FORTY POUNDS.

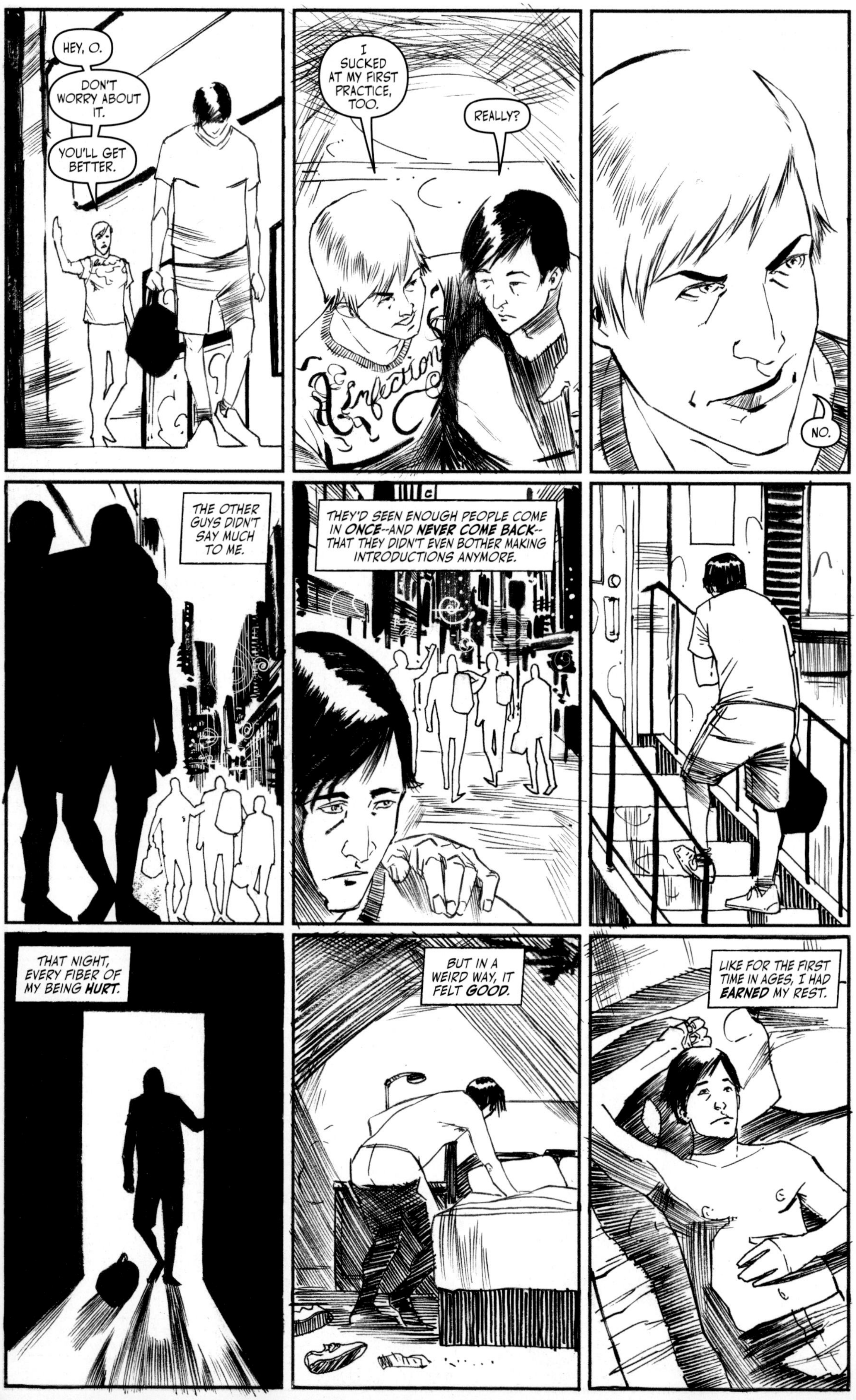

HEY, O.
DON'T WORRY ABOUT IT.
YOU'LL GET BETTER.
I SUCKED AT MY FIRST PRACTICE, TOO.
REALLY?
Infection
NO.
THE OTHER GUYS DIDN'T SAY MUCH TO ME.
THEY'D SEEN ENOUGH PEOPLE COME IN ONCE--AND NEVER COME BACK--THAT THEY DIDN'T EVEN BOTHER MAKING INTRODUCTIONS ANYMORE.
THAT NIGHT, EVERY FIBER OF MY BEING HURT.
BUT IN A WEIRD WAY, IT FELT GOOD.
LIKE FOR THE FIRST TIME IN AGES, I HAD EARNED MY REST.

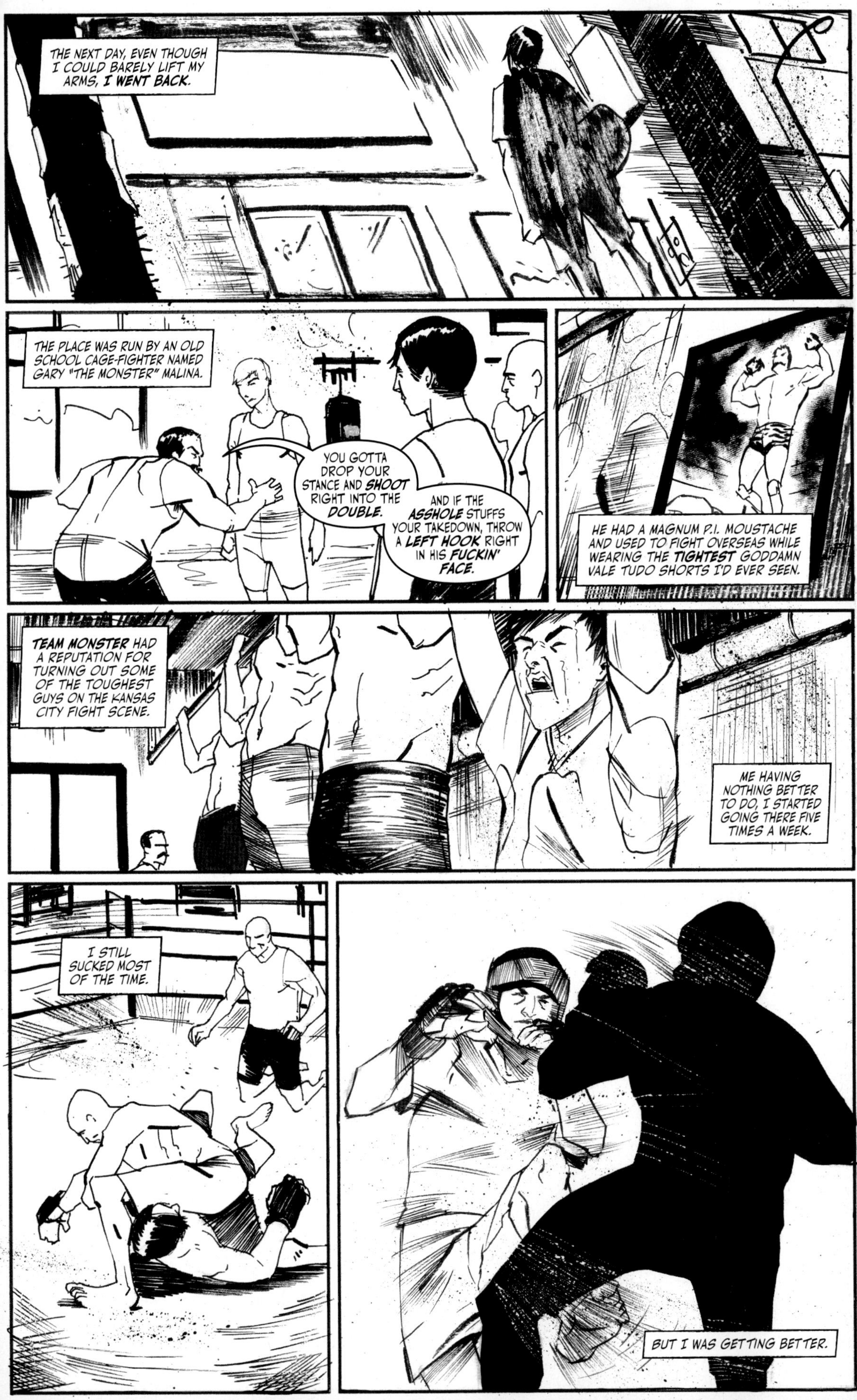
THE NEXT DAY, EVEN THOUGH I COULD BARELY LIFT MY ARMS, I WENT BACK.
THE PLACE WAS RUN BY AN OLD SCHOOL CAGE-FIGHTER NAMED GARY "THE MONSTER" MALINA.
YOU GOTTA DROP YOUR STANCE AND SHOOT RIGHT INTO THE DOUBLE.
AND IF THE ASSHOLE STUFFS YOUR TAKEDOWN, THROW A LEFT HOOK RIGHT IN HIS FUCKIN' FACE.
HE HAD A MAGNUM P.I. MOUSTACHE AND USED TO FIGHT OVERSEAS WHILE WEARING THE TIGHTEST GODDAMN VALE TUDO SHORTS I'D EVER SEEN.
TEAM MONSTER HAD A REPUTATION FOR TURNING OUT SOME OF THE TOUGHEST GUYS ON THE KANSAS CITY FIGHT SCENE.
ME HAVING NOTHING BETTER TO DO, I STARTED GOING THERE FIVE TIMES A WEEK.
I STILL SUCKED MOST OF THE TIME.
BUT I WAS GETTING BETTER.

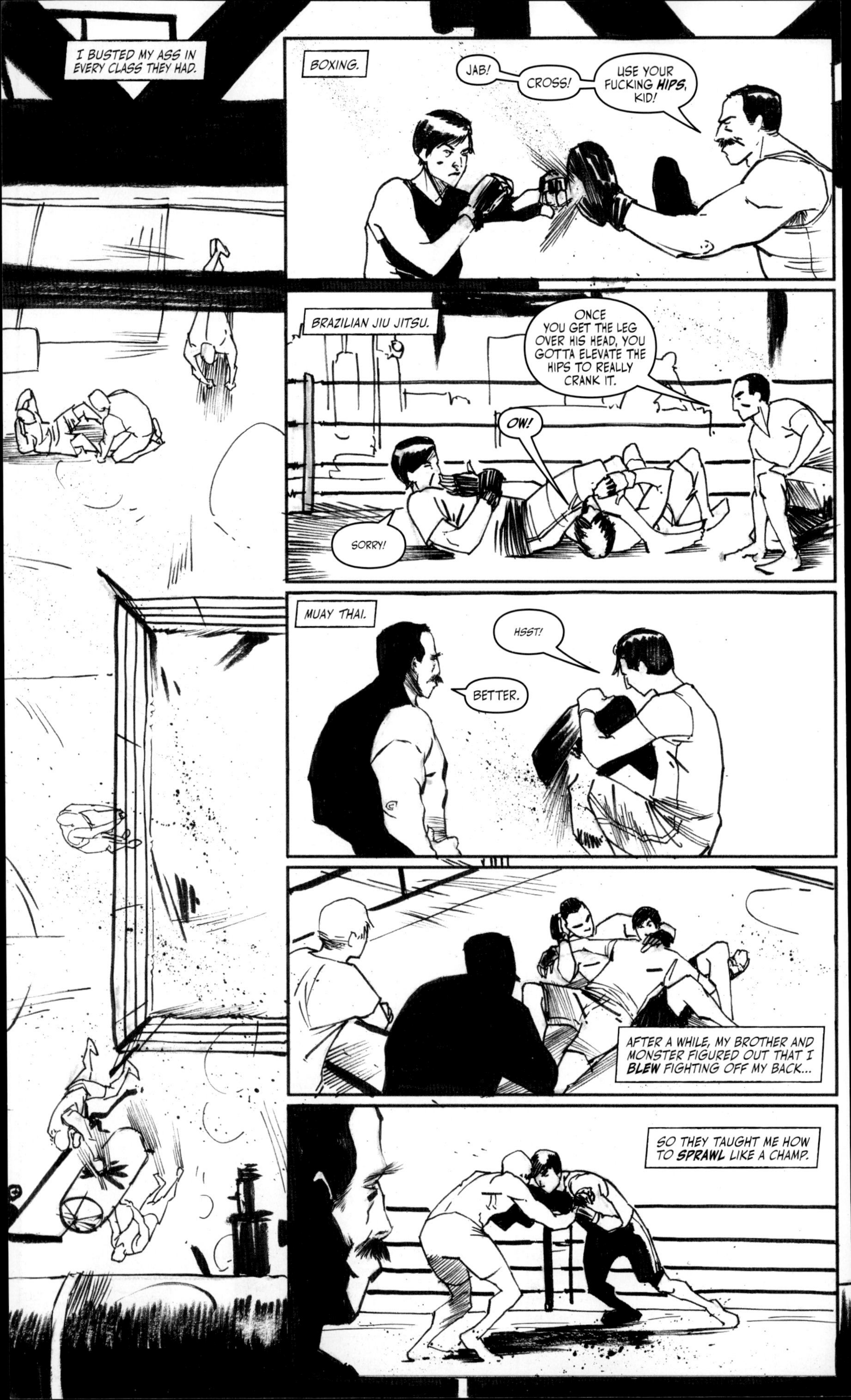
I BUSTED MY ASS IN EVERY CLASS THEY HAD.
BOXING.
JAB!
CROSS!
USE YOUR FUCKING HIPS, KID!
BRAZILIAN JIU JITSU.
ONCE YOU GET THE LEG OVER HIS HEAD, YOU GOTTA ELEVATE THE HIPS TO REALLY CRANK IT.
OW!
SORRY!
MUAY THAI.
HSST!
BETTER.
AFTER A WHILE, MY BROTHER AND MONSTER FIGURED OUT THAT I BLEW FIGHTING OFF MY BACK...
SO THEY TAUGHT ME HOW TO SPRAWL LIKE A CHAMP.

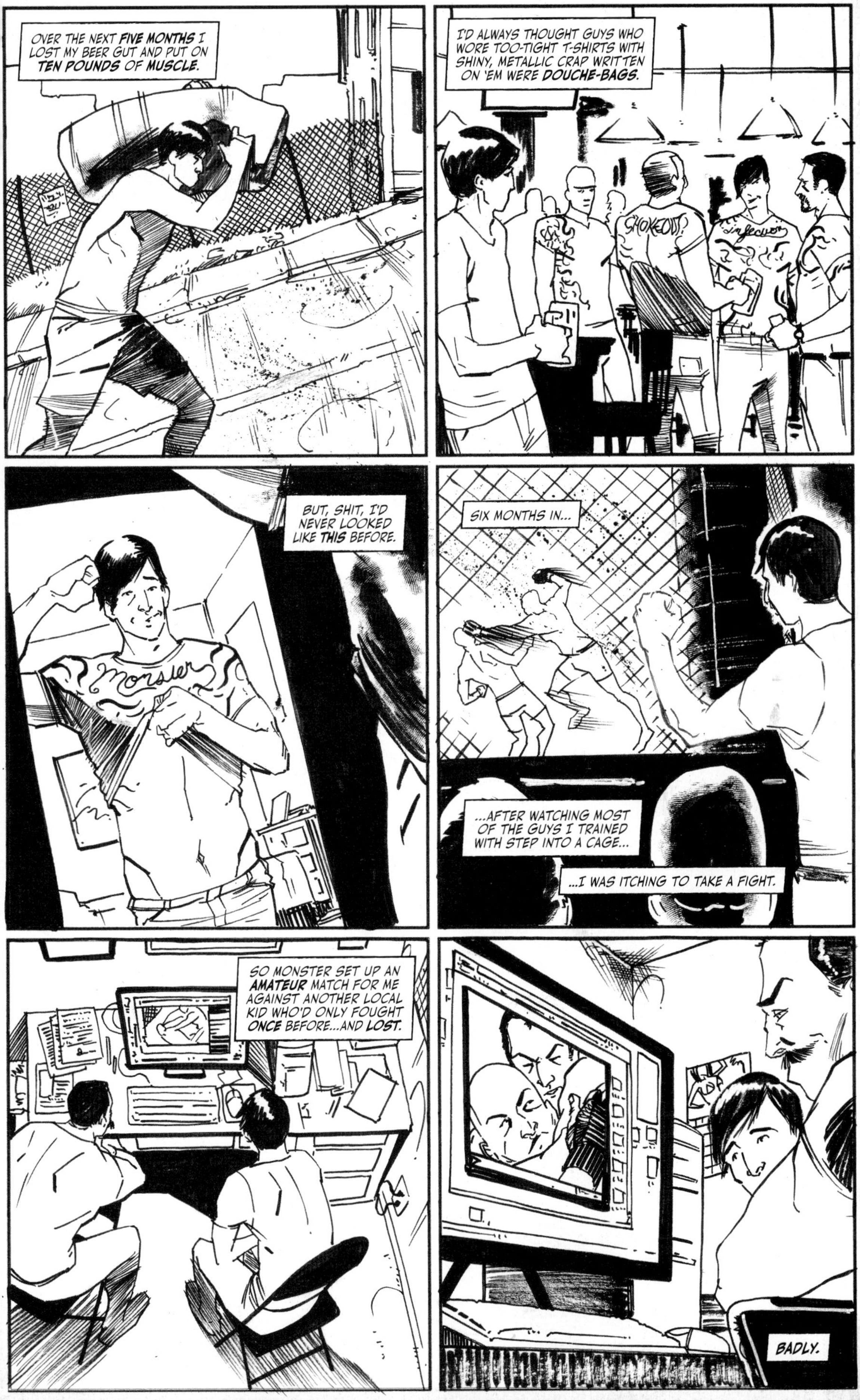
OVER THE NEXT **FIVE MONTHS** I LOST MY BEER GUT AND PUT ON **TEN POUNDS** OF **MUSCLE**.
I'D ALWAYS THOUGHT GUYS WHO WORE TOO-TIGHT T-SHIRTS WITH SHINY, METALLIC CRAP WRITTEN ON 'EM WERE **DOUCHE-BAGS**.
BUT, SHIT, I'D NEVER LOOKED LIKE **THIS** BEFORE.
Monster
SIX MONTHS IN...
...AFTER WATCHING MOST OF THE GUYS I TRAINED WITH STEP INTO A CAGE...
...I WAS ITCHING TO TAKE A FIGHT.
SO MONSTER SET UP AN **AMATEUR** MATCH FOR ME AGAINST ANOTHER LOCAL KID WHO'D ONLY FOUGHT **ONCE** BEFORE...AND **LOST**.
BADLY.

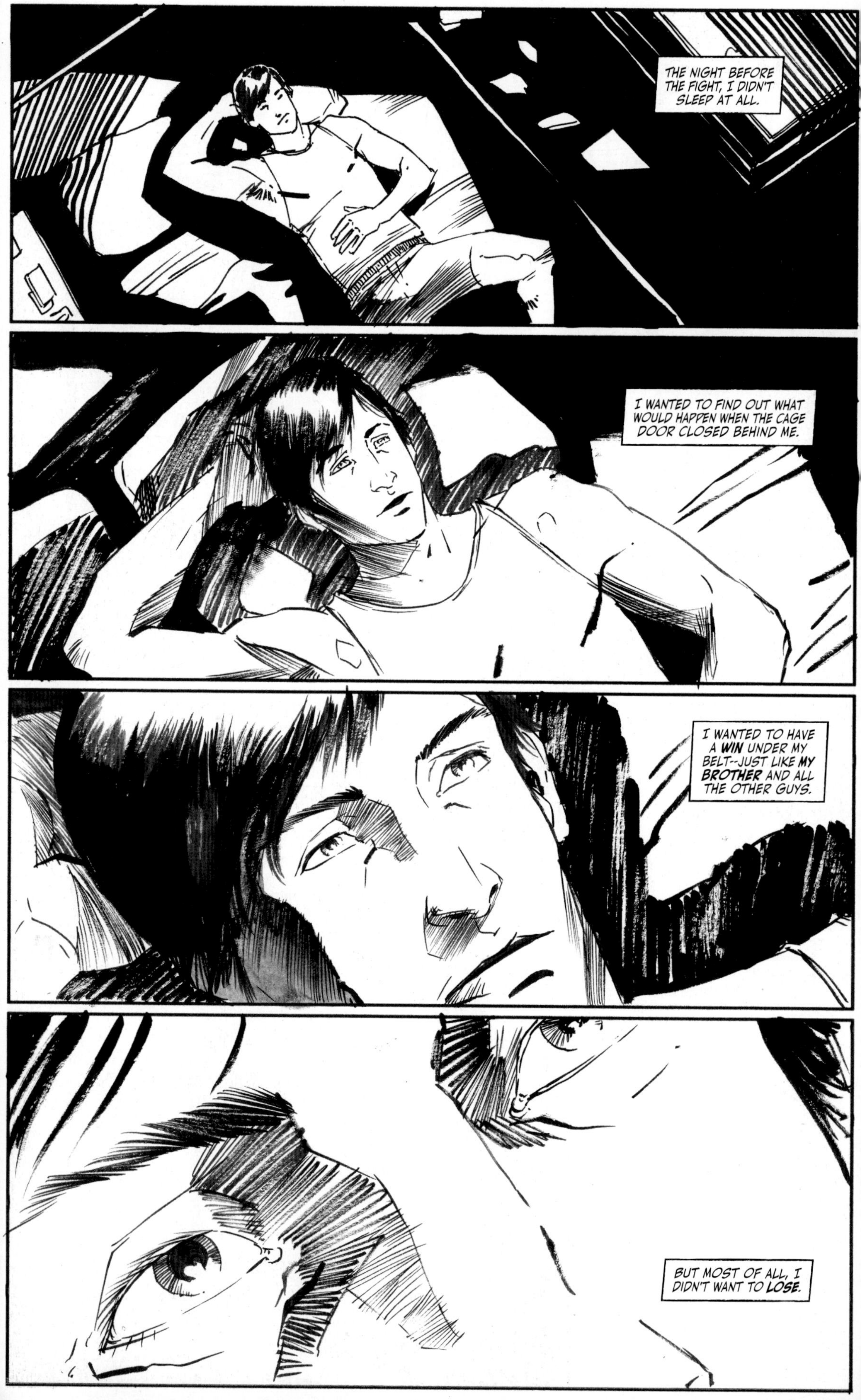
THE NIGHT BEFORE THE FIGHT, I DIDN'T SLEEP AT ALL.
I WANTED TO FIND OUT WHAT WOULD HAPPEN WHEN THE CAGE DOOR CLOSED BEHIND ME.
I WANTED TO HAVE A **WIN** UNDER MY BELT--JUST LIKE **MY BROTHER** AND ALL THE OTHER GUYS.
BUT MOST OF ALL, I DIDN'T WANT TO **LOSE**.

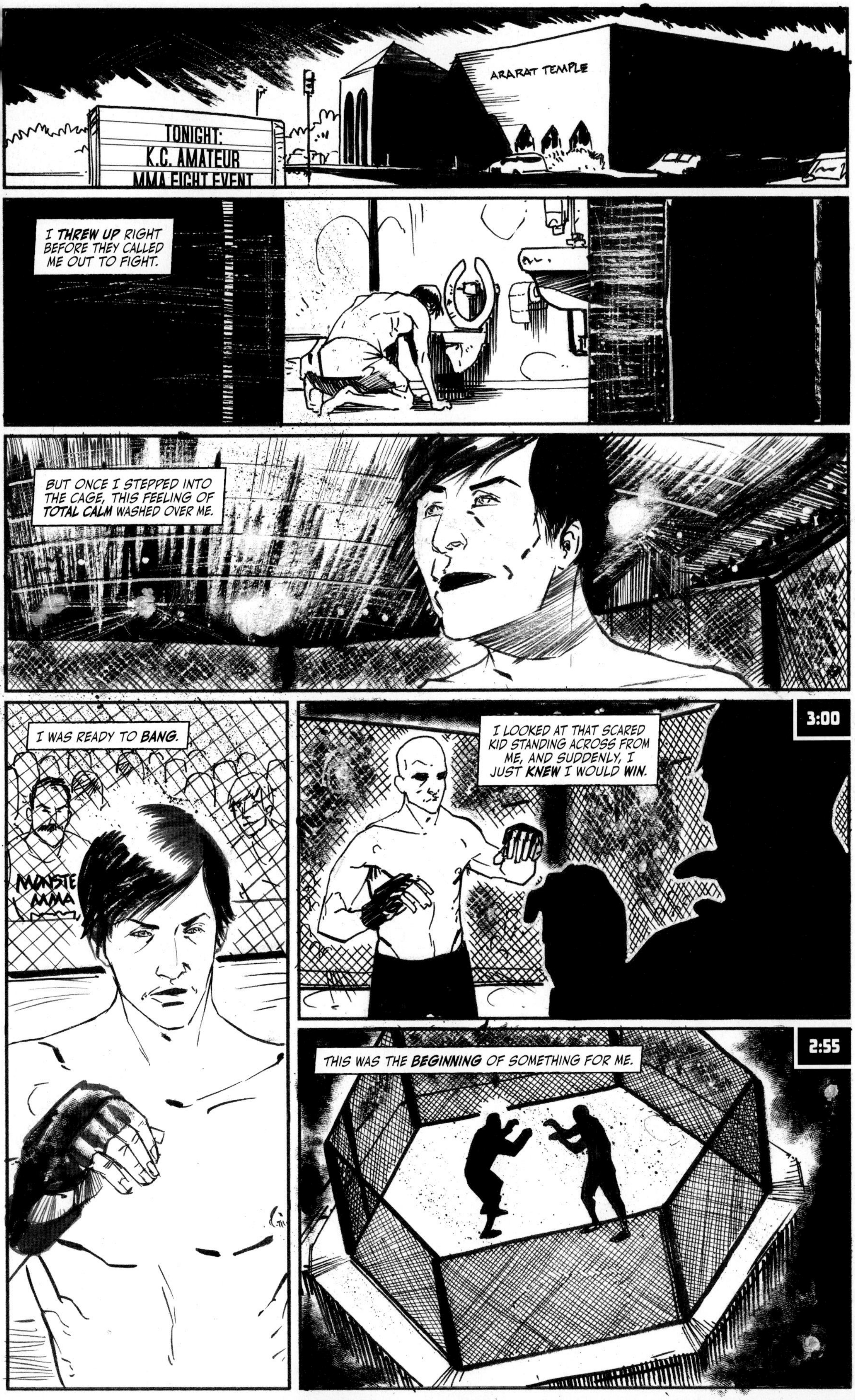

TONIGHT:
K.C. AMATEUR
MMA FIGHT EVENT
ARARAT TEMPLE
I THREW UP RIGHT BEFORE THEY CALLED ME OUT TO FIGHT.
BUT ONCE I STEPPED INTO THE CAGE, THIS FEELING OF TOTAL CALM WASHED OVER ME.
I WAS READY TO BANG.
3:00
I LOOKED AT THAT SCARED KID STANDING ACROSS FROM ME, AND SUDDENLY, I JUST KNEW I WOULD WIN.
2:55
THIS WAS THE BEGINNING OF SOMETHING FOR ME.

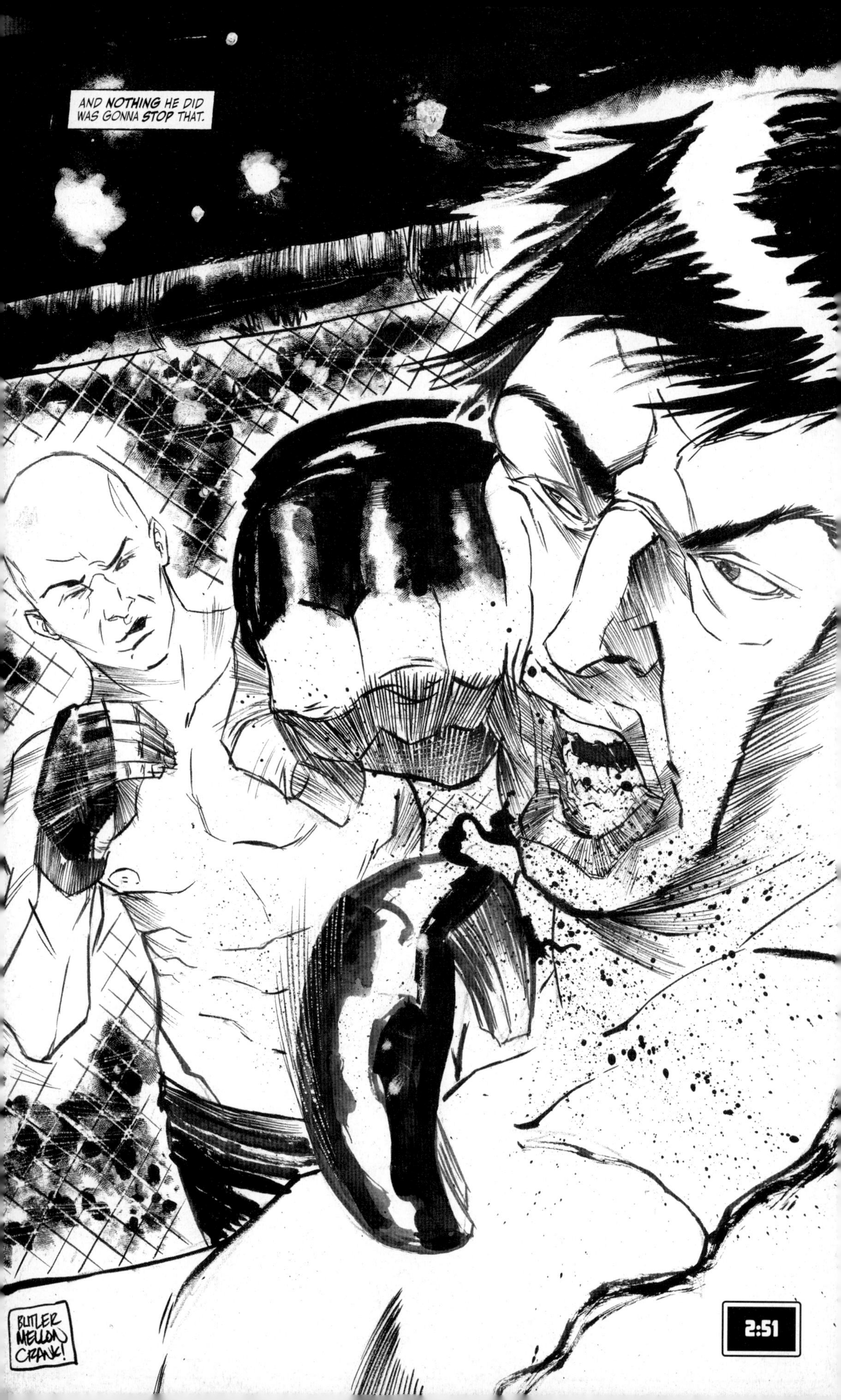
AND NOTHING HE DID WAS GONNA STOP THAT.
BUTLER MELLON CRANK!
2:51

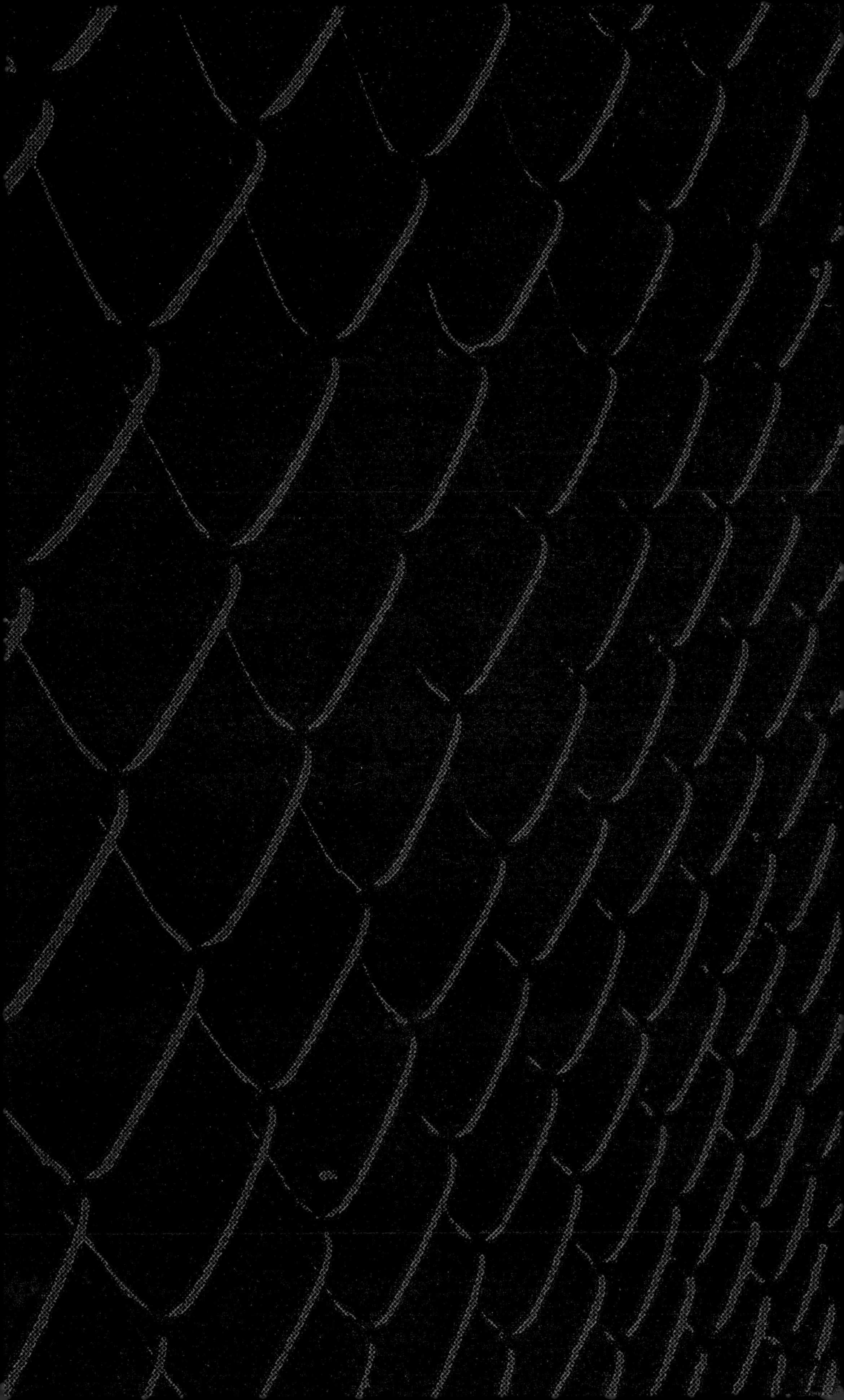

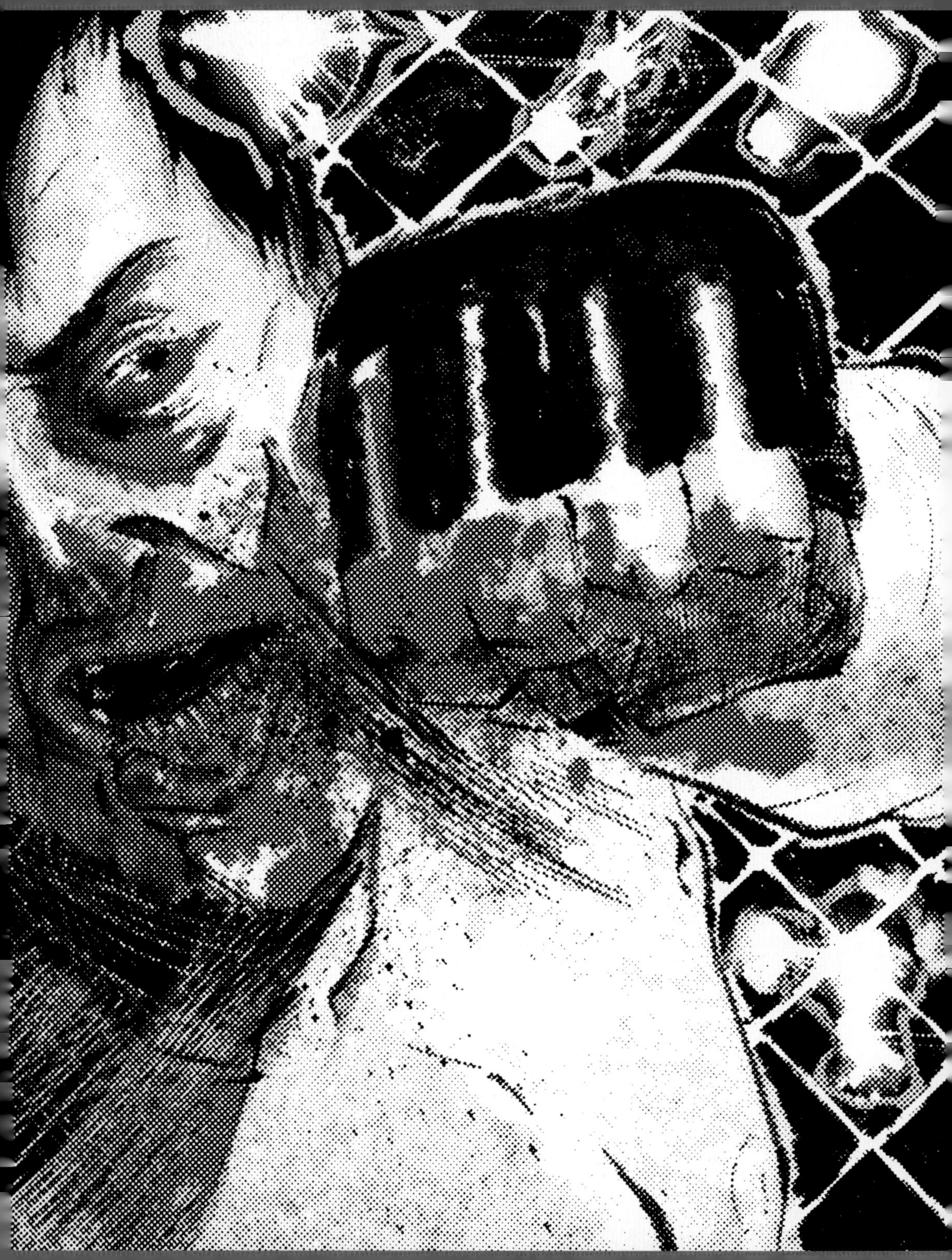

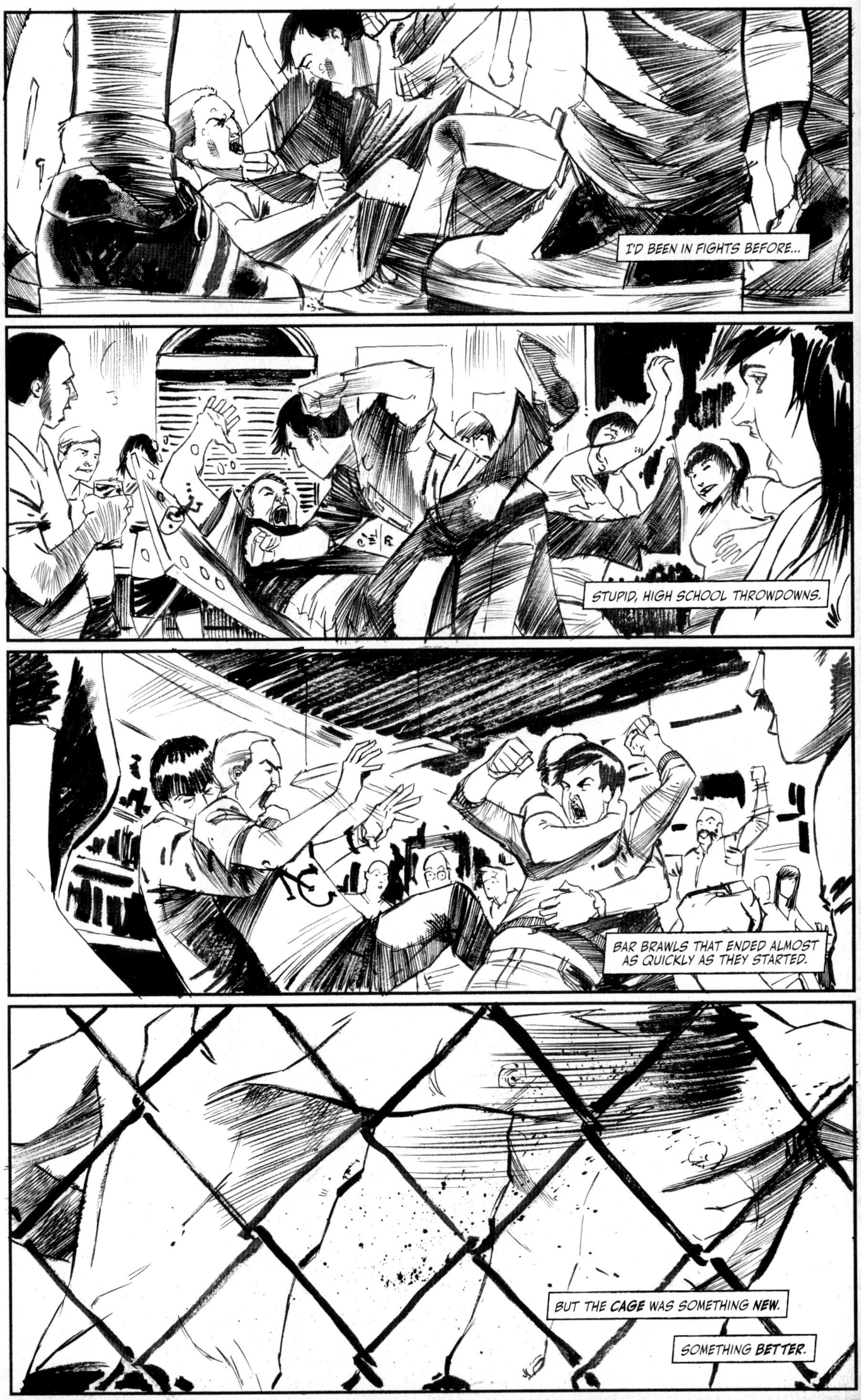
I'D BEEN IN FIGHTS BEFORE...
STUPID, HIGH SCHOOL THROWDOWNS.
BAR BRAWLS THAT ENDED ALMOST AS QUICKLY AS THEY STARTED.
BUT THE CAGE WAS SOMETHING NEW.
SOMETHING BETTER.

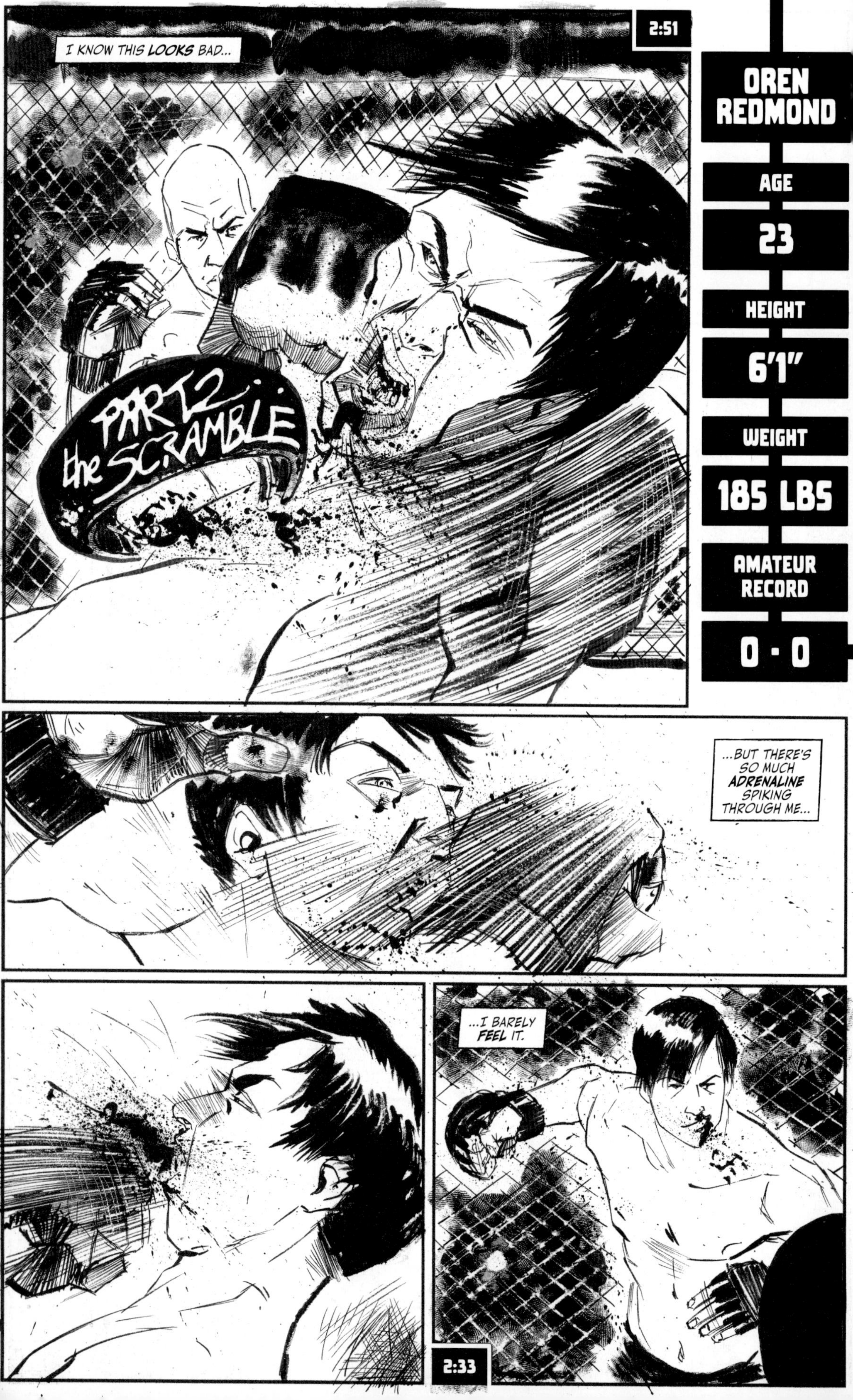
2:51
I KNOW THIS LOOKS BAD...
OREN REDMOND
AGE
23
HEIGHT
6'1"
WEIGHT
185 LBS
AMATEUR RECORD
0 - 0
PART 2 the SCRAMBLE
...BUT THERE'S SO MUCH ADRENALINE SPIKING THROUGH ME...
...I BARELY FEEL IT.
2:33

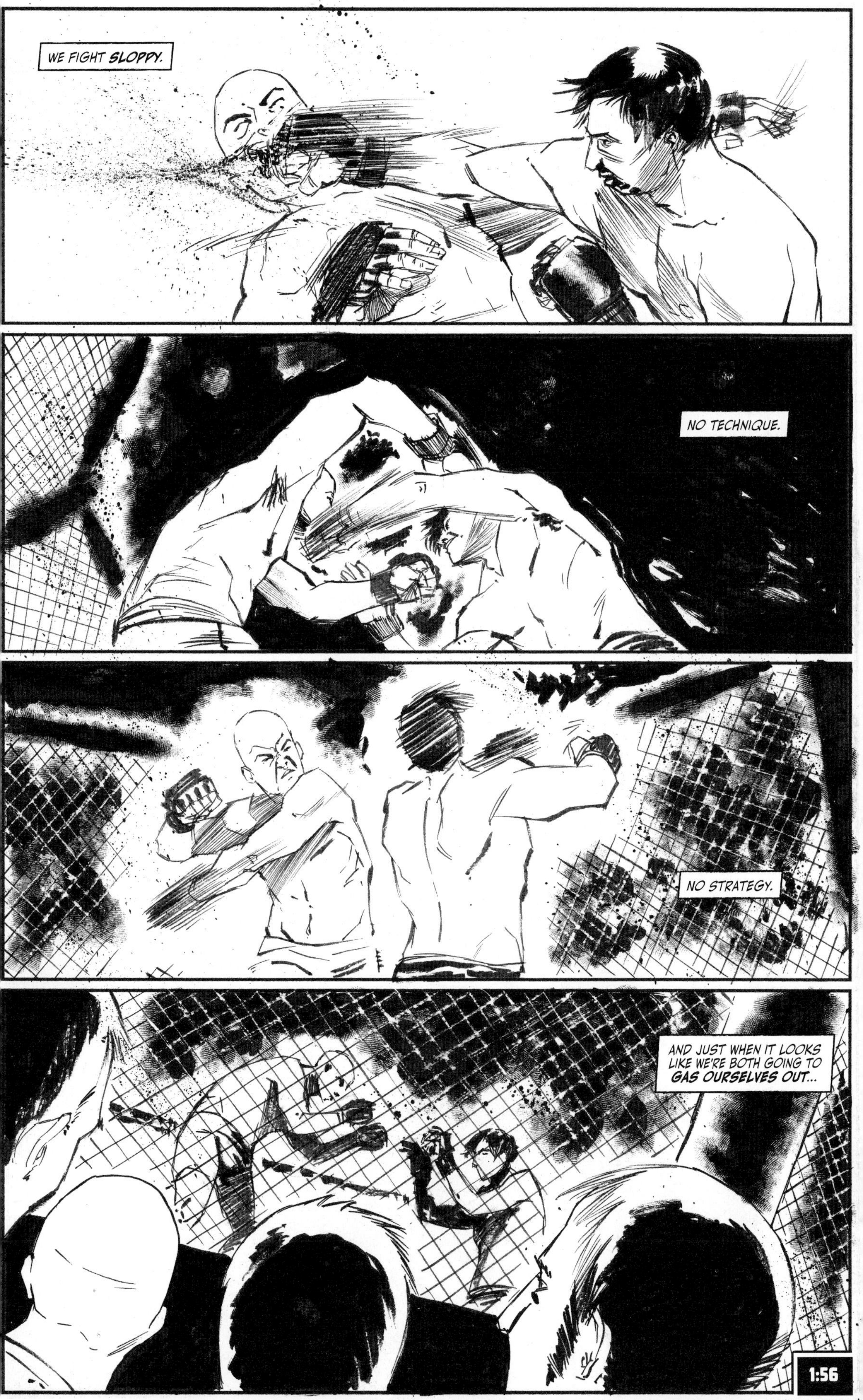
WE FIGHT SLOPPY.
NO TECHNIQUE.
NO STRATEGY.
AND JUST WHEN IT LOOKS LIKE WE'RE BOTH GOING TO GAS OURSELVES OUT...
1:56

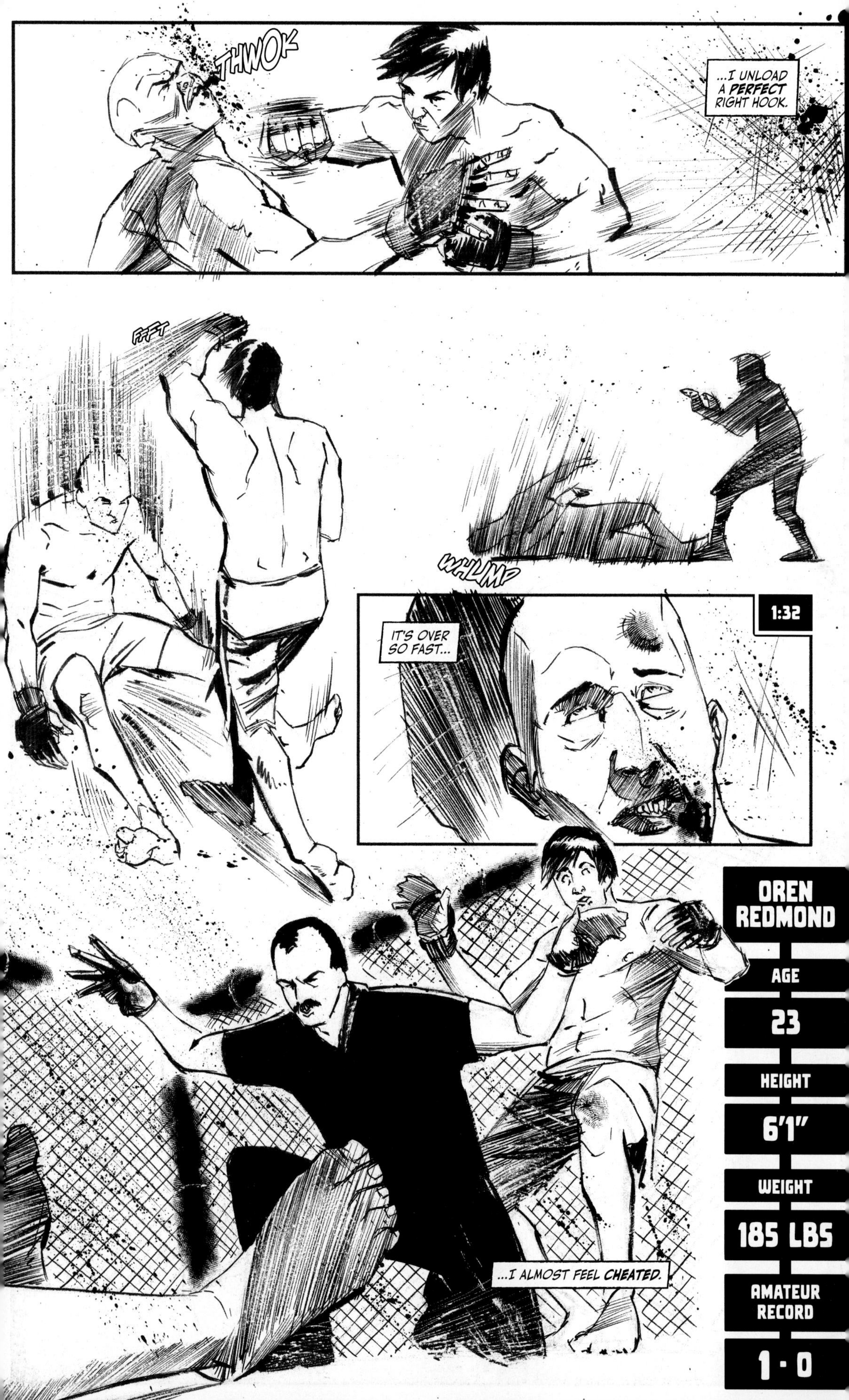
THWOK
...I UNLOAD A PERFECT RIGHT HOOK.
FFFT
WHUMP
1:32
IT'S OVER SO FAST...
...I ALMOST FEEL CHEATED.
OREN REDMOND
AGE
23
HEIGHT
6'1"
WEIGHT
185 LBS
AMATEUR RECORD
1 - 0

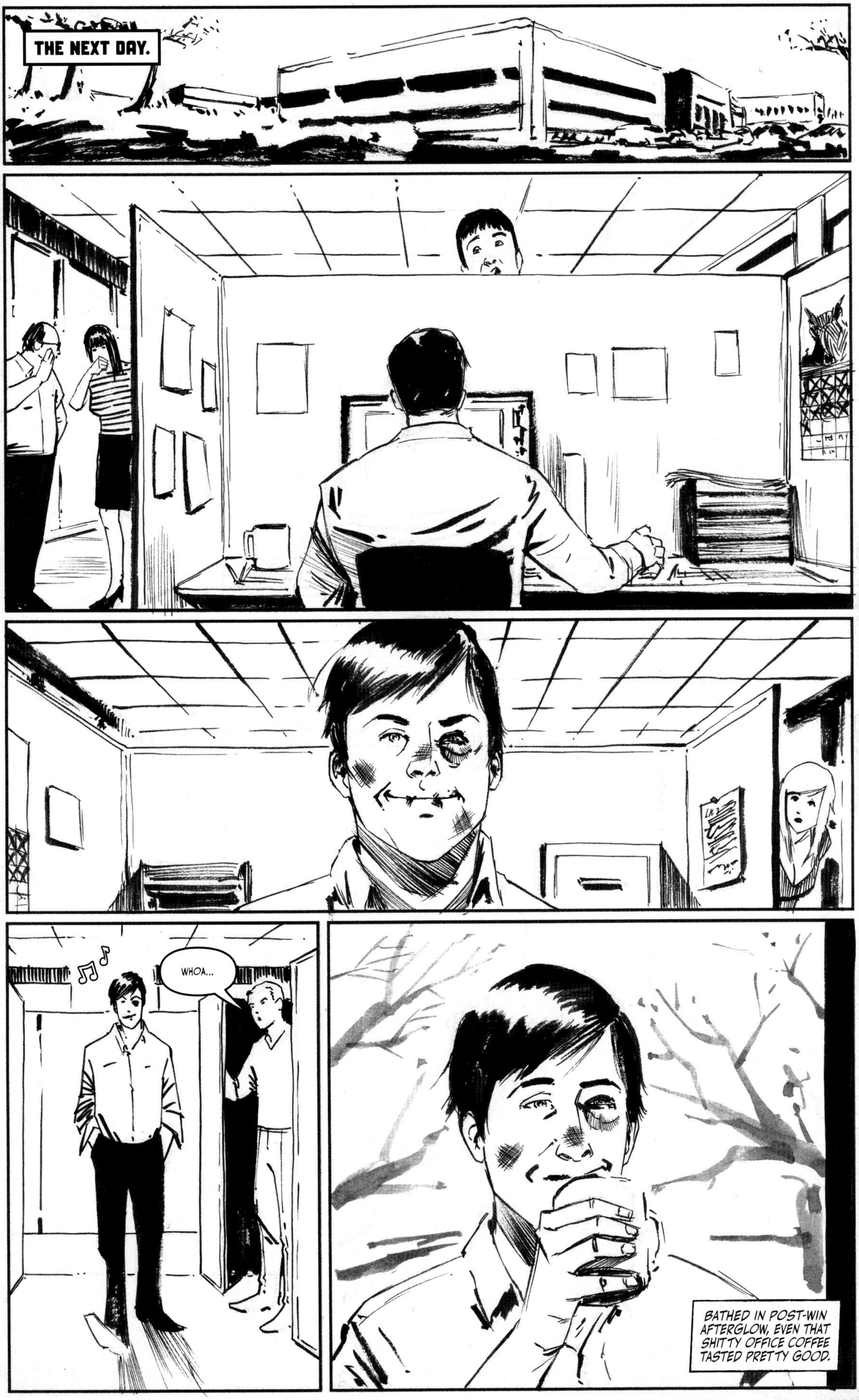

THE NEXT DAY.
WHOA...
BATHED IN POST-WIN AFTERGLOW, EVEN THAT SHITTY OFFICE COFFEE TASTED PRETTY GOOD.

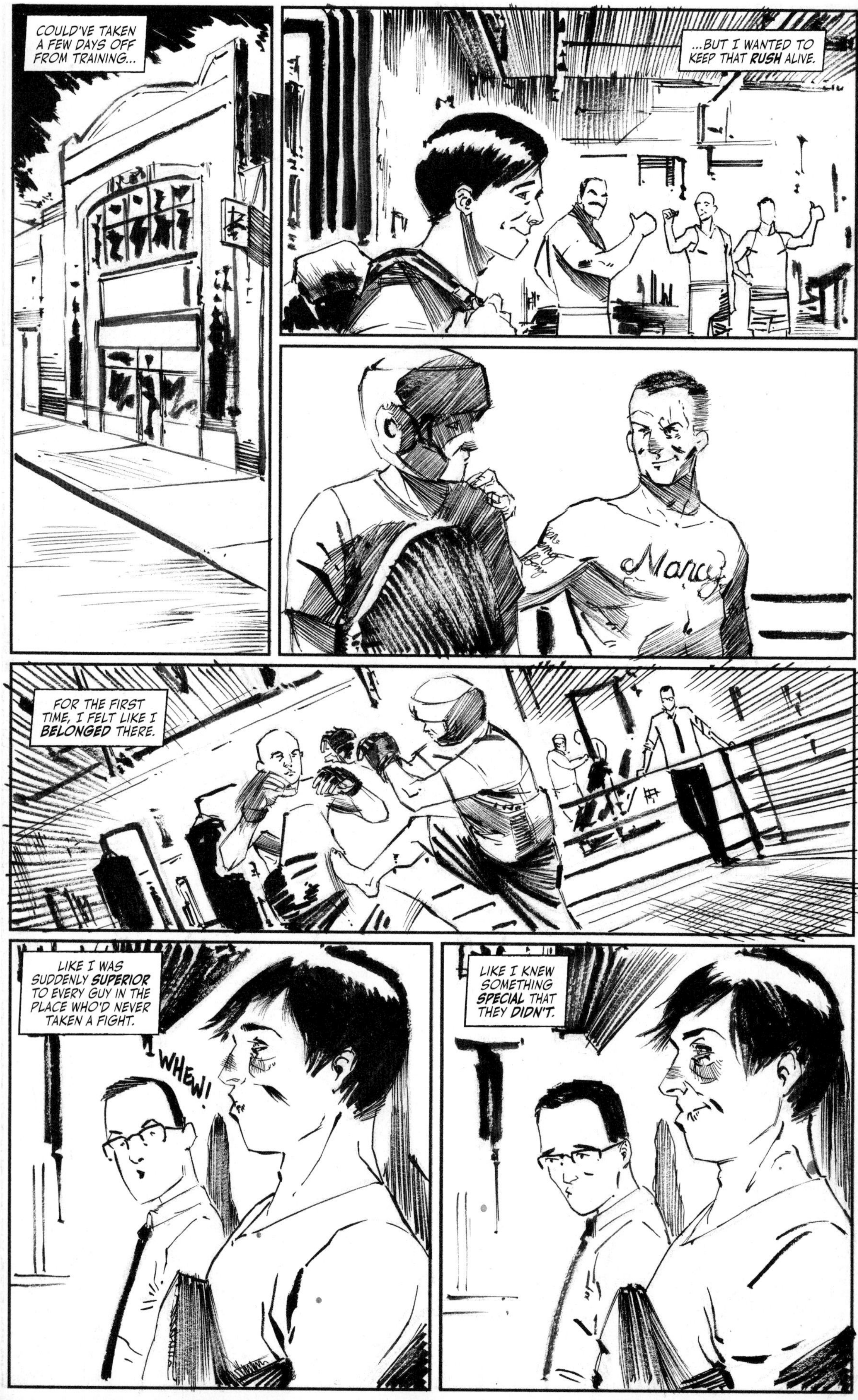
COULD'VE TAKEN A FEW DAYS OFF FROM TRAINING...
...BUT I WANTED TO KEEP THAT RUSH ALIVE.
FOR THE FIRST TIME, I FELT LIKE I BELONGED THERE.
LIKE I WAS SUDDENLY SUPERIOR TO EVERY GUY IN THE PLACE WHO'D NEVER TAKEN A FIGHT.
WHEW!
LIKE I KNEW SOMETHING SPECIAL THAT THEY DIDN'T.

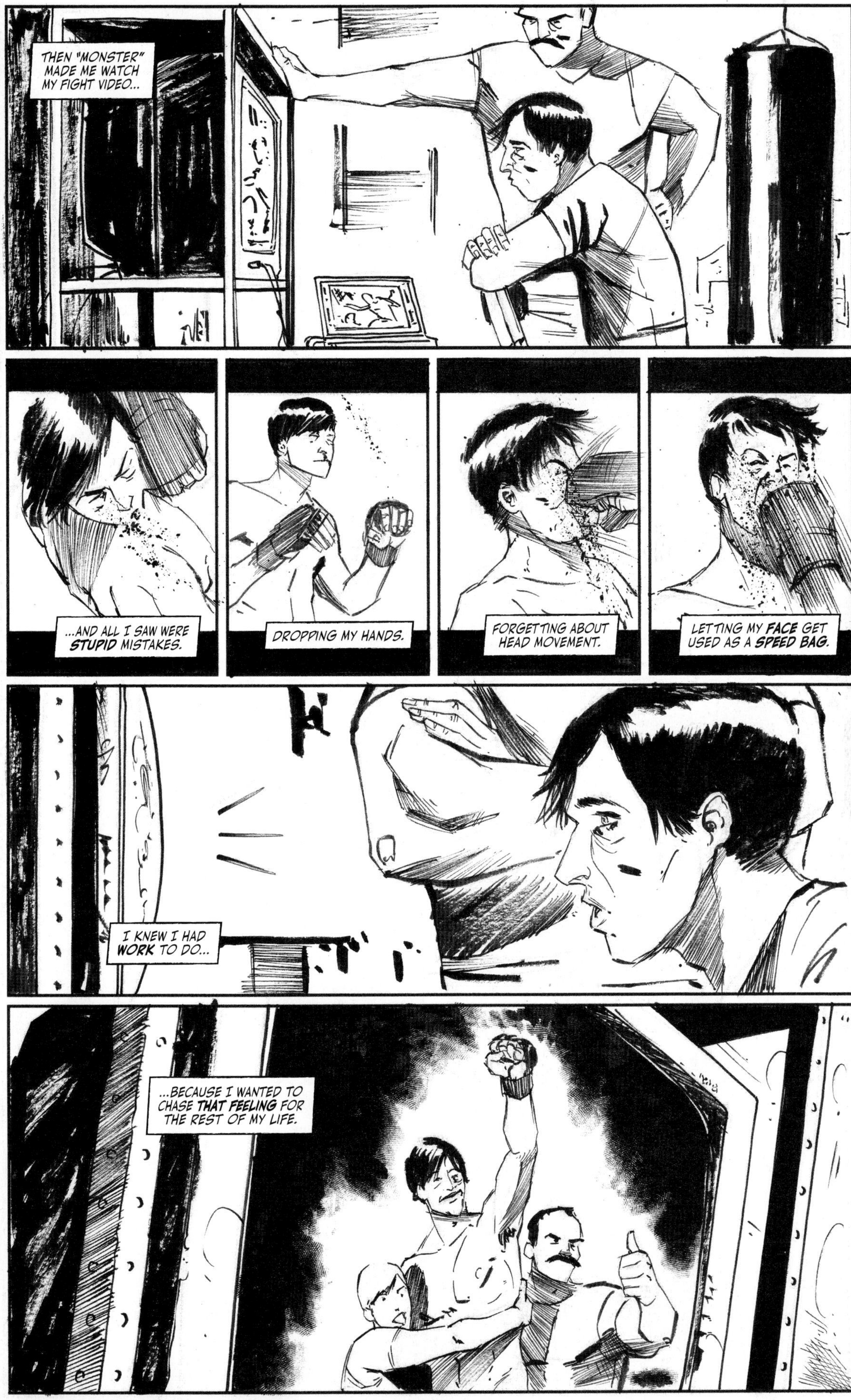
THEN "MONSTER" MADE ME WATCH MY FIGHT VIDEO...
...AND ALL I SAW WERE STUPID MISTAKES.
DROPPING MY HANDS.
FORGETTING ABOUT HEAD MOVEMENT.
LETTING MY FACE GET USED AS A SPEED BAG.
I KNEW I HAD WORK TO DO...
...BECAUSE I WANTED TO CHASE THAT FEELING FOR THE REST OF MY LIFE.

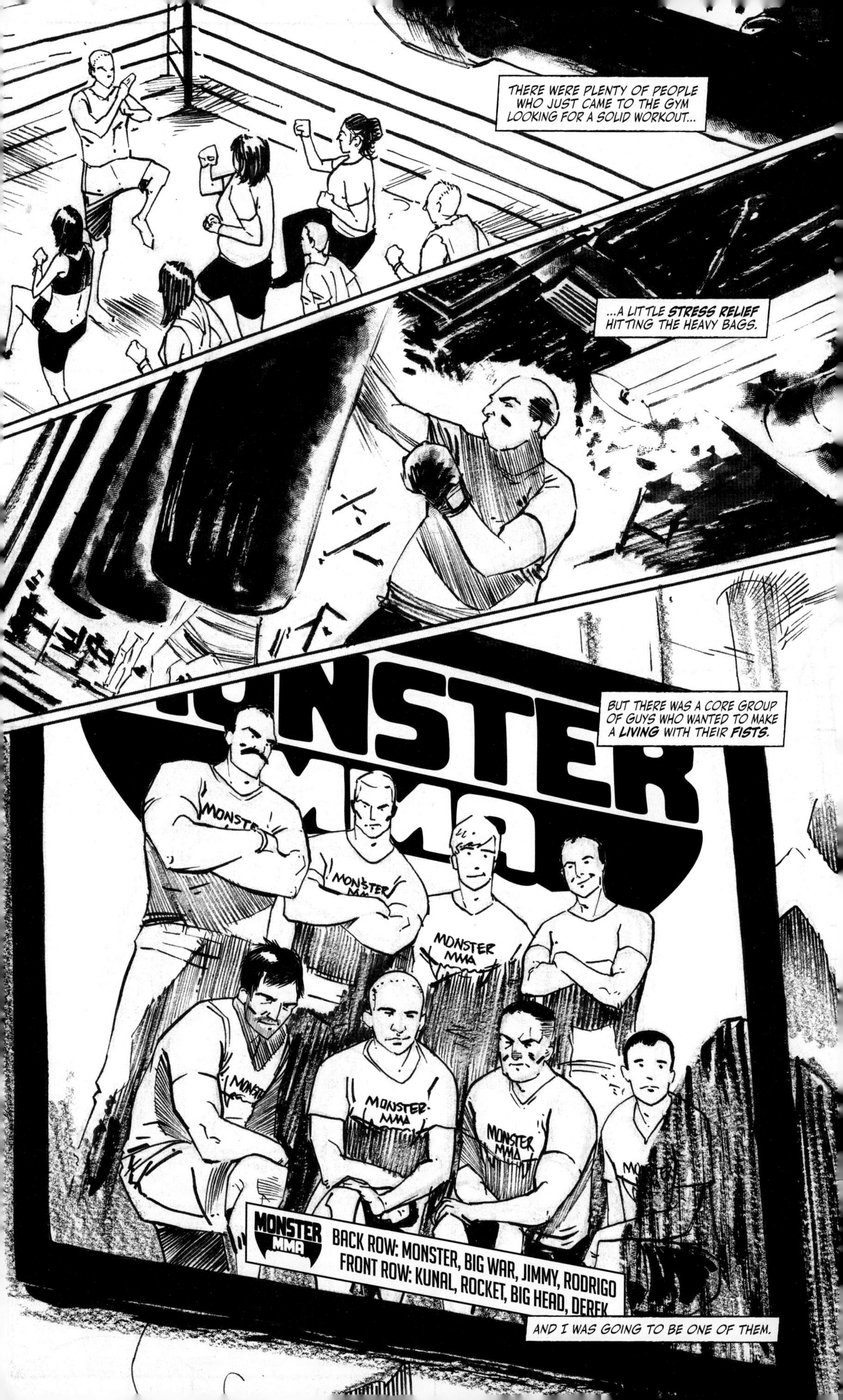
THERE WERE PLENTY OF PEOPLE WHO JUST CAME TO THE GYM LOOKING FOR A SOLID WORKOUT...
...A LITTLE **STRESS RELIEF** HITTING THE HEAVY BAGS.
BUT THERE WAS A CORE GROUP OF GUYS WHO WANTED TO MAKE A **LIVING** WITH THEIR **FISTS**.
MONSTER MMA
BACK ROW: MONSTER, BIG WAR, JIMMY, RODRIGO
FRONT ROW: KUNAL, ROCKET, BIG HEAD, DEREK
AND I WAS GOING TO BE ONE OF THEM.

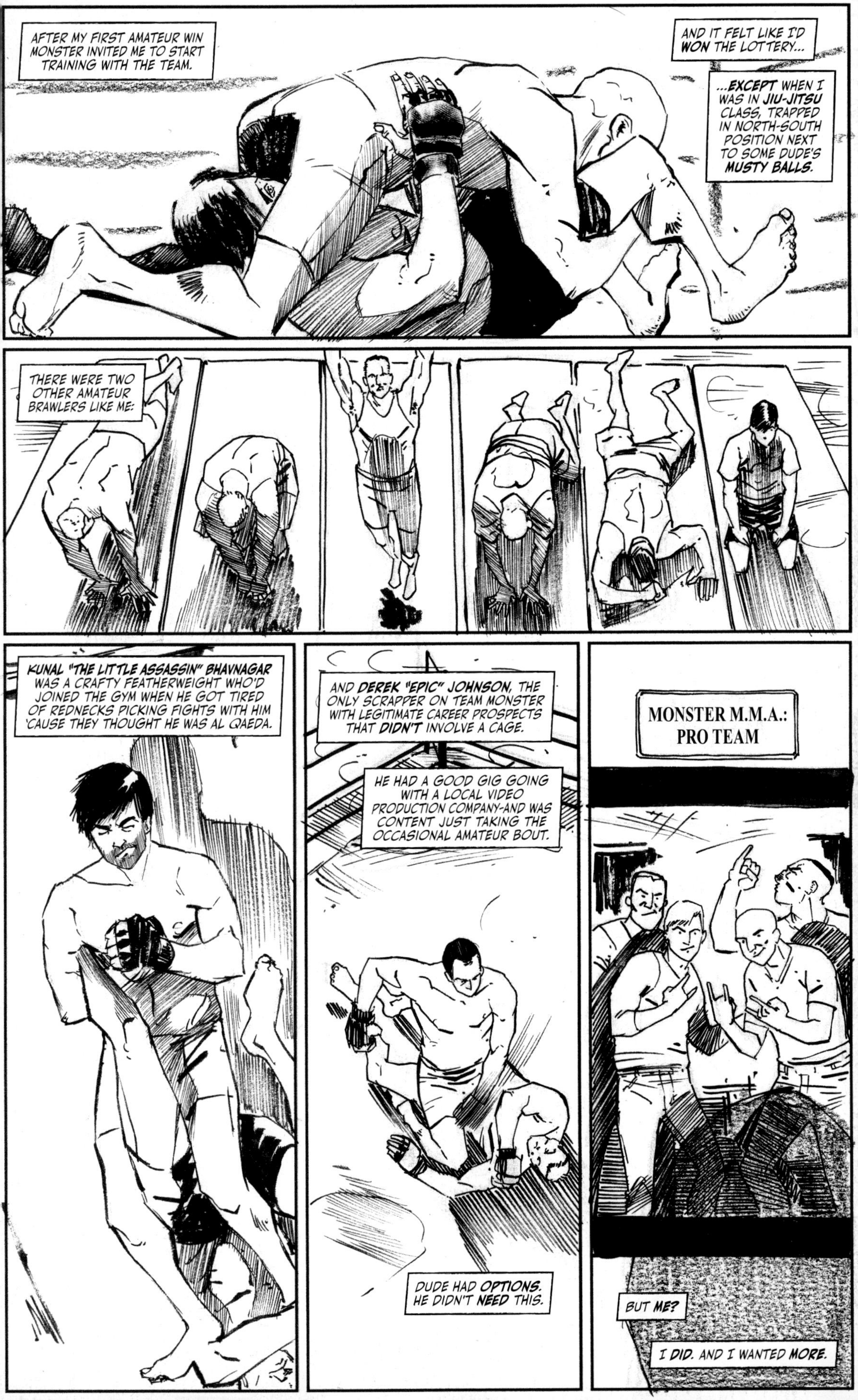
AFTER MY FIRST AMATEUR WIN MONSTER INVITED ME TO START TRAINING WITH THE TEAM.
AND IT FELT LIKE I'D WON THE LOTTERY...
...EXCEPT WHEN I WAS IN JIU-JITSU CLASS, TRAPPED IN NORTH-SOUTH POSITION NEXT TO SOME DUDE'S MUSTY BALLS.
THERE WERE TWO OTHER AMATEUR BRAWLERS LIKE ME:
KUNAL "THE LITTLE ASSASSIN" BHAVNAGAR WAS A CRAFTY FEATHERWEIGHT WHO'D JOINED THE GYM WHEN HE GOT TIRED OF REDNECKS PICKING FIGHTS WITH HIM 'CAUSE THEY THOUGHT HE WAS AL QAEDA.
AND DEREK "EPIC" JOHNSON, THE ONLY SCRAPPER ON TEAM MONSTER WITH LEGITIMATE CAREER PROSPECTS THAT DIDN'T INVOLVE A CAGE.
HE HAD A GOOD GIG GOING WITH A LOCAL VIDEO PRODUCTION COMPANY-AND WAS CONTENT JUST TAKING THE OCCASIONAL AMATEUR BOUT.
DUDE HAD OPTIONS. HE DIDN'T NEED THIS.
MONSTER M.M.A.: PRO TEAM
BUT ME?
I DID. AND I WANTED MORE.

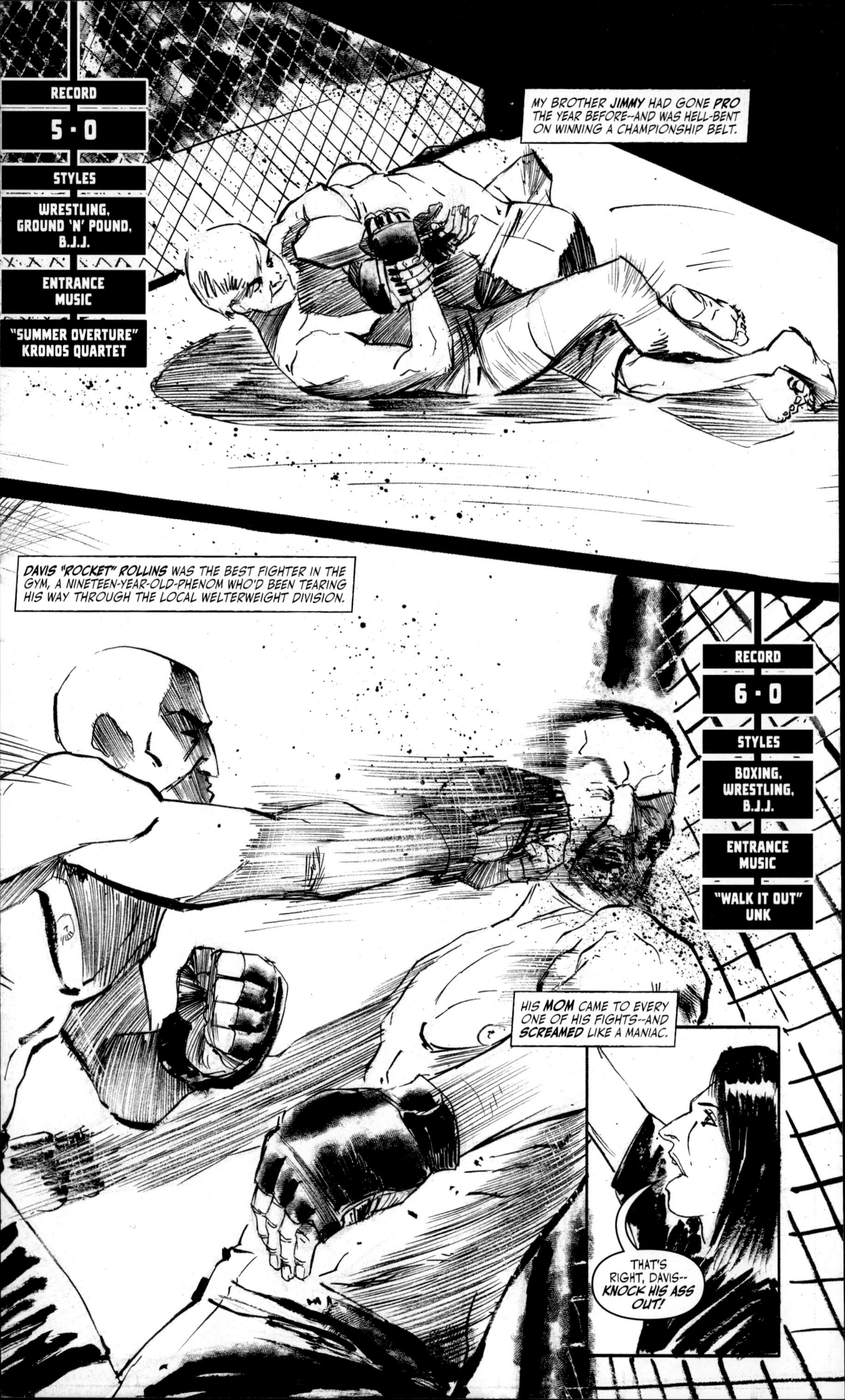

RECORD
5 - 0
STYLES
WRESTLING, GROUND 'N' POUND, B.J.J.
ENTRANCE MUSIC
"SUMMER OVERTURE" KRONOS QUARTET
MY BROTHER JIMMY HAD GONE PRO THE YEAR BEFORE--AND WAS HELL-BENT ON WINNING A CHAMPIONSHIP BELT.
DAVIS "ROCKET" ROLLINS WAS THE BEST FIGHTER IN THE GYM, A NINETEEN-YEAR-OLD-PHENOM WHO'D BEEN TEARING HIS WAY THROUGH THE LOCAL WELTERWEIGHT DIVISION.
RECORD
6 - 0
STYLES
BOXING, WRESTLING, B.J.J.
ENTRANCE MUSIC
"WALK IT OUT" UNK
HIS MOM CAME TO EVERY ONE OF HIS FIGHTS--AND SCREAMED LIKE A MANIAC.
THAT'S RIGHT, DAVIS-- KNOCK HIS ASS OUT!

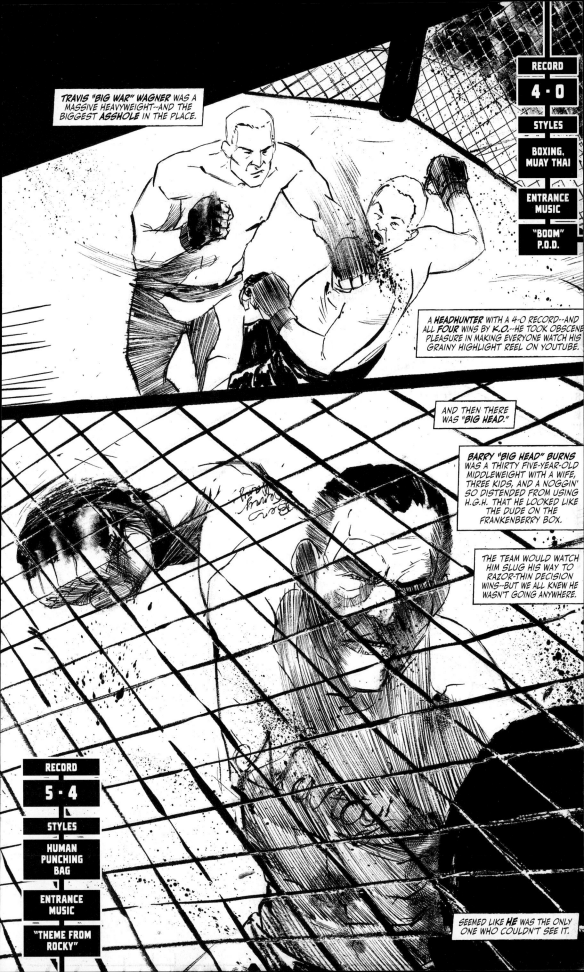

TRAVIS "BIG WAR" WAGNER WAS A MASSIVE HEAVYWEIGHT--AND THE BIGGEST **ASSHOLE** IN THE PLACE.

RECORD

4 - 0

STYLES

BOXING, MUAY THAI

ENTRANCE MUSIC

"BOOM" P.O.D.

A **HEADHUNTER** WITH A 4-0 RECORD--AND ALL **FOUR** WINS BY **K.O.**--HE TOOK OBSCENE PLEASURE IN MAKING EVERYONE WATCH HIS GRAINY HIGHLIGHT REEL ON YOUTUBE.

AND THEN THERE WAS *"BIG HEAD."*

BARRY "BIG HEAD" BURNS WAS A THIRTY FIVE-YEAR-OLD MIDDLEWEIGHT WITH A WIFE, THREE KIDS, AND A NOGGIN' SO DISTENDED FROM USING H.G.H. THAT HE LOOKED LIKE THE DUDE ON THE FRANKENBERRY BOX.

THE TEAM WOULD WATCH HIM SLUG HIS WAY TO RAZOR-THIN DECISION WINS--BUT WE ALL KNEW HE WASN'T GOING ANYWHERE.

RECORD

5 - 4

STYLES

HUMAN PUNCHING BAG

ENTRANCE MUSIC

"THEME FROM ROCKY"

SEEMED LIKE **HE** WAS THE ONLY ONE WHO COULDN'T SEE IT.

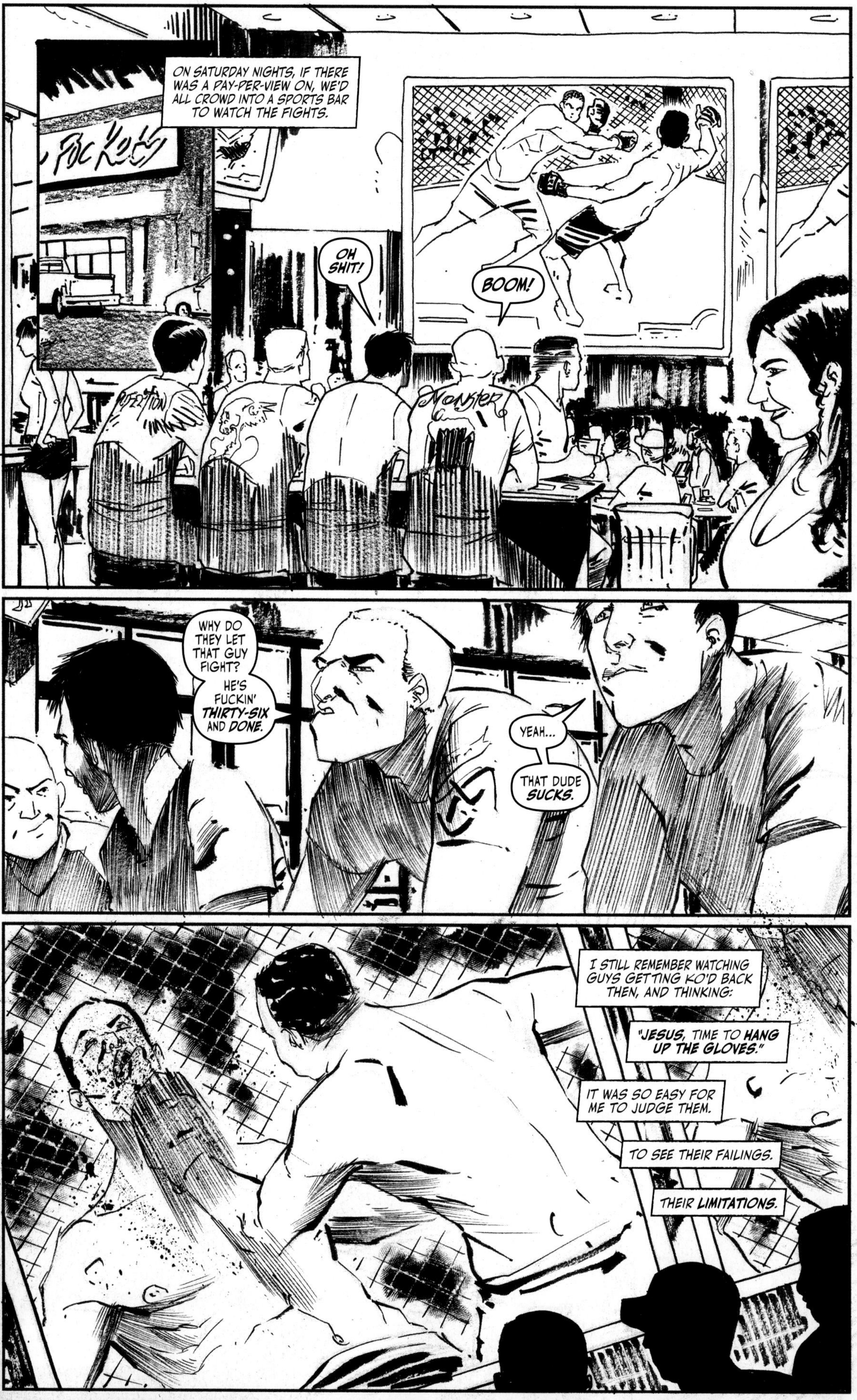

ON SATURDAY NIGHTS, IF THERE WAS A PAY-PER-VIEW ON, WE'D ALL CROWD INTO A SPORTS BAR TO WATCH THE FIGHTS.
OH SHIT!
BOOM!
WHY DO THEY LET THAT GUY FIGHT?
HE'S FUCKIN' THIRTY-SIX AND DONE.
YEAH...
THAT DUDE SUCKS.
I STILL REMEMBER WATCHING GUYS GETTING KO'D BACK THEN, AND THINKING:
"JESUS, TIME TO HANG UP THE GLOVES."
IT WAS SO EASY FOR ME TO JUDGE THEM.
TO SEE THEIR FAILINGS.
THEIR LIMITATIONS.

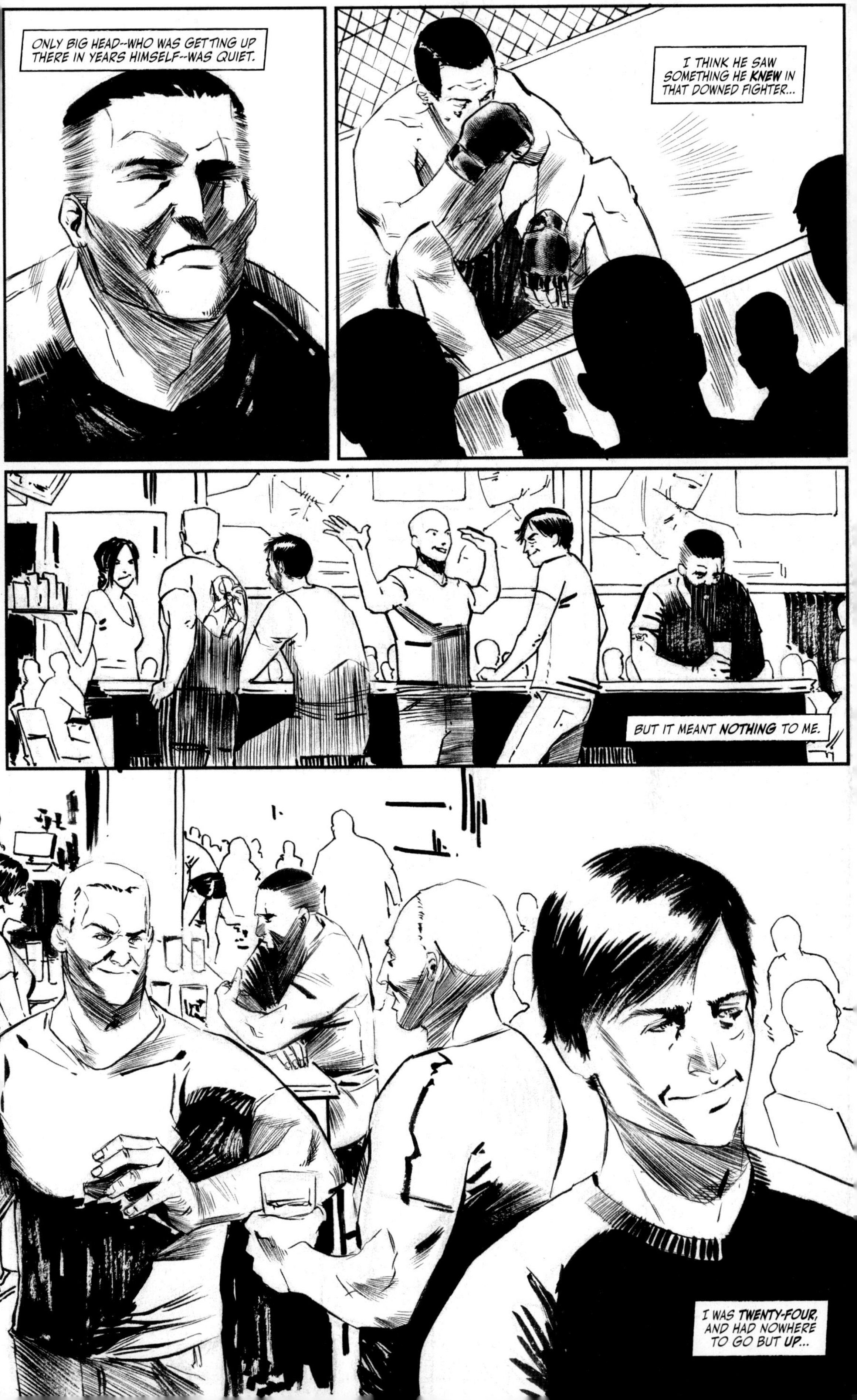
ONLY BIG HEAD--WHO WAS GETTING UP THERE IN YEARS HIMSELF--WAS QUIET.
I THINK HE SAW SOMETHING HE KNEW IN THAT DOWNED FIGHTER...
BUT IT MEANT NOTHING TO ME.
I WAS TWENTY-FOUR, AND HAD NOWHERE TO GO BUT UP...

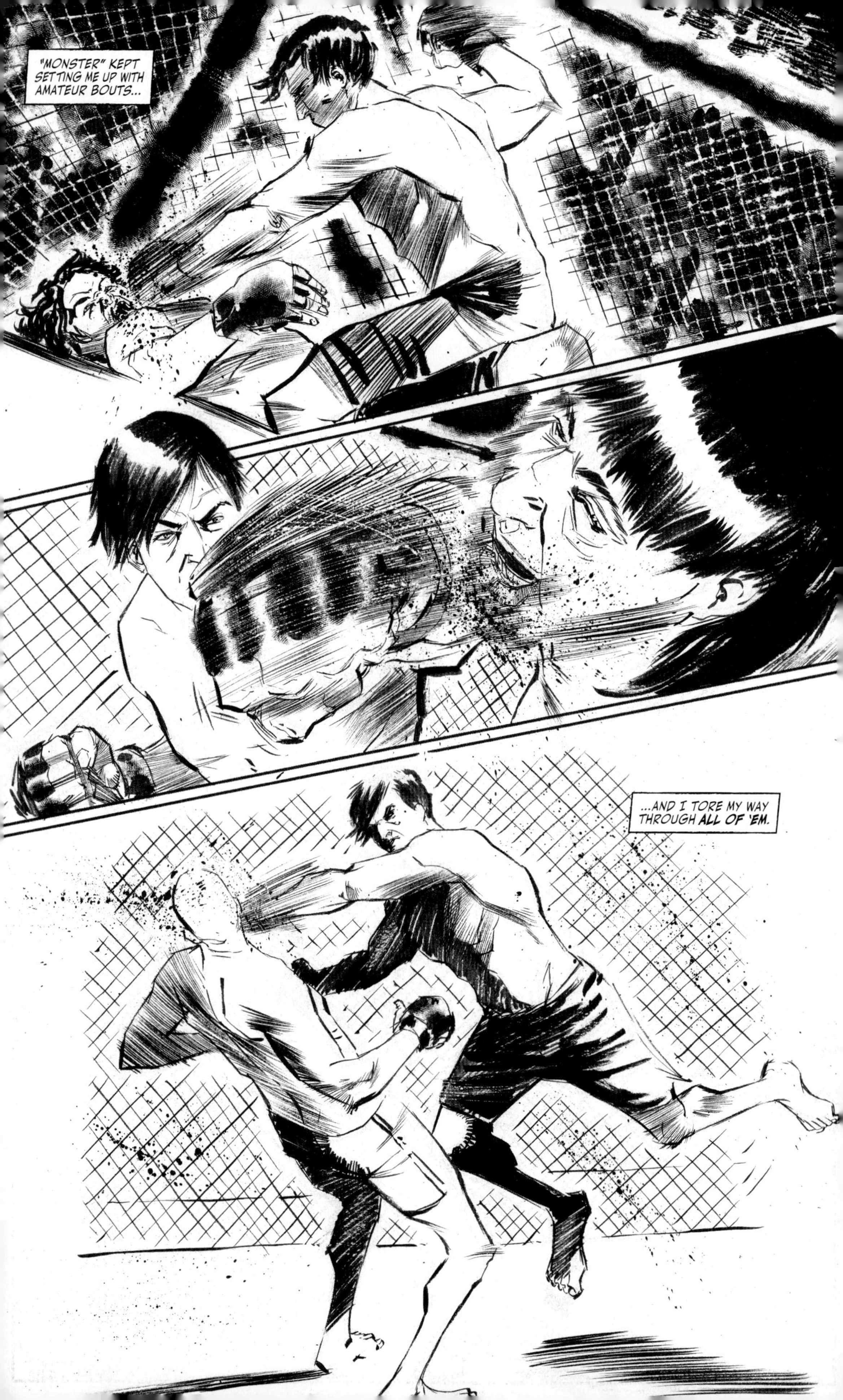
"MONSTER" KEPT SETTING ME UP WITH AMATEUR BOUTS...
...AND I TORE MY WAY THROUGH **ALL OF 'EM**.

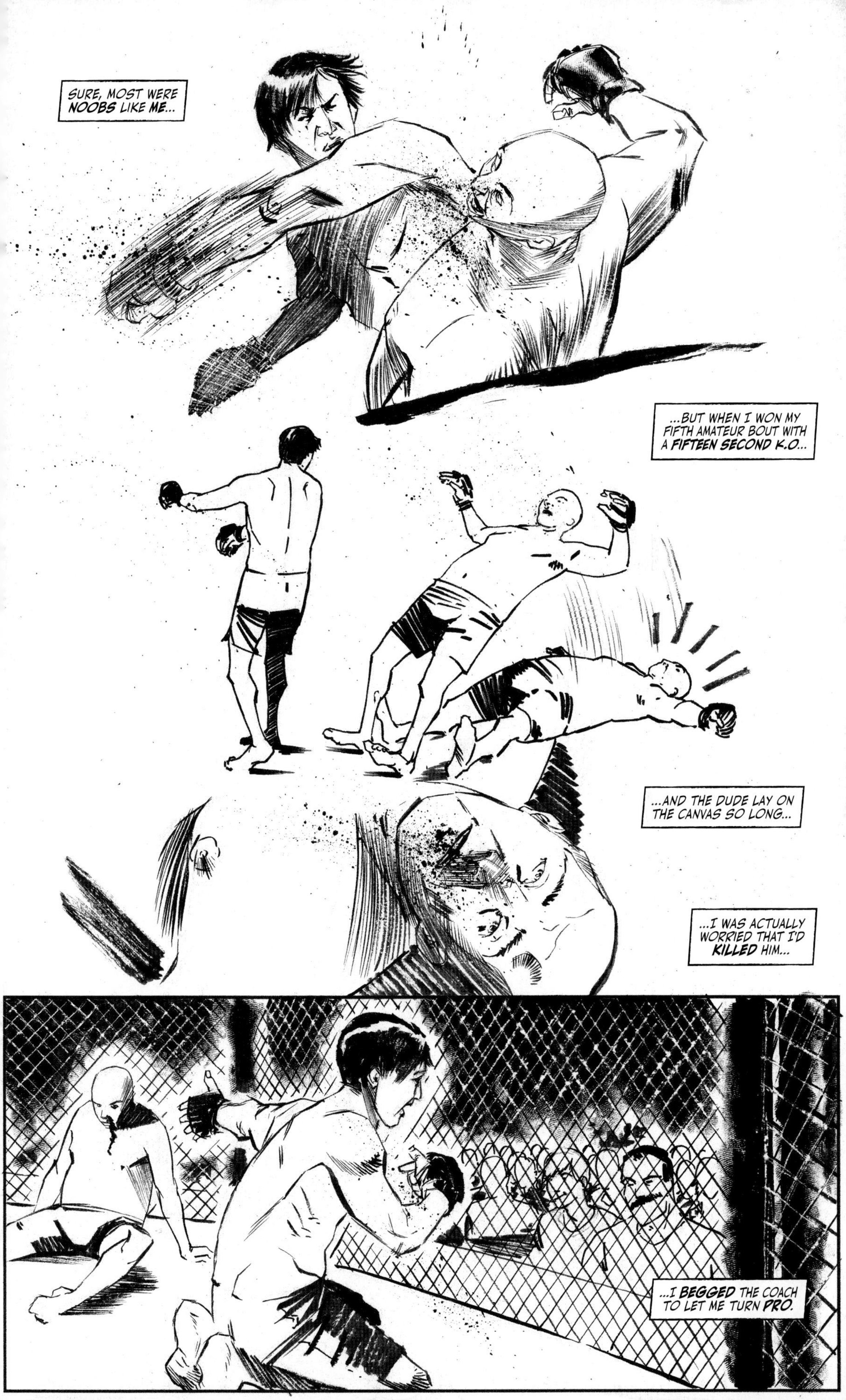
SURE, MOST WERE NOOBS LIKE ME...
...BUT WHEN I WON MY FIFTH AMATEUR BOUT WITH A FIFTEEN SECOND K.O...
...AND THE DUDE LAY ON THE CANVAS SO LONG...
...I WAS ACTUALLY WORRIED THAT I'D KILLED HIM...
...I BEGGED THE COACH TO LET ME TURN PRO.

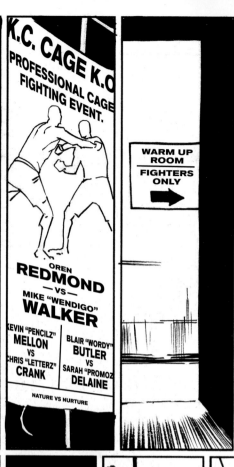

K.C. CAGE K.O.

PROFESSIONAL CAGE FIGHTING EVENT.

OREN
REDMOND
— VS —
MIKE "WENDIGO"
WALKER

KEVIN "PENCILZ"
MELLON
VS
CHRIS "LETTERZ"
CRANK

BLAIR "WORDY"
BUTLER
VS
SARAH "PROMOZ"
DELAINE

NATURE VS NURTURE

WARM UP
ROOM

FIGHTERS
ONLY

➡

MONSTER
MMA

MONSTER
MMA

MONST
MM

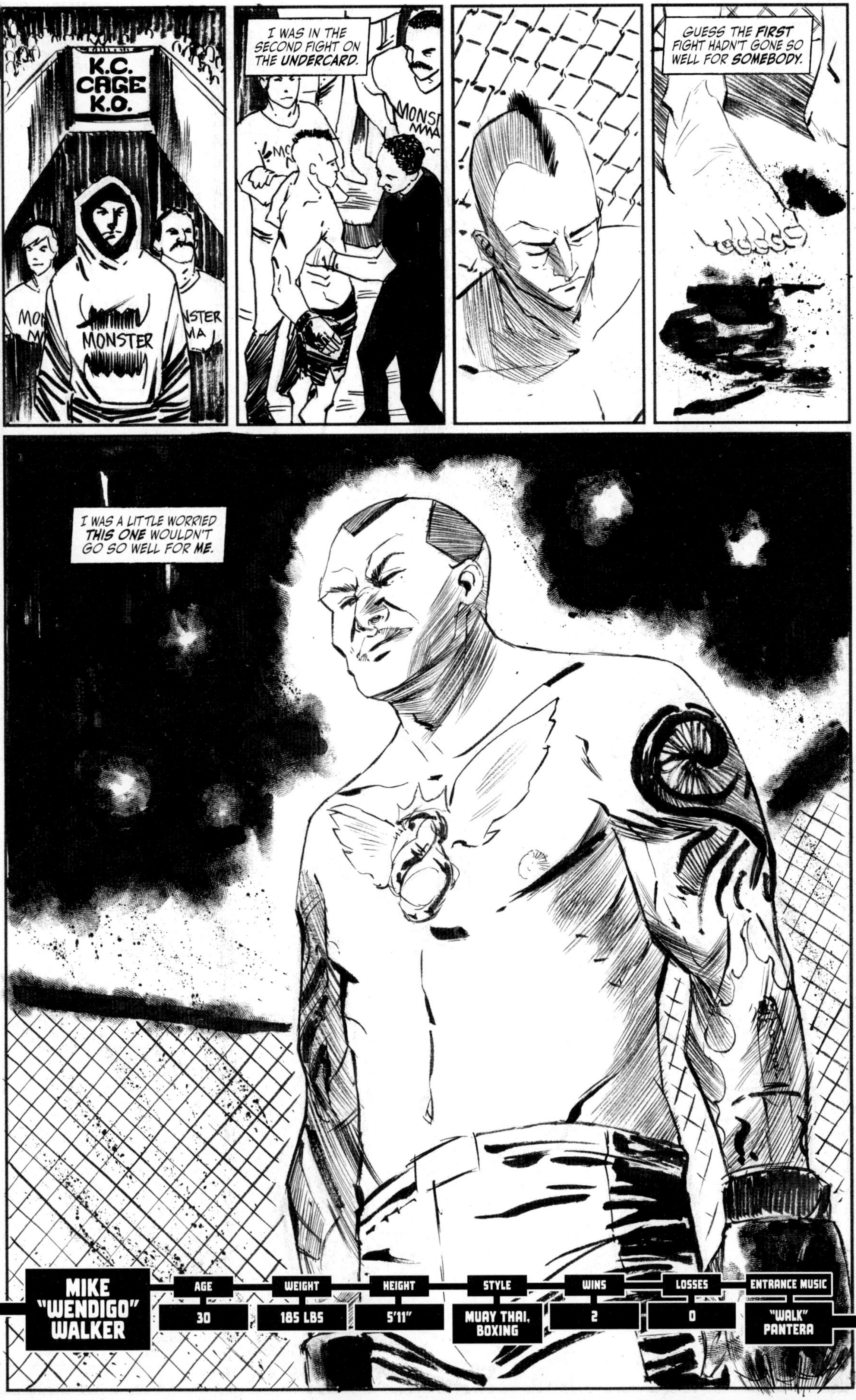
K.C. CAGE K.O.
MONSTER
MONSTER MMA
I WAS IN THE SECOND FIGHT ON THE **UNDERCARD**.
MONSTER MMA
GUESS THE **FIRST** FIGHT HADN'T GONE SO WELL FOR **SOMEBODY**.
I WAS A LITTLE WORRIED **THIS ONE** WOULDN'T GO SO WELL FOR **ME**.
MIKE "WENDIGO" WALKER
AGE 30
WEIGHT 185 LBS
HEIGHT 5'11"
STYLE MUAY THAI, BOXING
WINS 2
LOSSES 0
ENTRANCE MUSIC "WALK" PANTERA

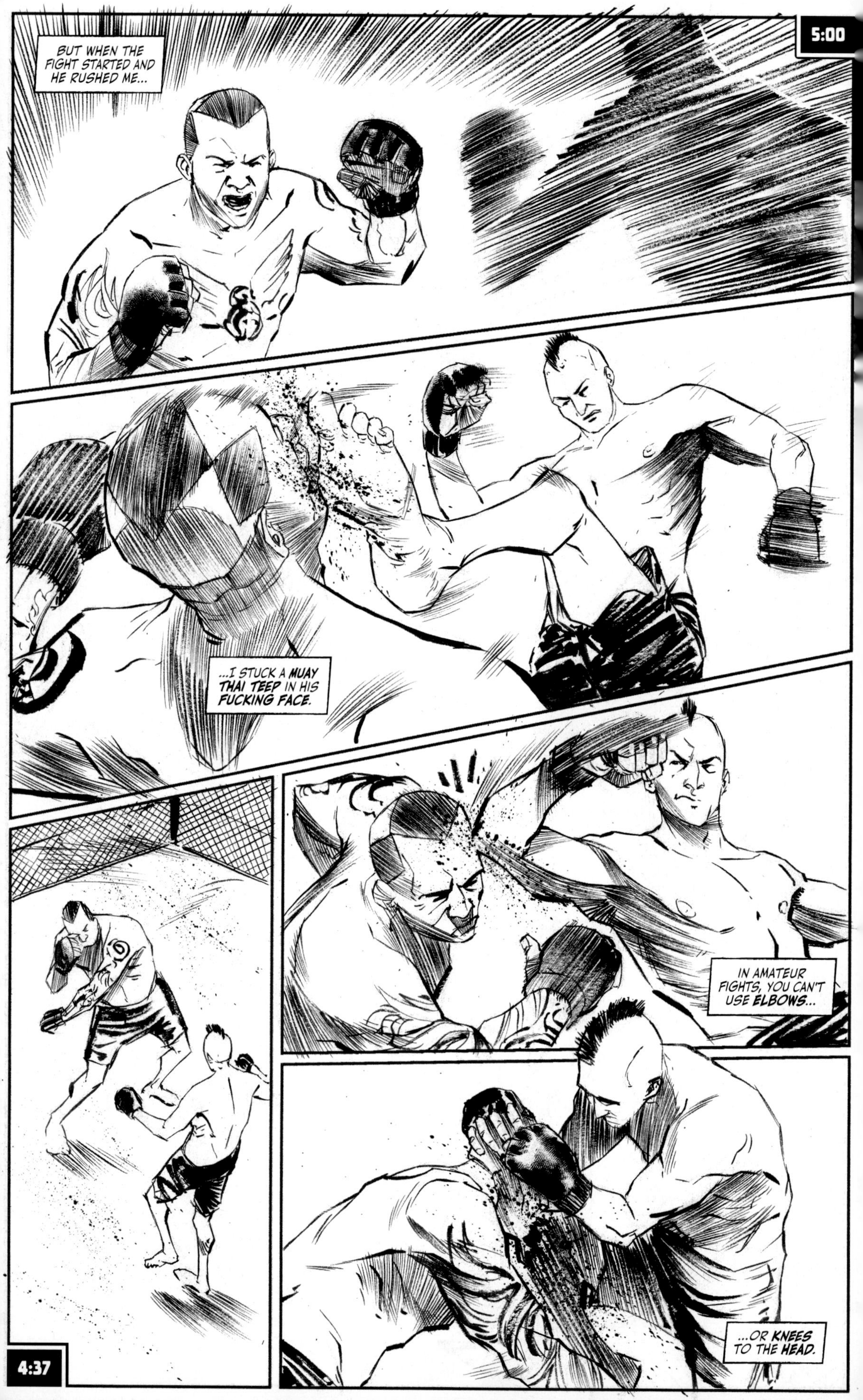
5:00
BUT WHEN THE FIGHT STARTED AND HE RUSHED ME...
...I STUCK A MUAY THAI TEEP IN HIS FUCKING FACE.
IN AMATEUR FIGHTS, YOU CAN'T USE ELBOWS...
...OR KNEES TO THE HEAD.
4:37

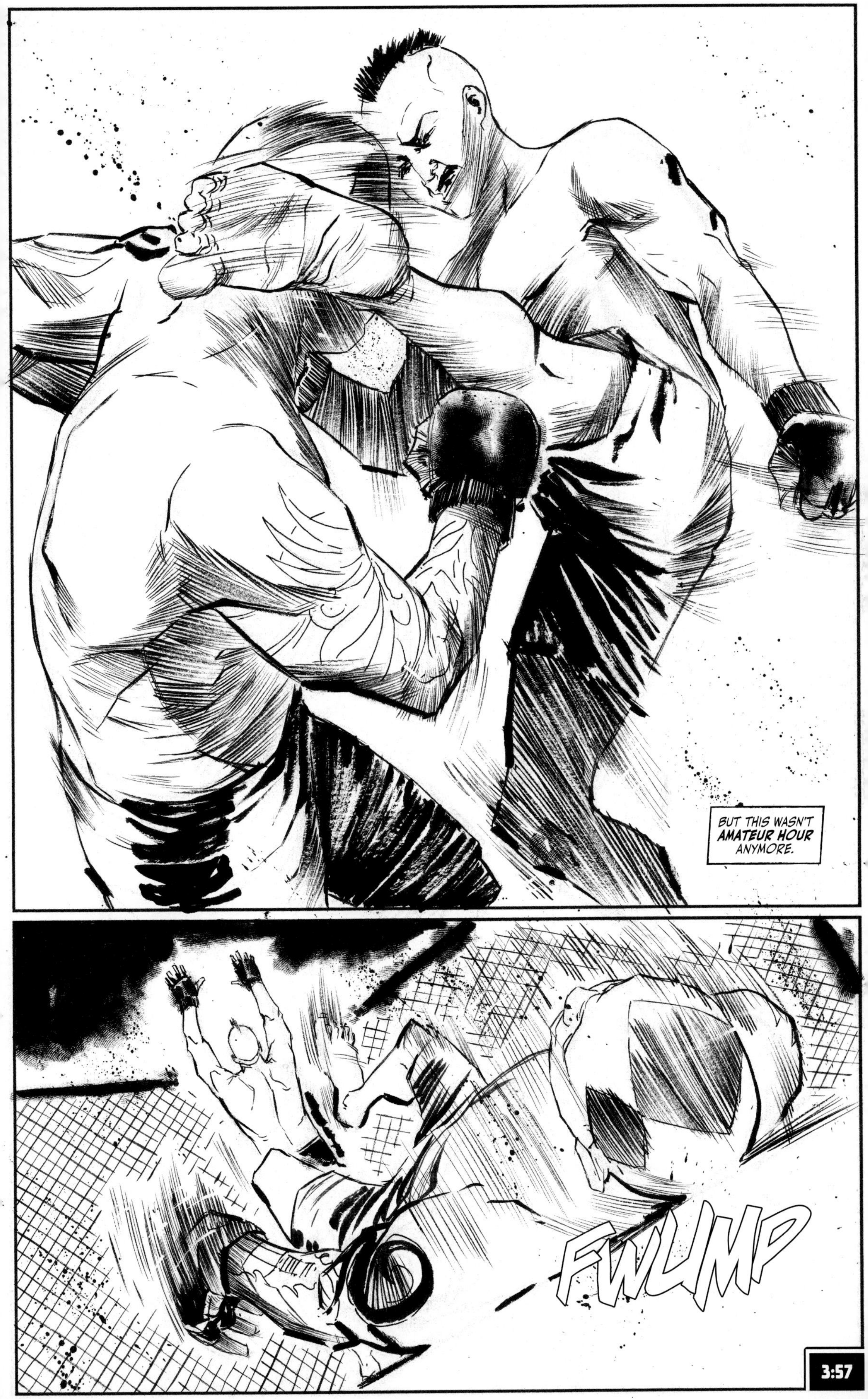
BUT THIS WASN'T **AMATEUR HOUR** ANYMORE.
FWUMP
3:57

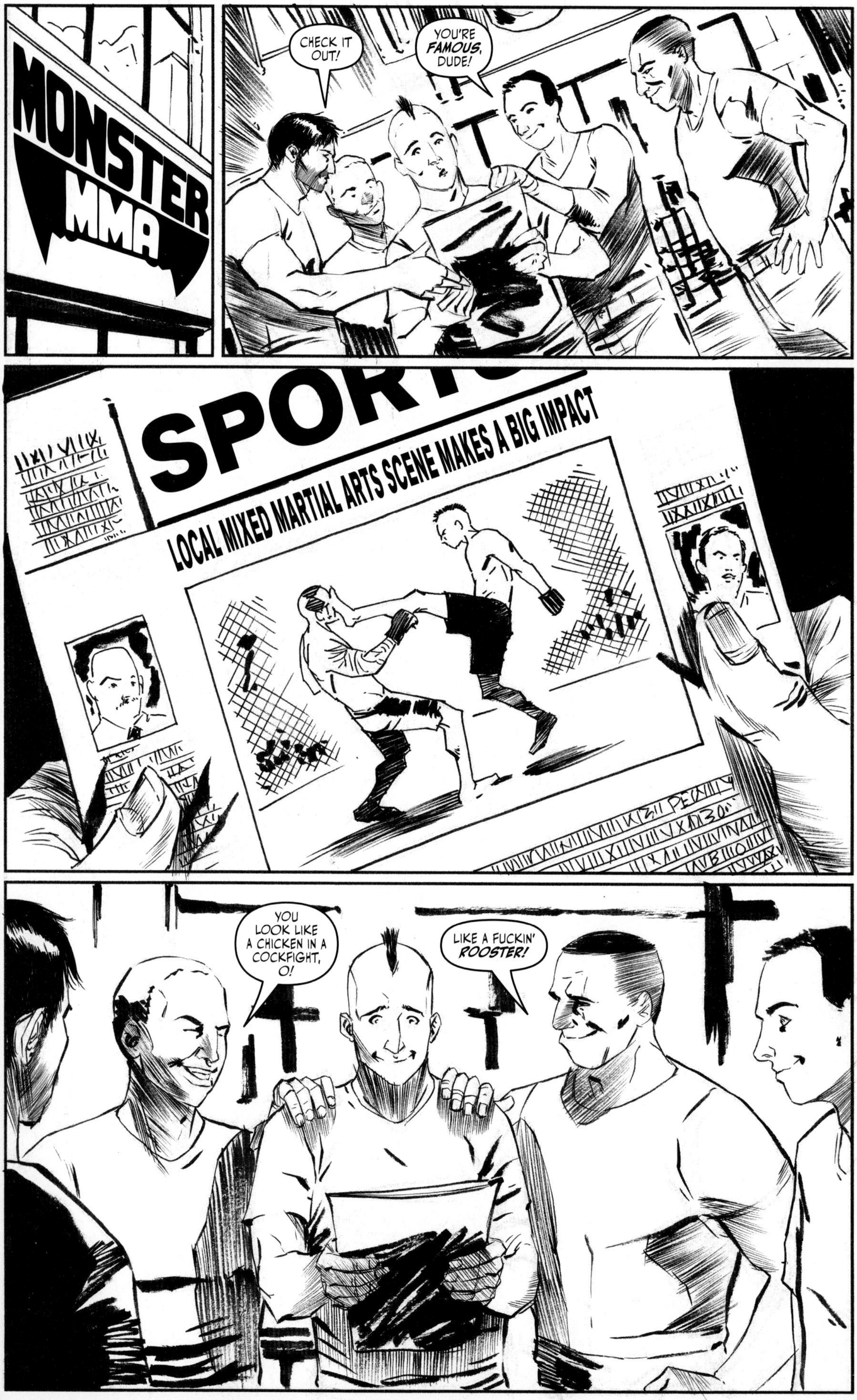
MONSTER MMA
CHECK IT OUT!
YOU'RE FAMOUS, DUDE!
SPORTS
LOCAL MIXED MARTIAL ARTS SCENE MAKES A BIG IMPACT
YOU LOOK LIKE A CHICKEN IN A COCKFIGHT, O!
LIKE A FUCKIN' ROOSTER!

AND THAT WAS *THAT*...

...THE NAME JUST STUCK.

OREN "ROOSTER" **REDMOND**

HOURS
MONDAY - SATURD
12PM - 10PM
SUNDAY
12PM - 6PM

I USED ALL THE MONEY I WON...

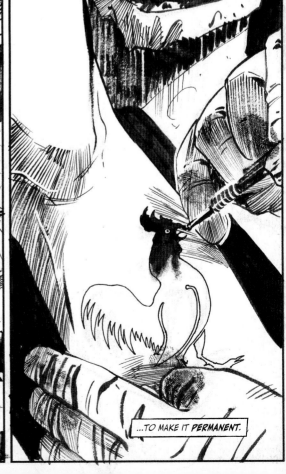

...TO MAKE IT *PERMANENT.*

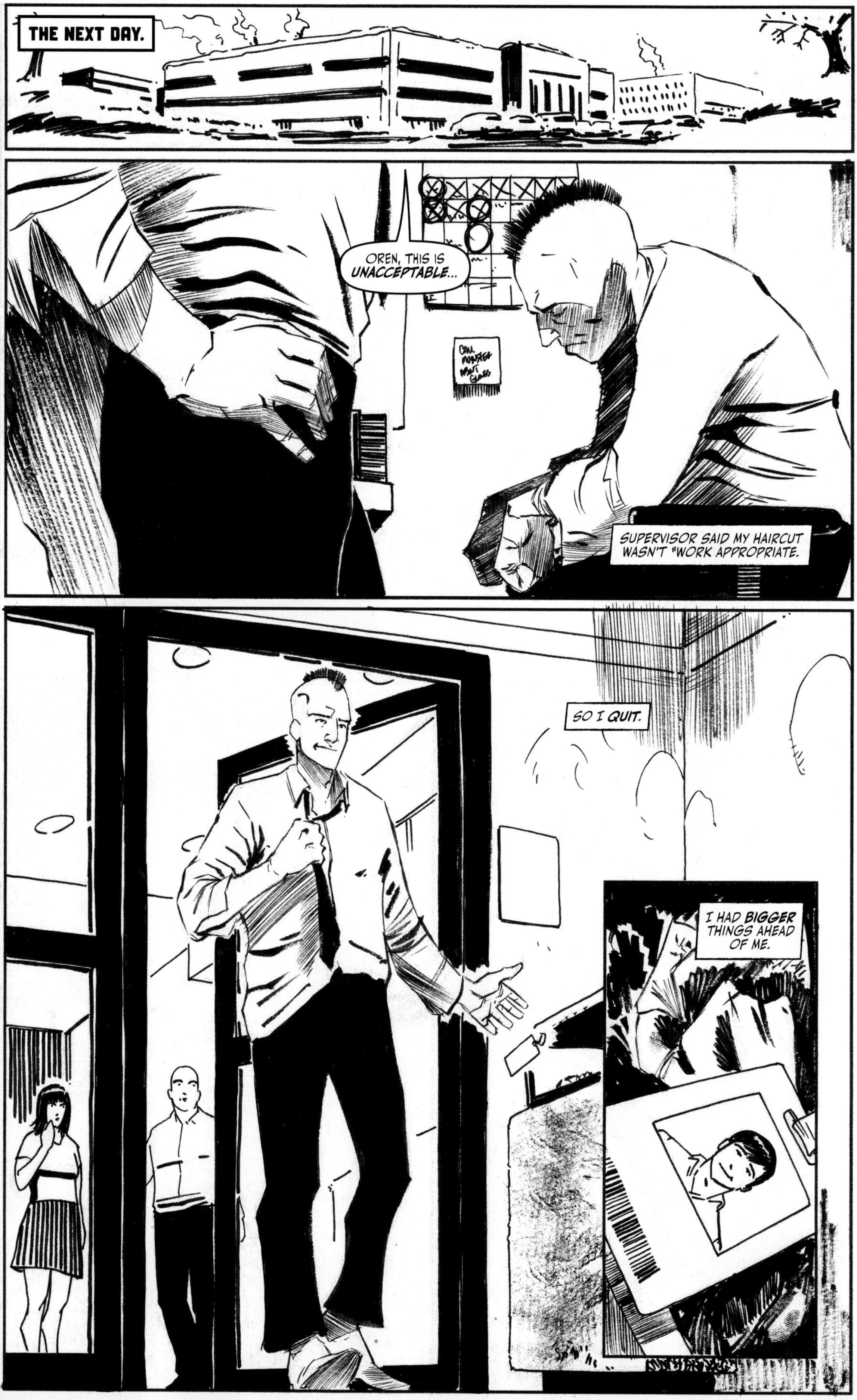
THE NEXT DAY.
OREN, THIS IS UNACCEPTABLE...
SUPERVISOR SAID MY HAIRCUT WASN'T "WORK APPROPRIATE.
SO I QUIT.
I HAD BIGGER THINGS AHEAD OF ME.

WALKING OUT THE DOOR, I KNEW THAT I'D NEVER GO BACK TO BEING A *SHEEP*.

IN THAT MOMENT I HAD A TREMENDOUS FEELING OF *CONVICTION*.

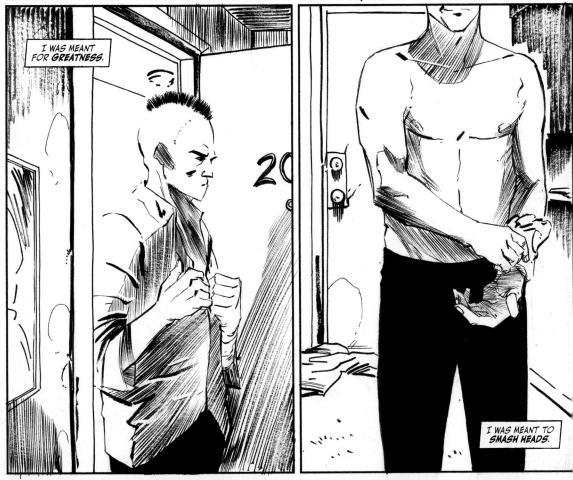

I WAS MEANT FOR *GREATNESS*.

I WAS MEANT TO *SMASH HEADS*.

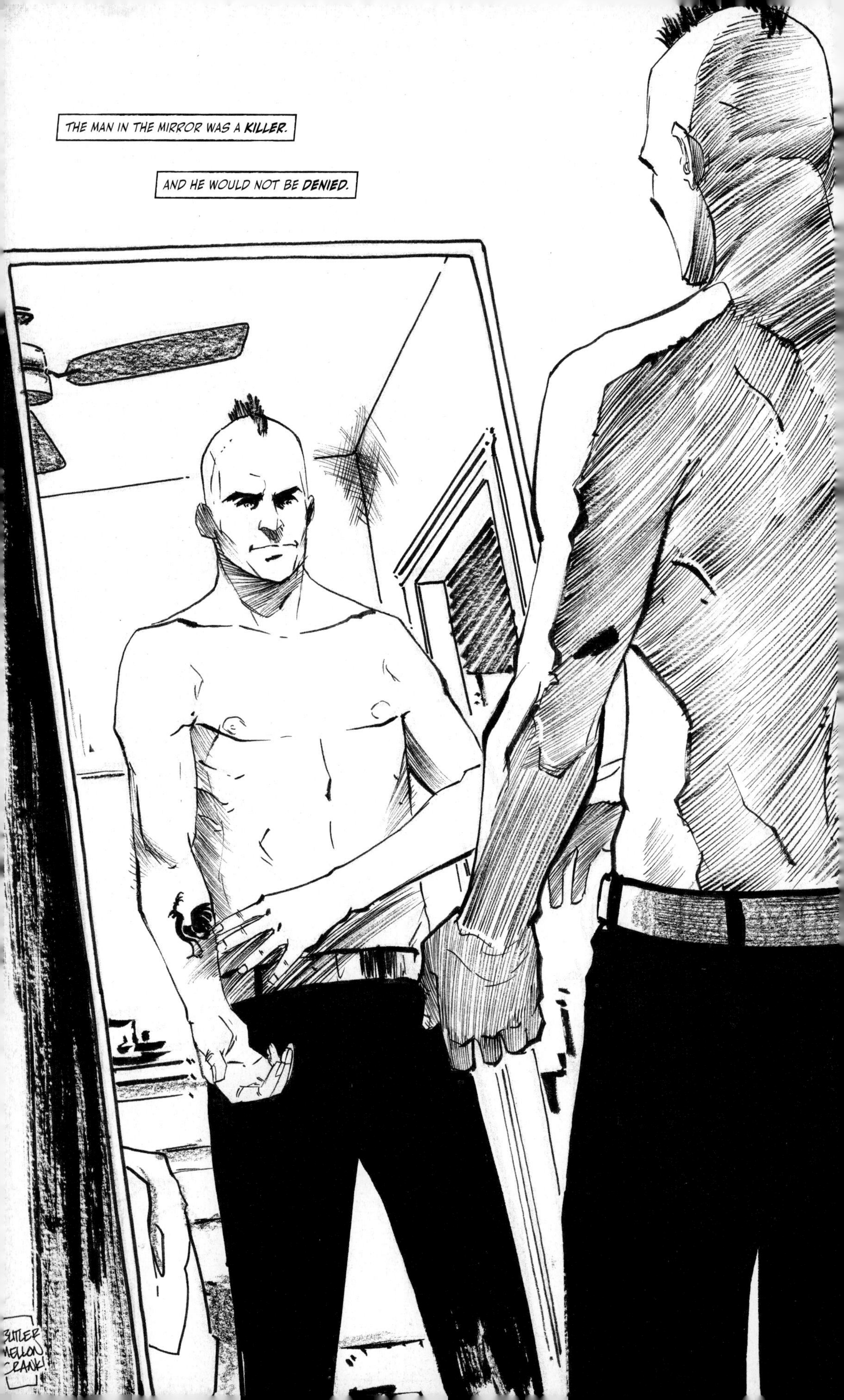
THE MAN IN THE MIRROR WAS A KILLER.
AND HE WOULD NOT BE DENIED.
BUTLER MELLON CRANK!

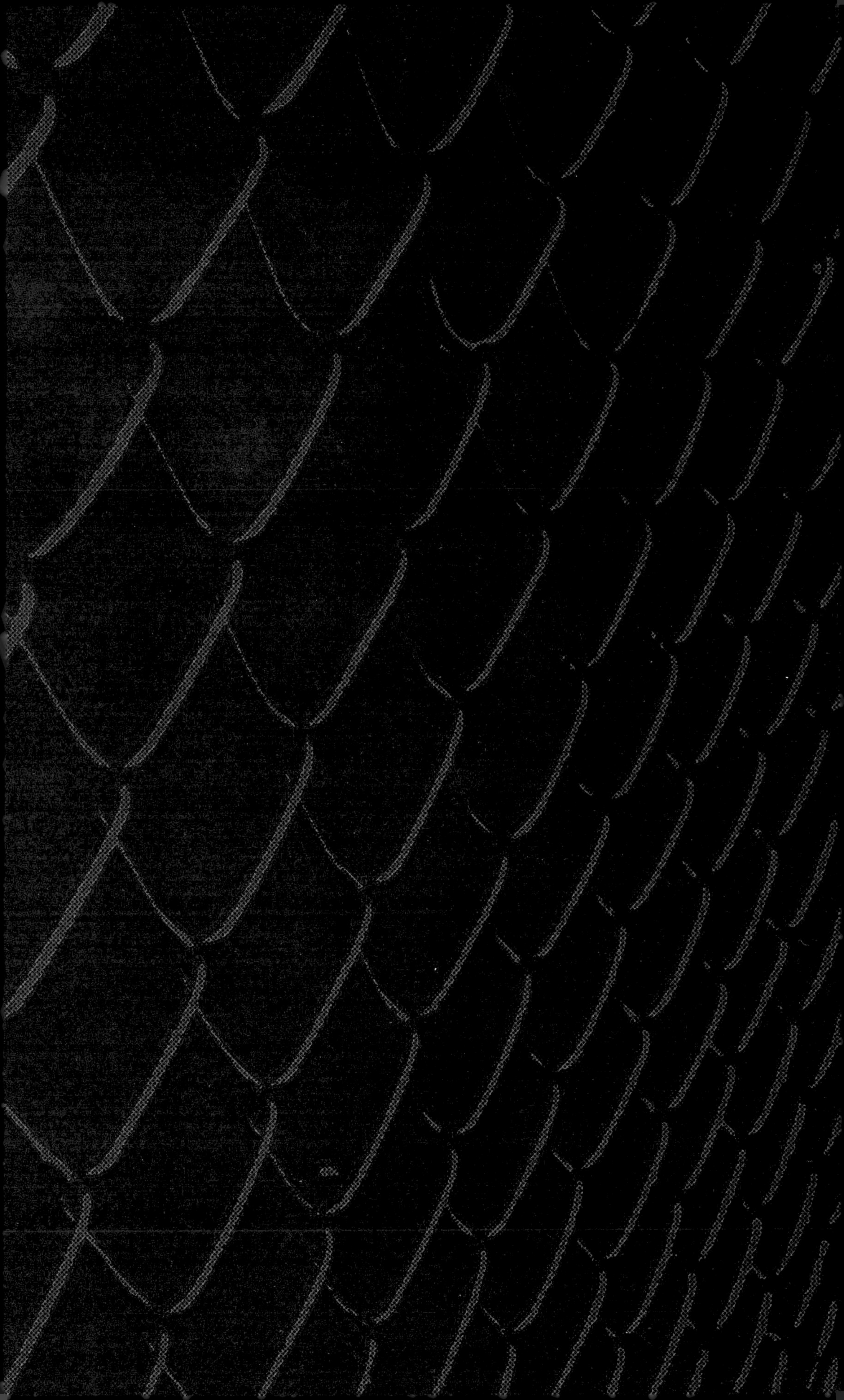

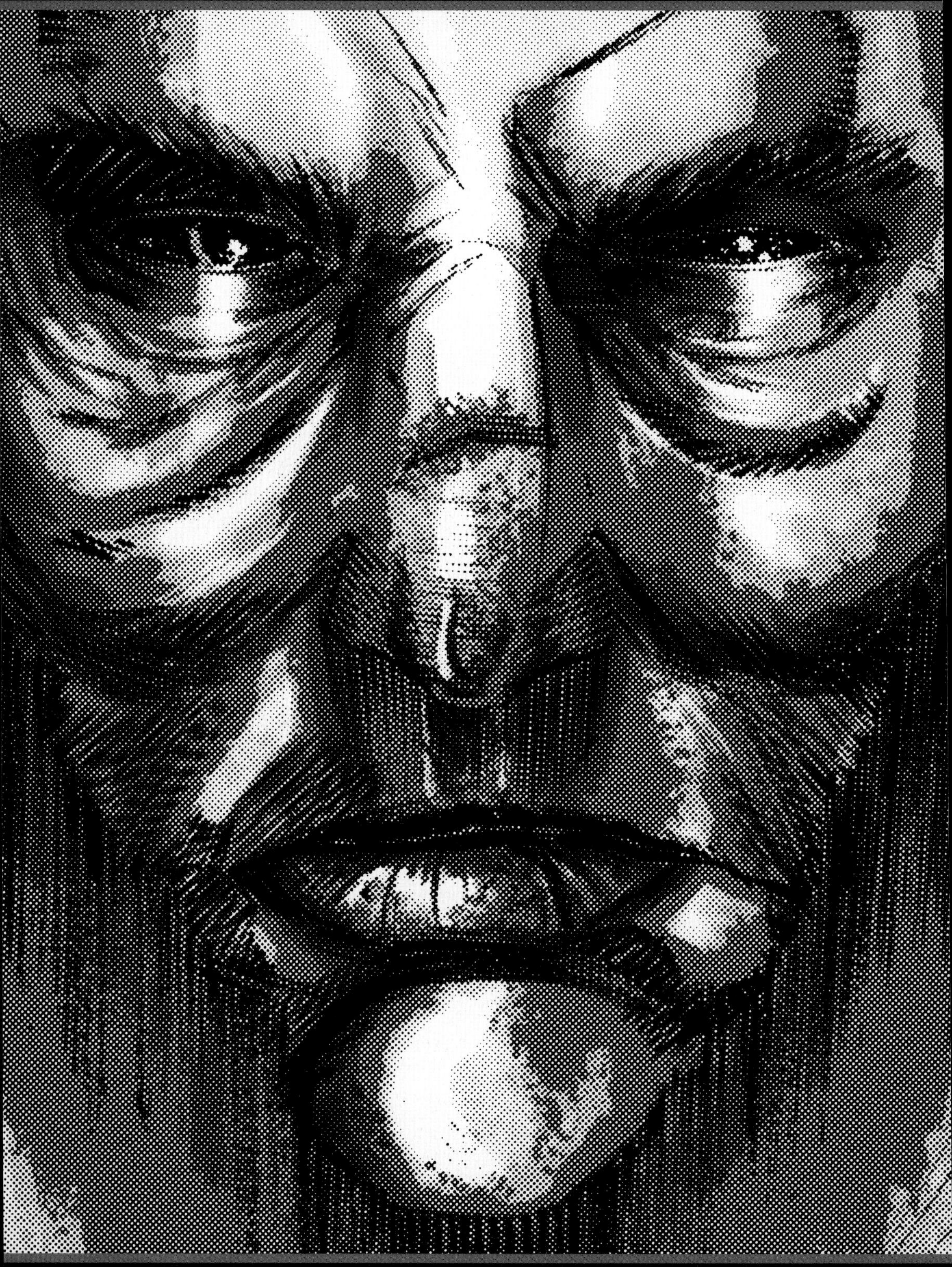

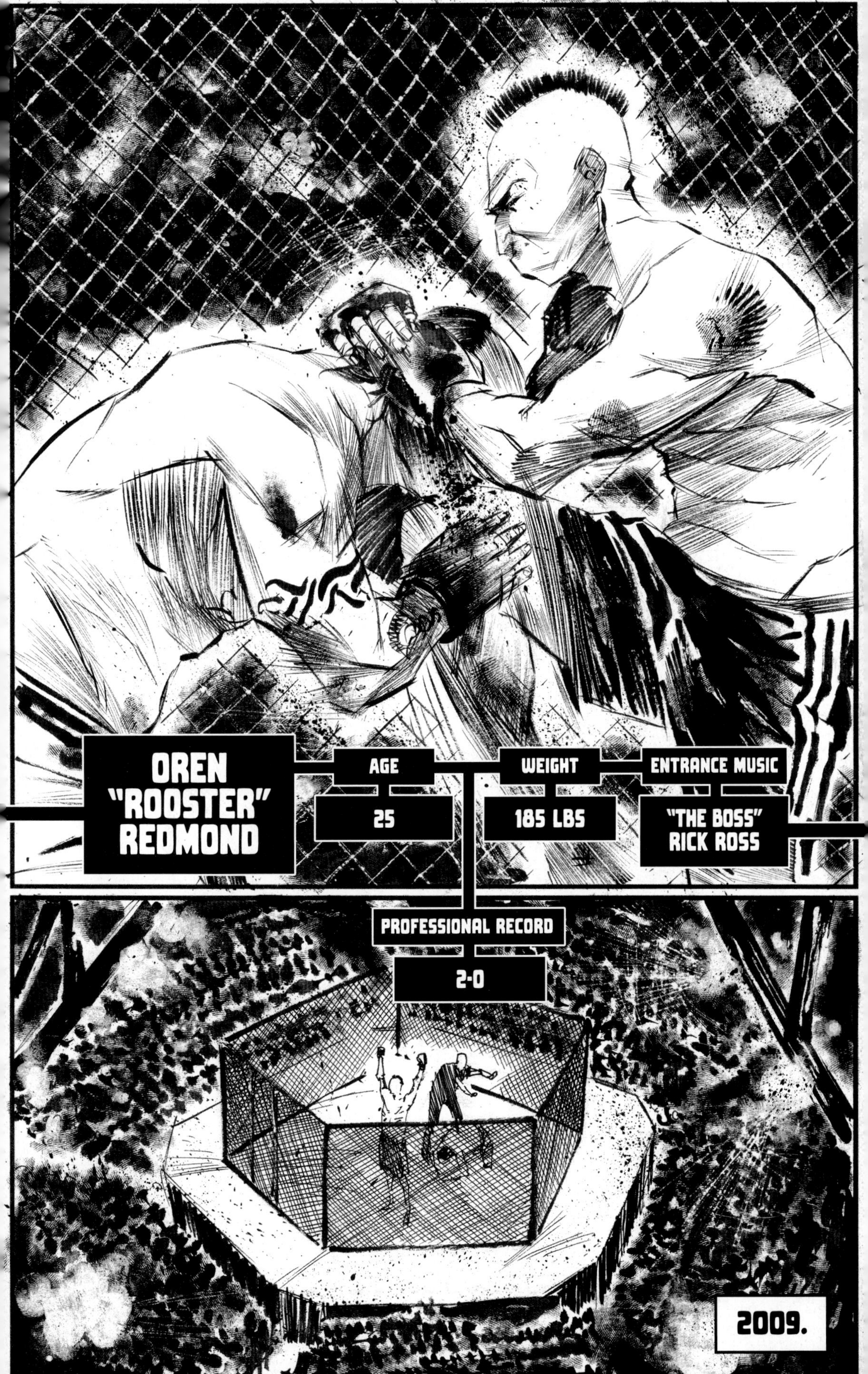
OREN "ROOSTER" REDMOND
AGE
25
WEIGHT
185 LBS
ENTRANCE MUSIC
"THE BOSS" RICK ROSS
PROFESSIONAL RECORD
2-0
2009.

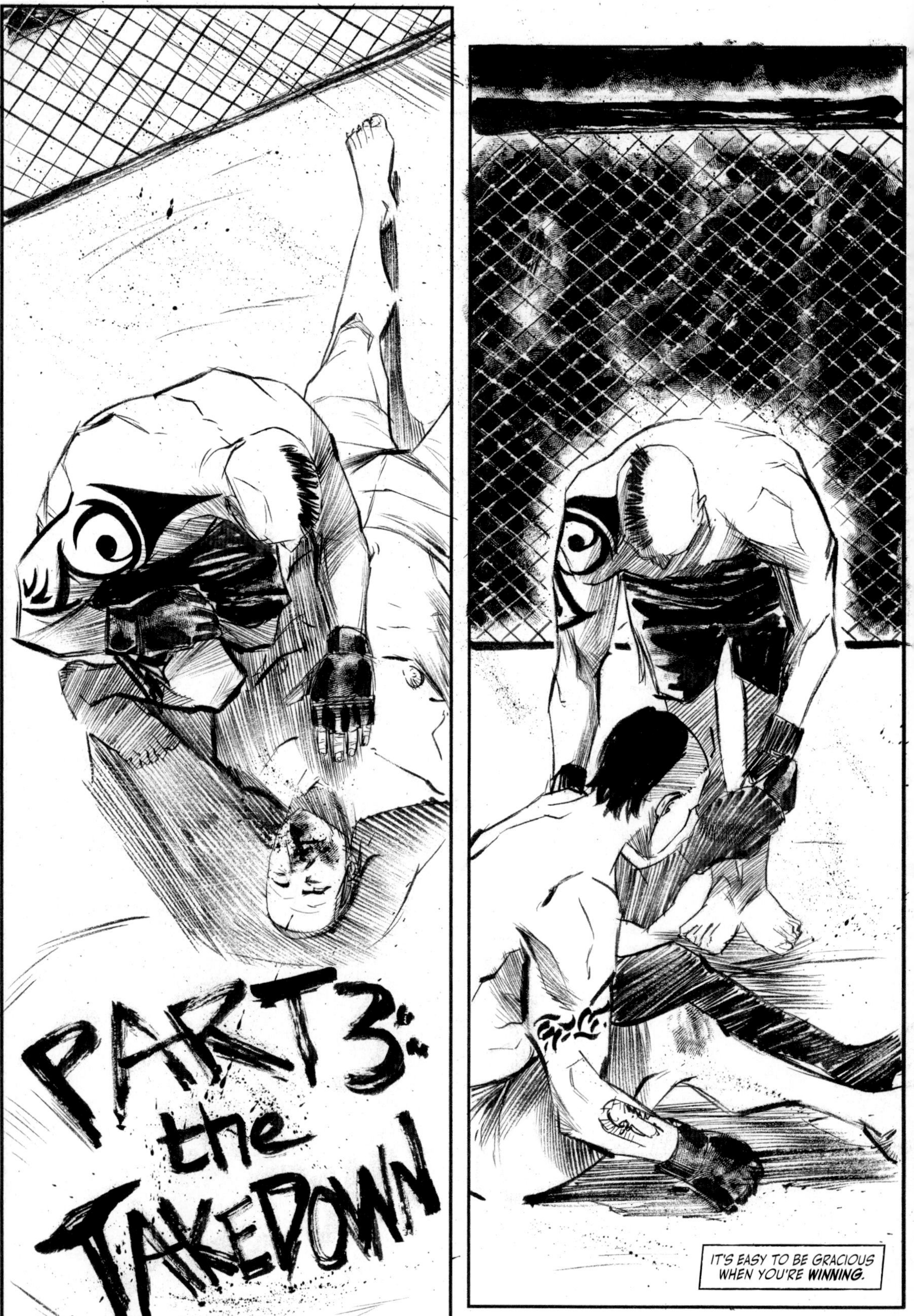
PART 3: the TAKEDOWN
IT'S EASY TO BE GRACIOUS WHEN YOU'RE **WINNING**.

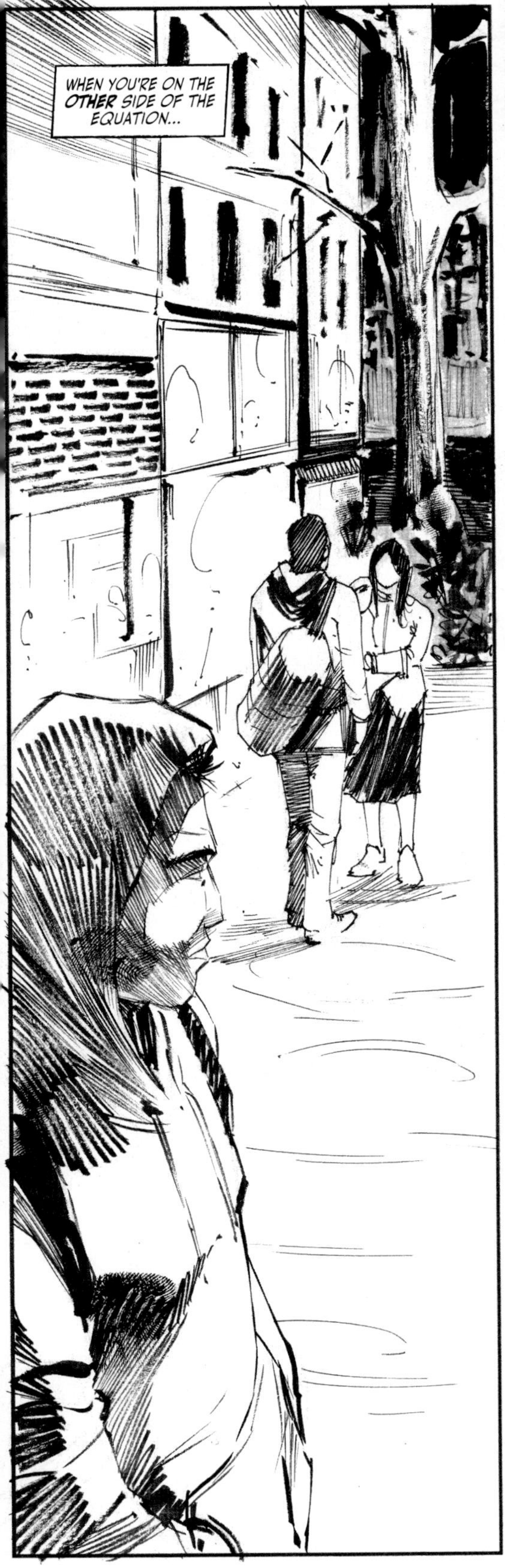
WHEN YOU'RE ON THE OTHER SIDE OF THE EQUATION...

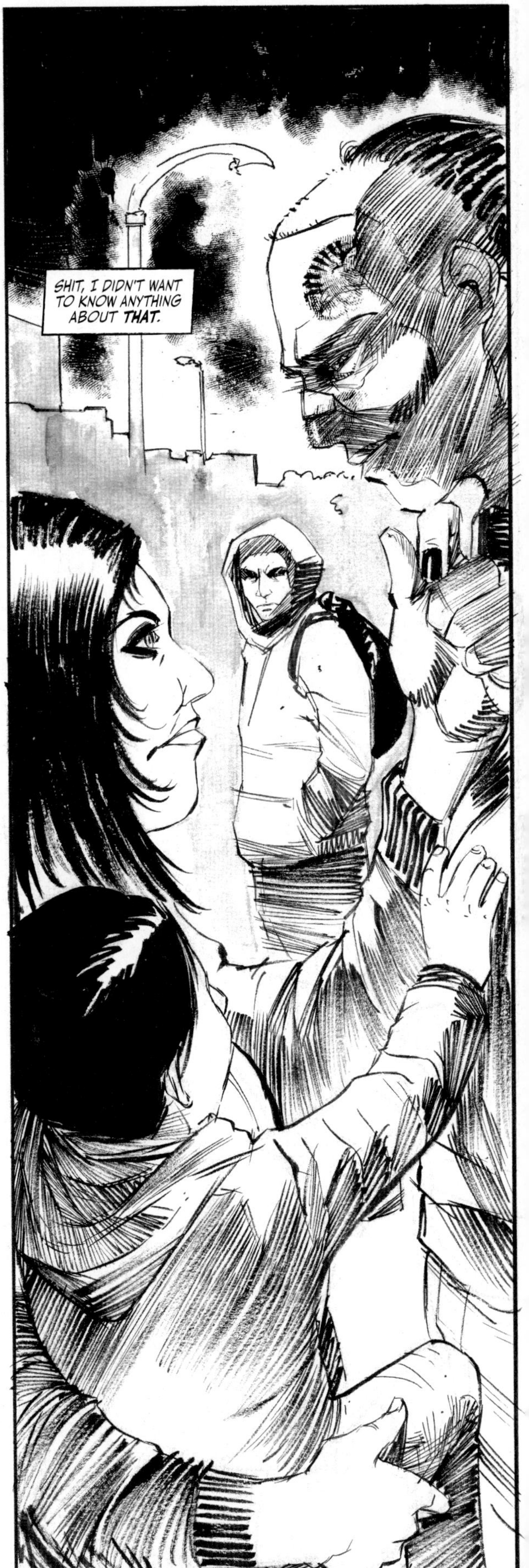
SHIT, I DIDN'T WANT TO KNOW ANYTHING ABOUT THAT.

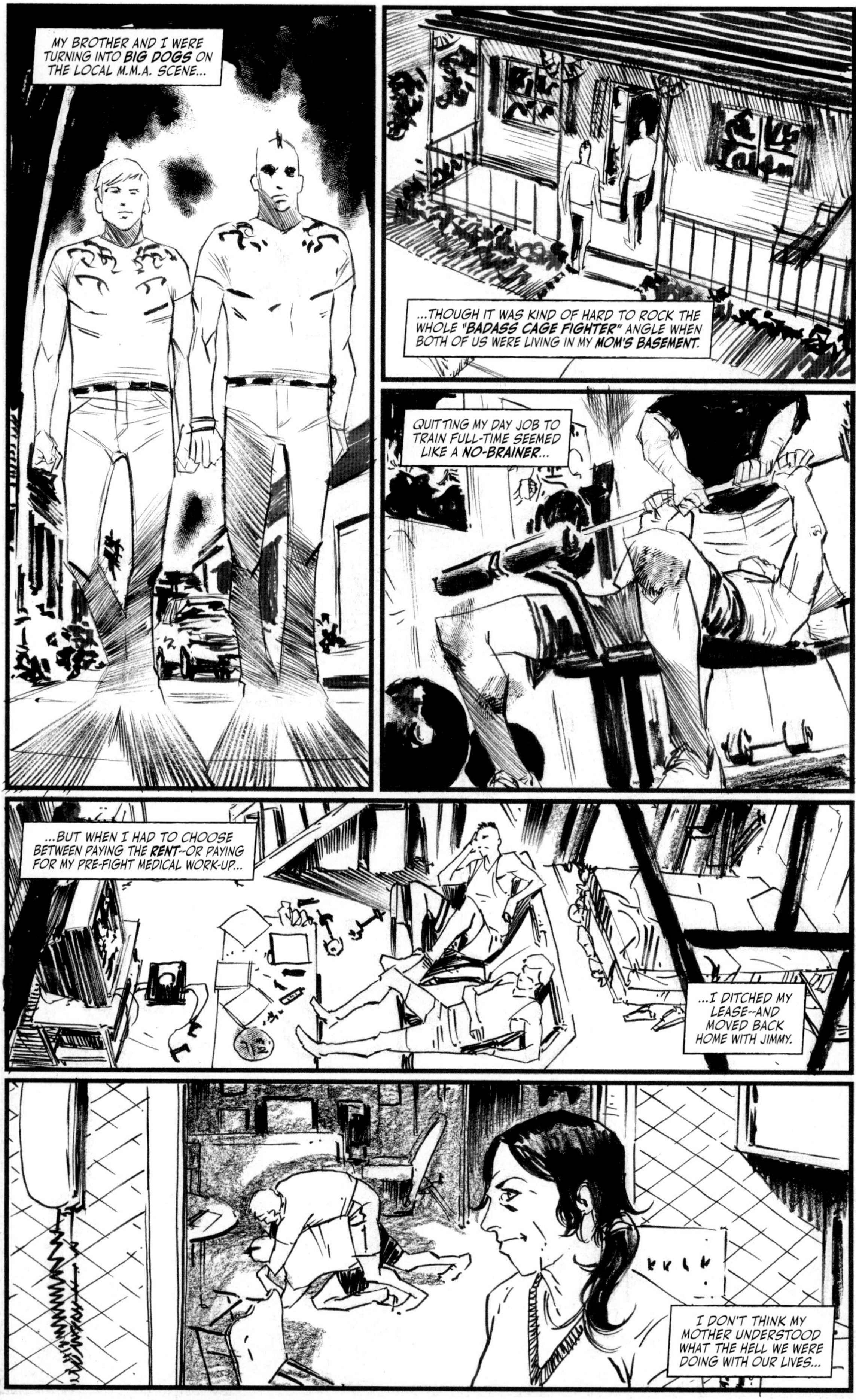
MY BROTHER AND I WERE TURNING INTO BIG DOGS ON THE LOCAL M.M.A. SCENE...
...THOUGH IT WAS KIND OF HARD TO ROCK THE WHOLE "BADASS CAGE FIGHTER" ANGLE WHEN BOTH OF US WERE LIVING IN MY MOM'S BASEMENT.
QUITTING MY DAY JOB TO TRAIN FULL-TIME SEEMED LIKE A NO-BRAINER...
...BUT WHEN I HAD TO CHOOSE BETWEEN PAYING THE RENT--OR PAYING FOR MY PRE-FIGHT MEDICAL WORK-UP...
...I DITCHED MY LEASE--AND MOVED BACK HOME WITH JIMMY.
I DON'T THINK MY MOTHER UNDERSTOOD WHAT THE HELL WE WERE DOING WITH OUR LIVES...

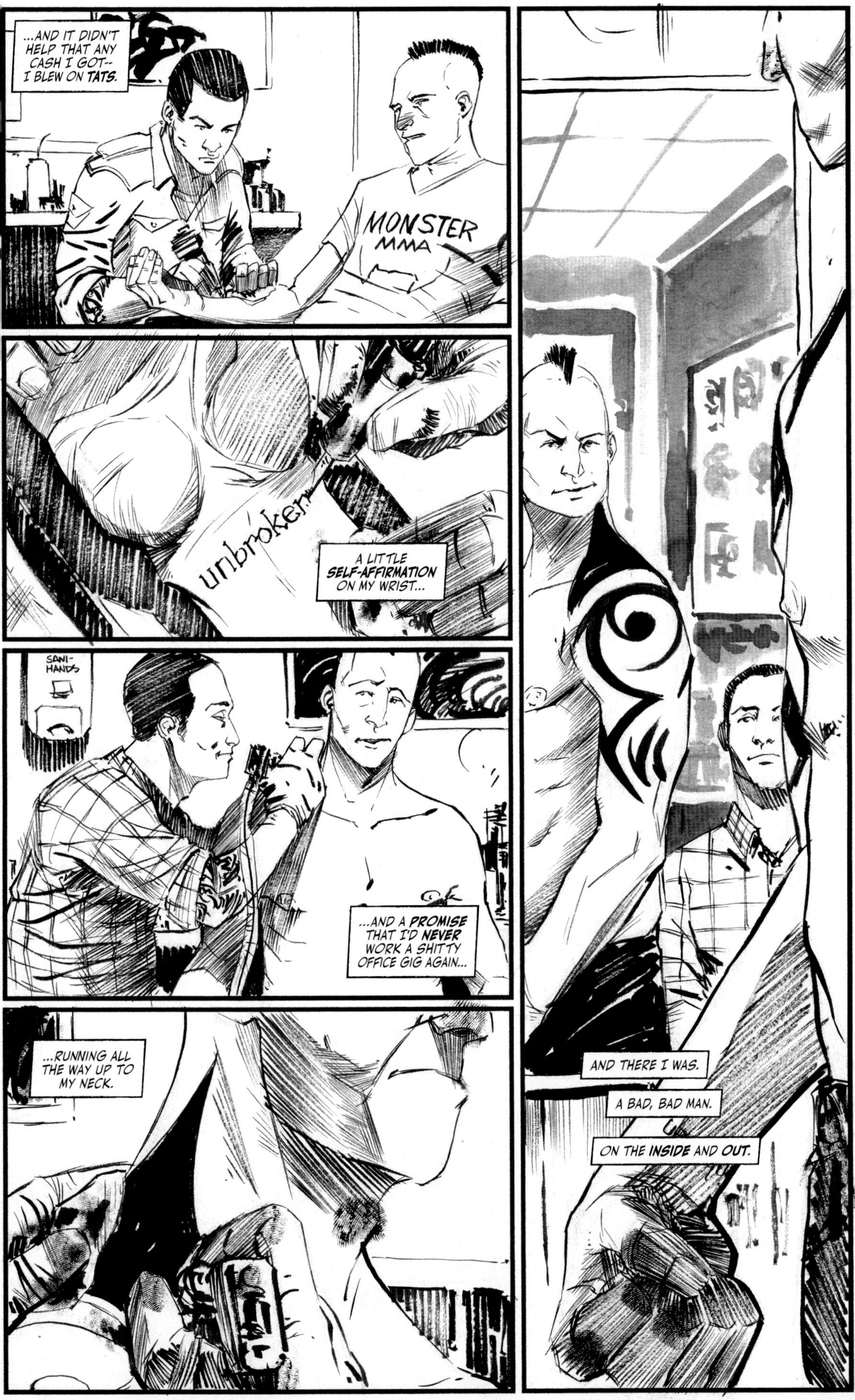
...AND IT DIDN'T HELP THAT ANY CASH I GOT-- I BLEW ON TATS.
MONSTER MMA
unbroken
A LITTLE SELF-AFFIRMATION ON MY WRIST...
SANI-HANDS
...AND A PROMISE THAT I'D NEVER WORK A SHITTY OFFICE GIG AGAIN...
...RUNNING ALL THE WAY UP TO MY NECK.
AND THERE I WAS.
A BAD, BAD MAN.
ON THE INSIDE AND OUT.

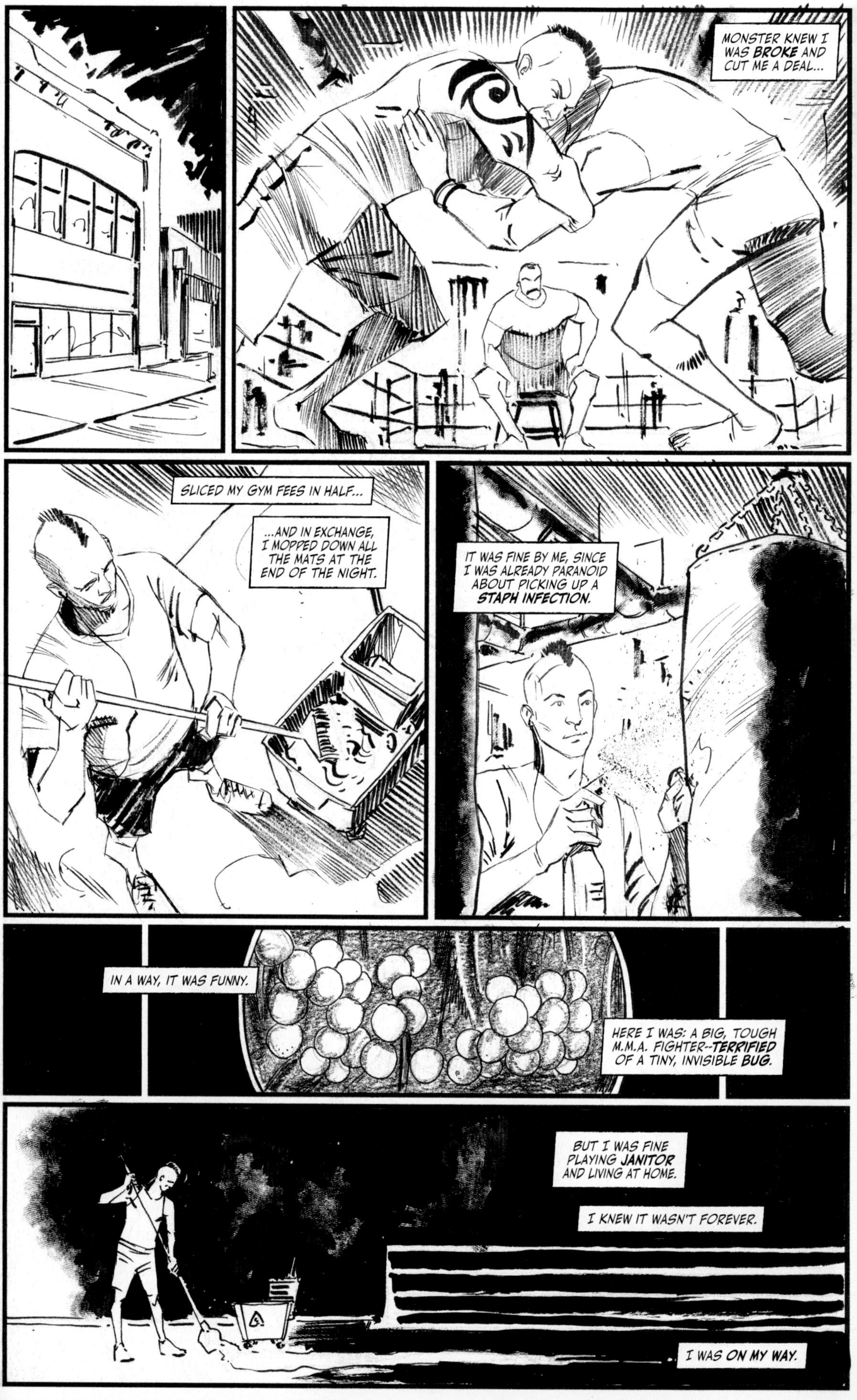
MONSTER KNEW I WAS BROKE AND CUT ME A DEAL...
SLICED MY GYM FEES IN HALF...
...AND IN EXCHANGE, I MOPPED DOWN ALL THE MATS AT THE END OF THE NIGHT.
IT WAS FINE BY ME, SINCE I WAS ALREADY PARANOID ABOUT PICKING UP A STAPH INFECTION.
IN A WAY, IT WAS FUNNY.
HERE I WAS: A BIG, TOUGH M.M.A. FIGHTER--TERRIFIED OF A TINY, INVISIBLE BUG.
BUT I WAS FINE PLAYING JANITOR AND LIVING AT HOME.
I KNEW IT WASN'T FOREVER.
I WAS ON MY WAY.

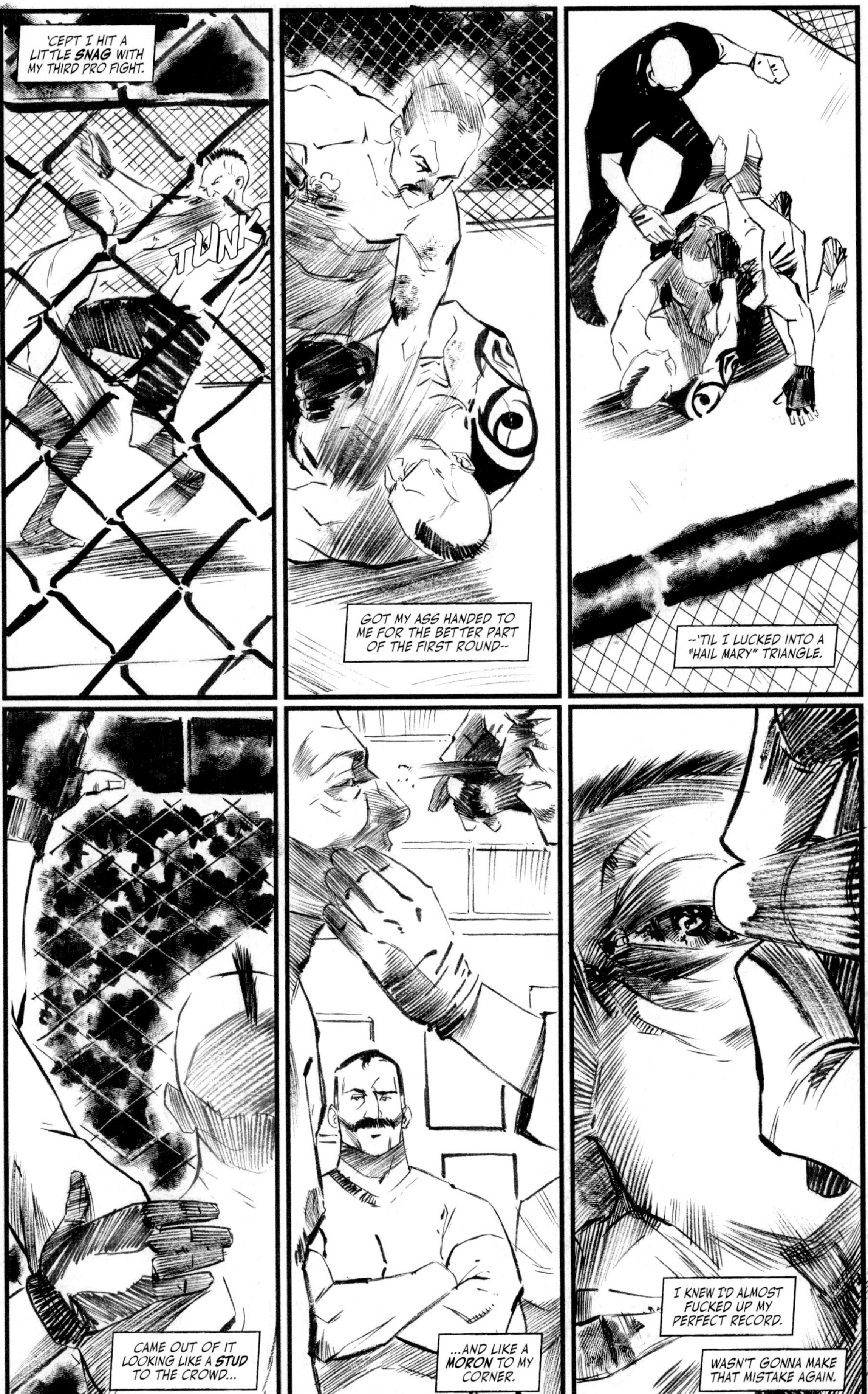
'CEPT I HIT A LITTLE SNAG WITH MY THIRD PRO FIGHT.
TUNK
GOT MY ASS HANDED TO ME FOR THE BETTER PART OF THE FIRST ROUND--
--'TIL I LUCKED INTO A "HAIL MARY" TRIANGLE.
CAME OUT OF IT LOOKING LIKE A STUD TO THE CROWD...
...AND LIKE A MORON TO MY CORNER.
I KNEW I'D ALMOST FUCKED UP MY PERFECT RECORD.
WASN'T GONNA MAKE THAT MISTAKE AGAIN.

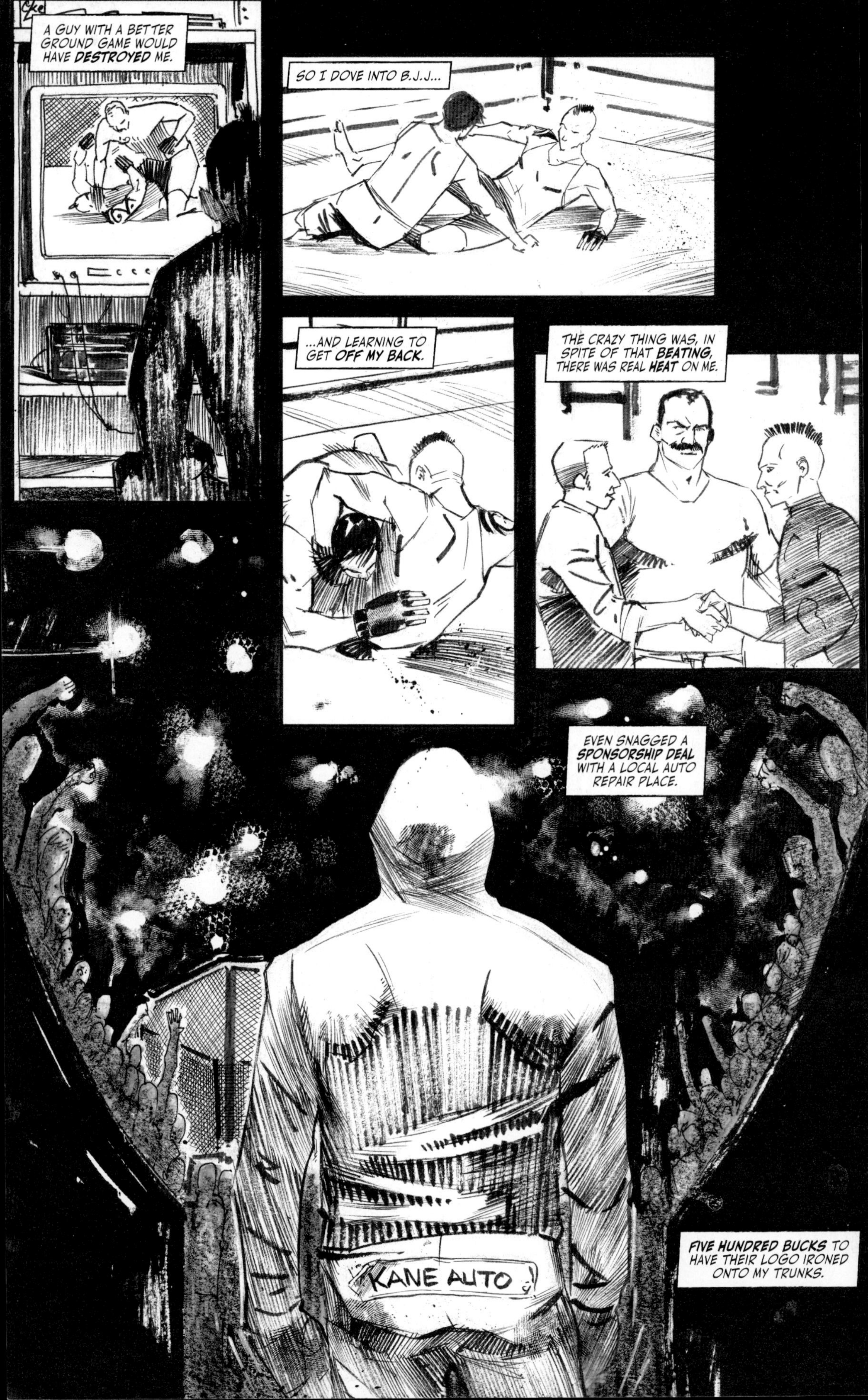
A GUY WITH A BETTER GROUND GAME WOULD HAVE DESTROYED ME.
SO I DOVE INTO B.J.J...
...AND LEARNING TO GET OFF MY BACK.
THE CRAZY THING WAS, IN SPITE OF THAT BEATING, THERE WAS REAL HEAT ON ME.
EVEN SNAGGED A SPONSORSHIP DEAL WITH A LOCAL AUTO REPAIR PLACE.
KANE AUTO
FIVE HUNDRED BUCKS TO HAVE THEIR LOGO IRONED ONTO MY TRUNKS.

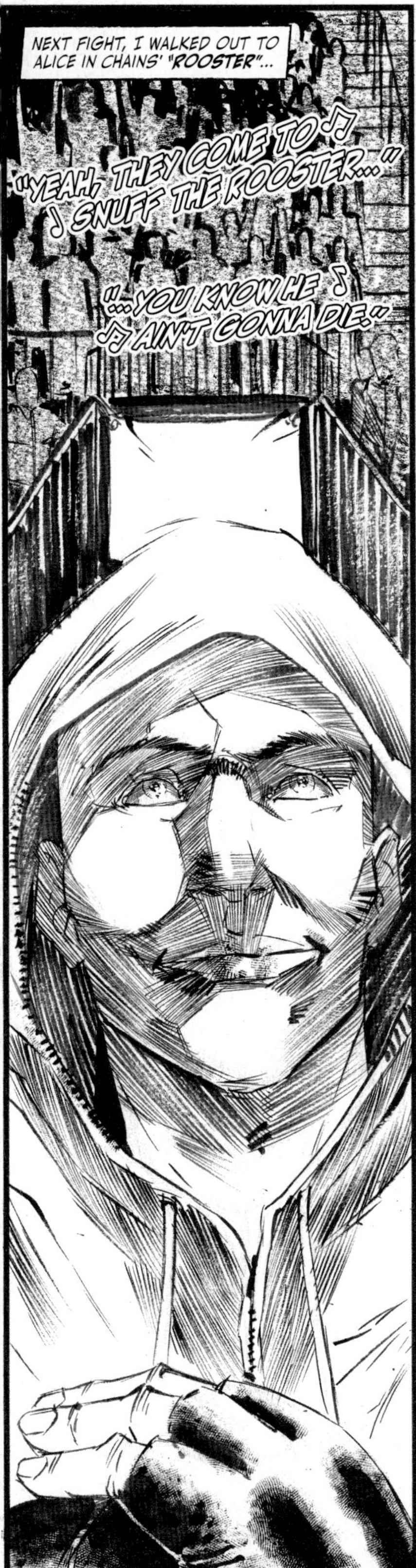
NEXT FIGHT, I WALKED OUT TO ALICE IN CHAINS' "ROOSTER"...
"YEAH, THEY COME TO ♫ ♪ SNUFF THE ROOSTER..."
"...YOU KNOW HE ♪ ♫ AIN'T GONNA DIE."

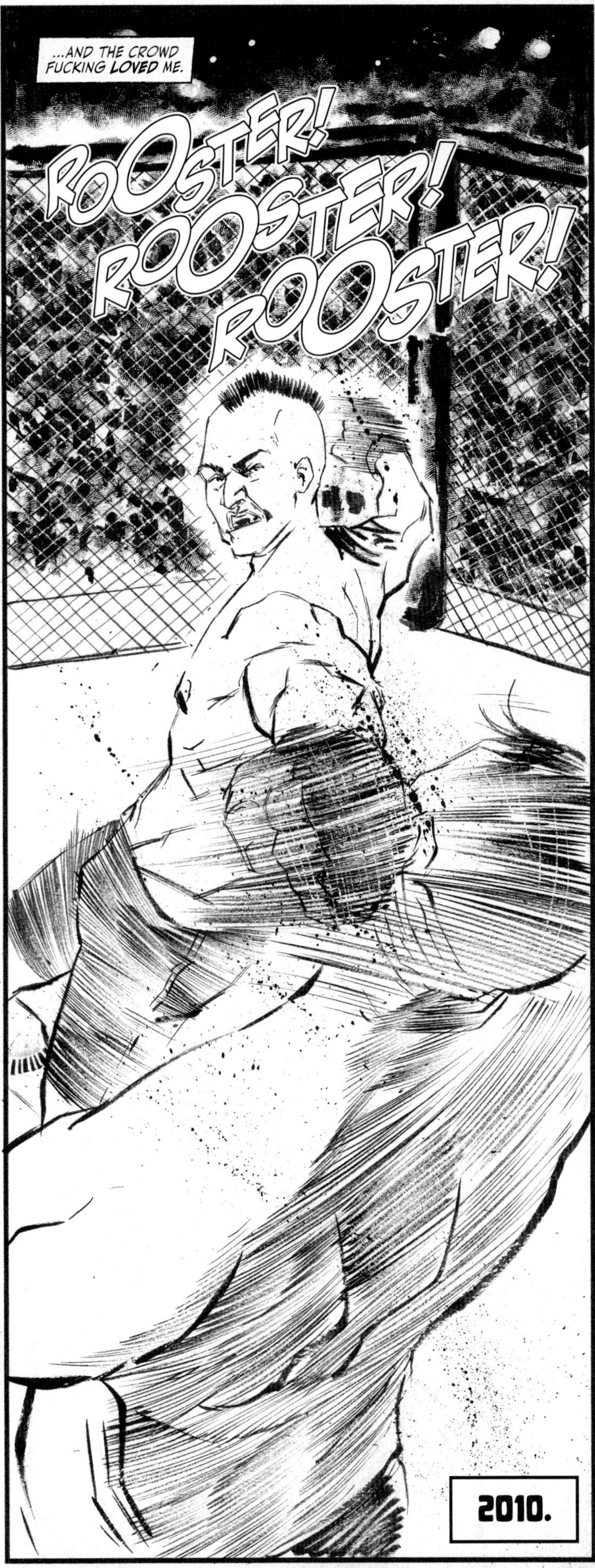
...AND THE CROWD FUCKING LOVED ME.
ROOSTER!
ROOSTER!
ROOSTER!
2010.

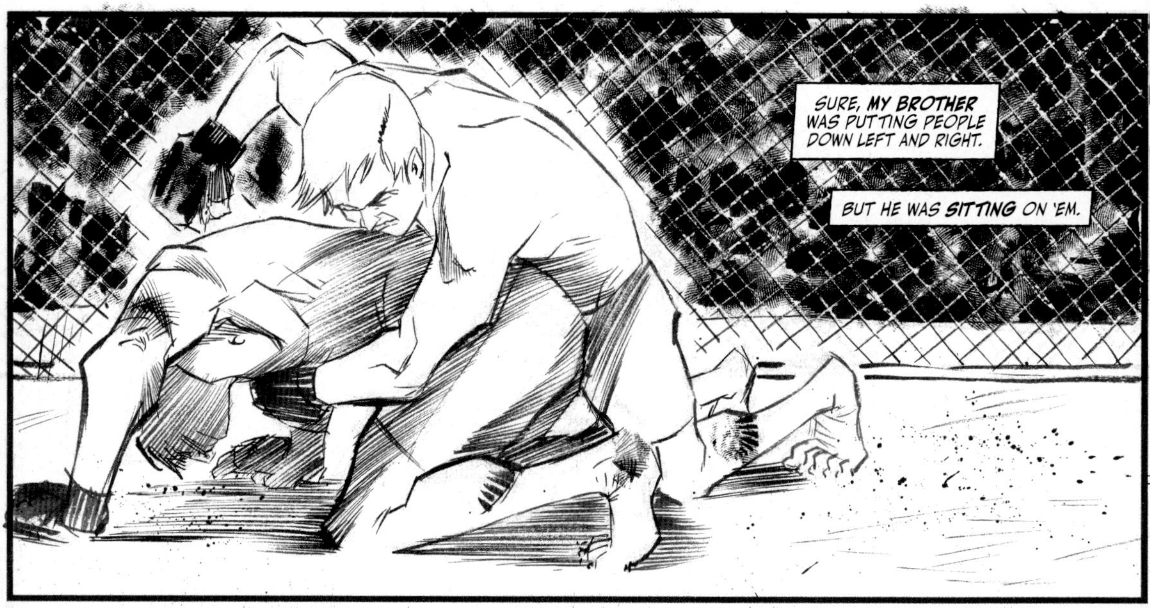
SURE, MY BROTHER WAS PUTTING PEOPLE DOWN LEFT AND RIGHT.
BUT HE WAS SITTING ON 'EM.

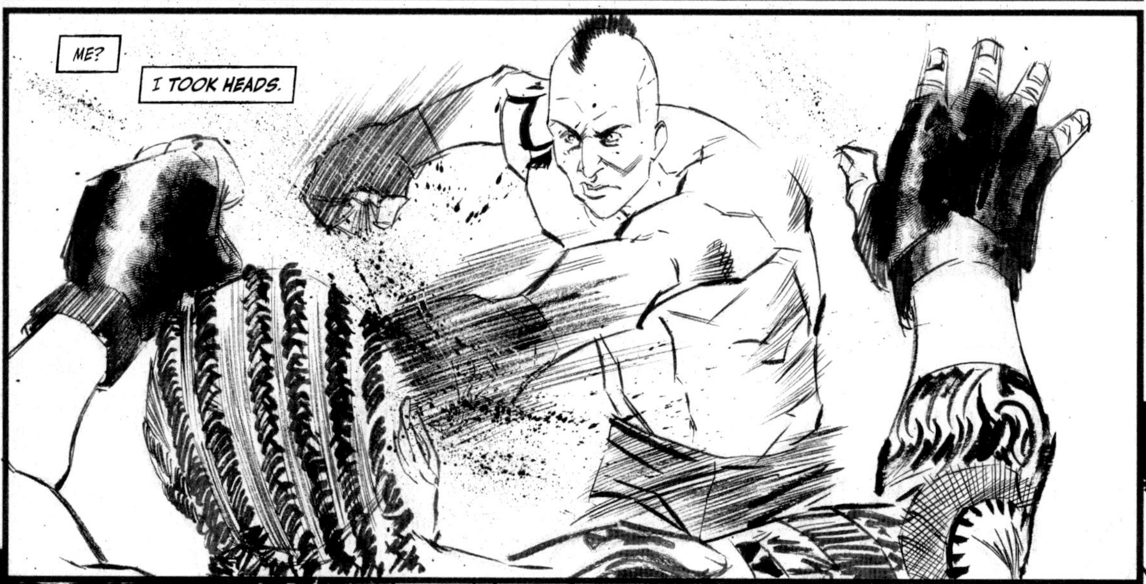
ME?
I TOOK HEADS.

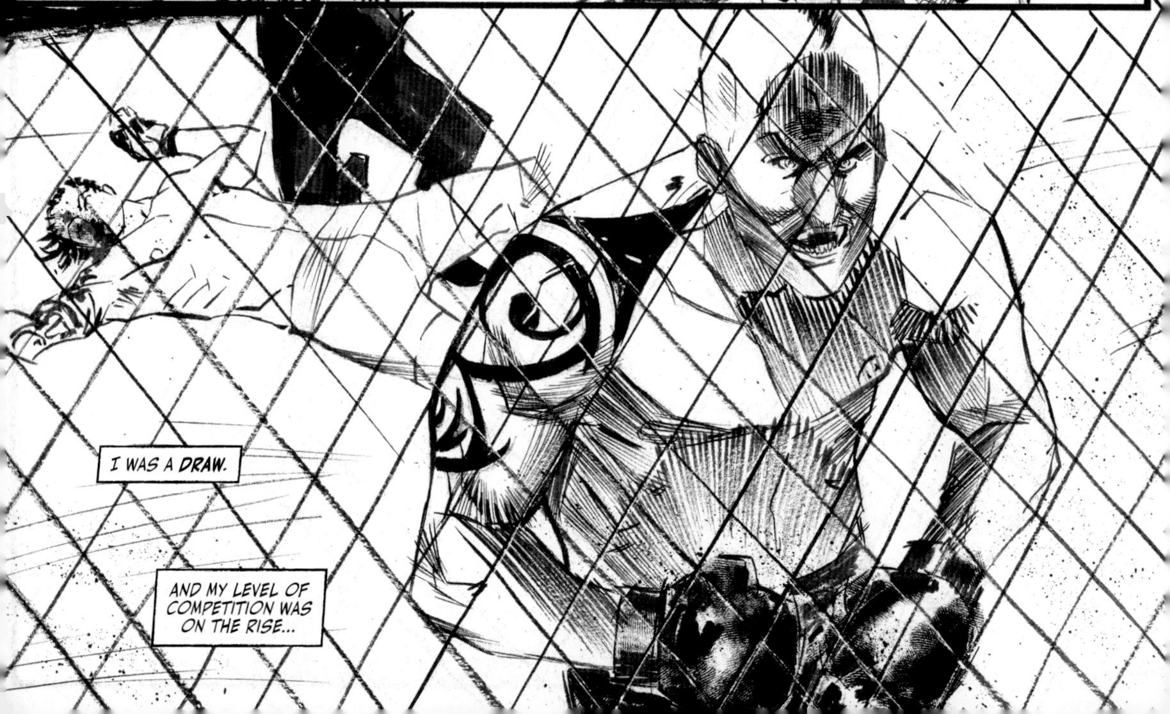
I WAS A DRAW.
AND MY LEVEL OF COMPETITION WAS ON THE RISE...

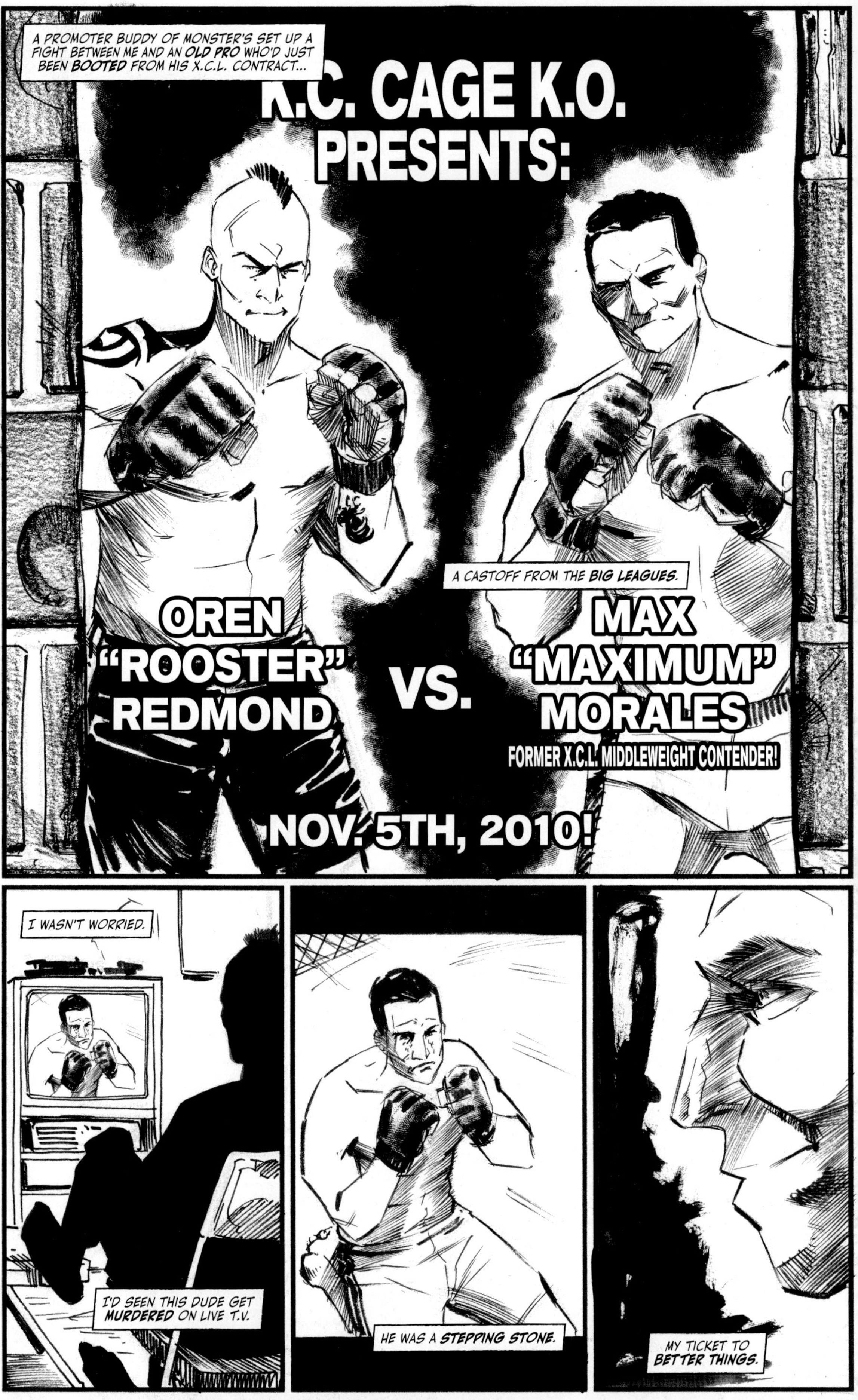

A PROMOTER BUDDY OF MONSTER'S SET UP A FIGHT BETWEEN ME AND AN OLD PRO WHO'D JUST BEEN BOOTED FROM HIS X.C.L. CONTRACT...
K.C. CAGE K.O. PRESENTS:
A CASTOFF FROM THE BIG LEAGUES.
OREN "ROOSTER" REDMOND
VS.
MAX "MAXIMUM" MORALES
FORMER X.C.L. MIDDLEWEIGHT CONTENDER!
NOV. 5TH, 2010!
I WASN'T WORRIED.
I'D SEEN THIS DUDE GET MURDERED ON LIVE T.V.
HE WAS A STEPPING STONE.
MY TICKET TO BETTER THINGS.

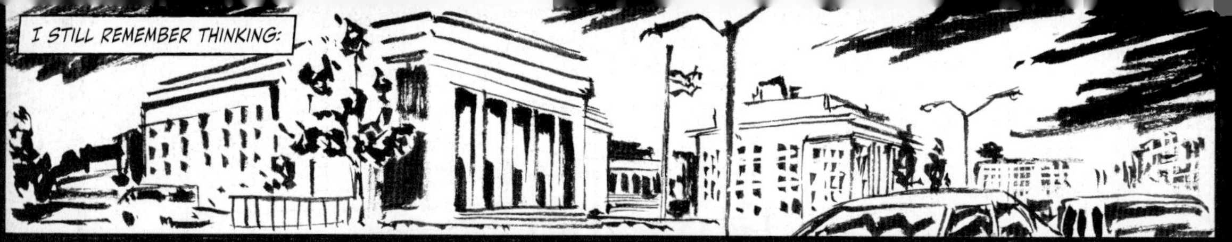
I STILL REMEMBER THINKING:

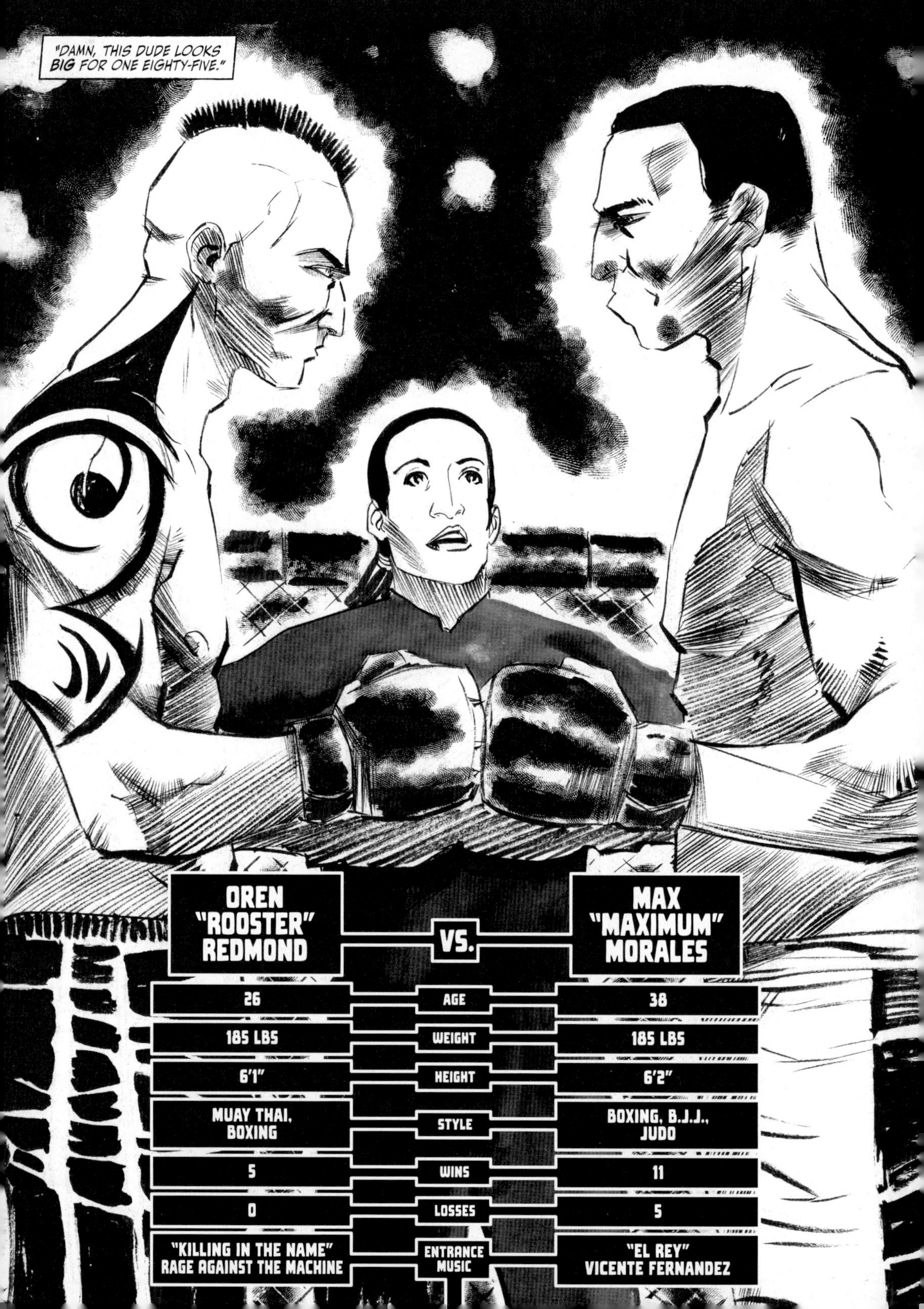
"DAMN, THIS DUDE LOOKS BIG FOR ONE EIGHTY-FIVE."

OREN "ROOSTER" REDMOND	VS.	MAX "MAXIMUM" MORALES
26	AGE	38
185 LBS	WEIGHT	185 LBS
6'1"	HEIGHT	6'2"
MUAY THAI, BOXING	STYLE	BOXING, B.J.J., JUDO
5	WINS	11
0	LOSSES	5
"KILLING IN THE NAME" RAGE AGAINST THE MACHINE	ENTRANCE MUSIC	"EL REY" VICENTE FERNANDEZ

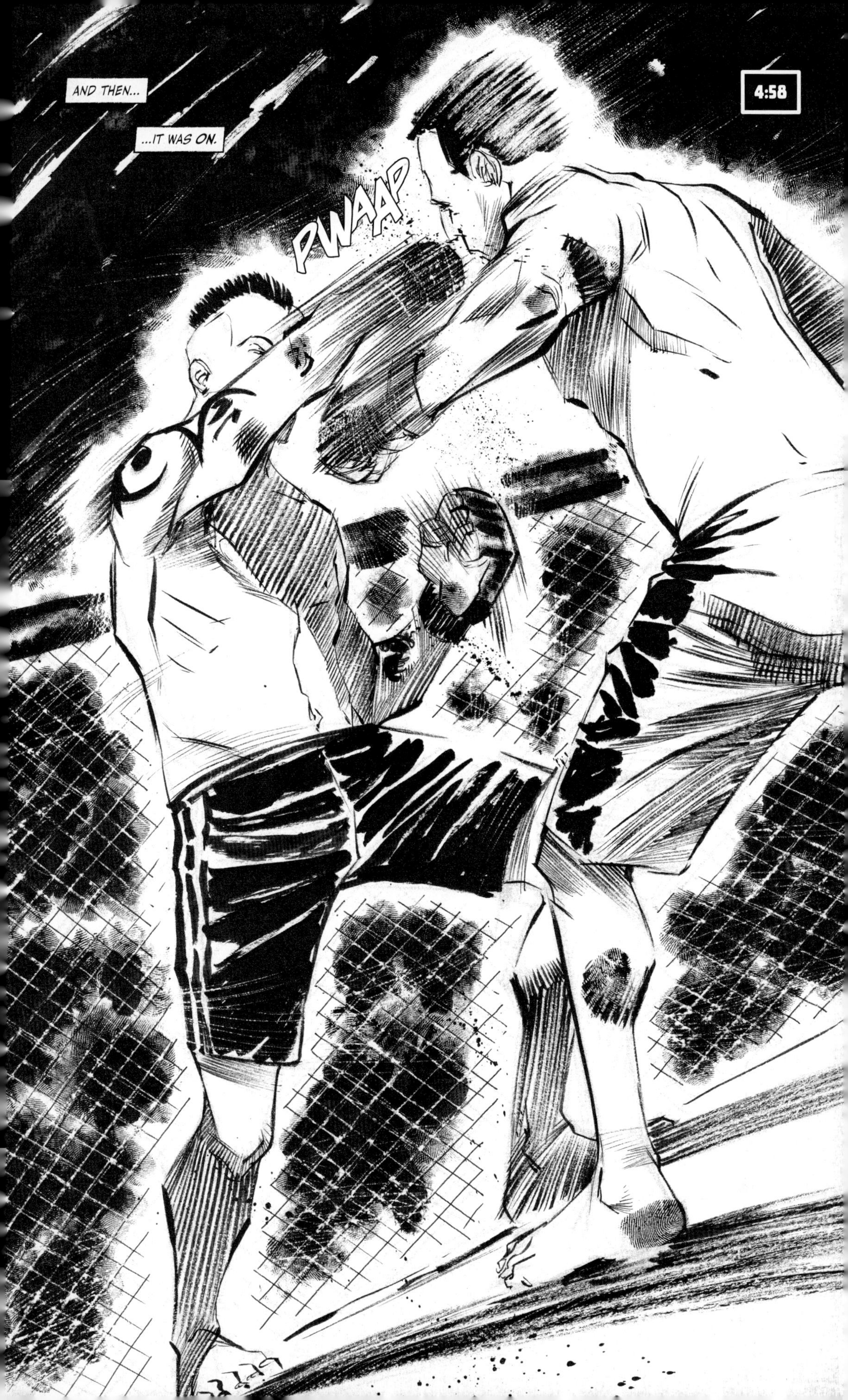
AND THEN...
...IT WAS ON.
4:58
PWAAP

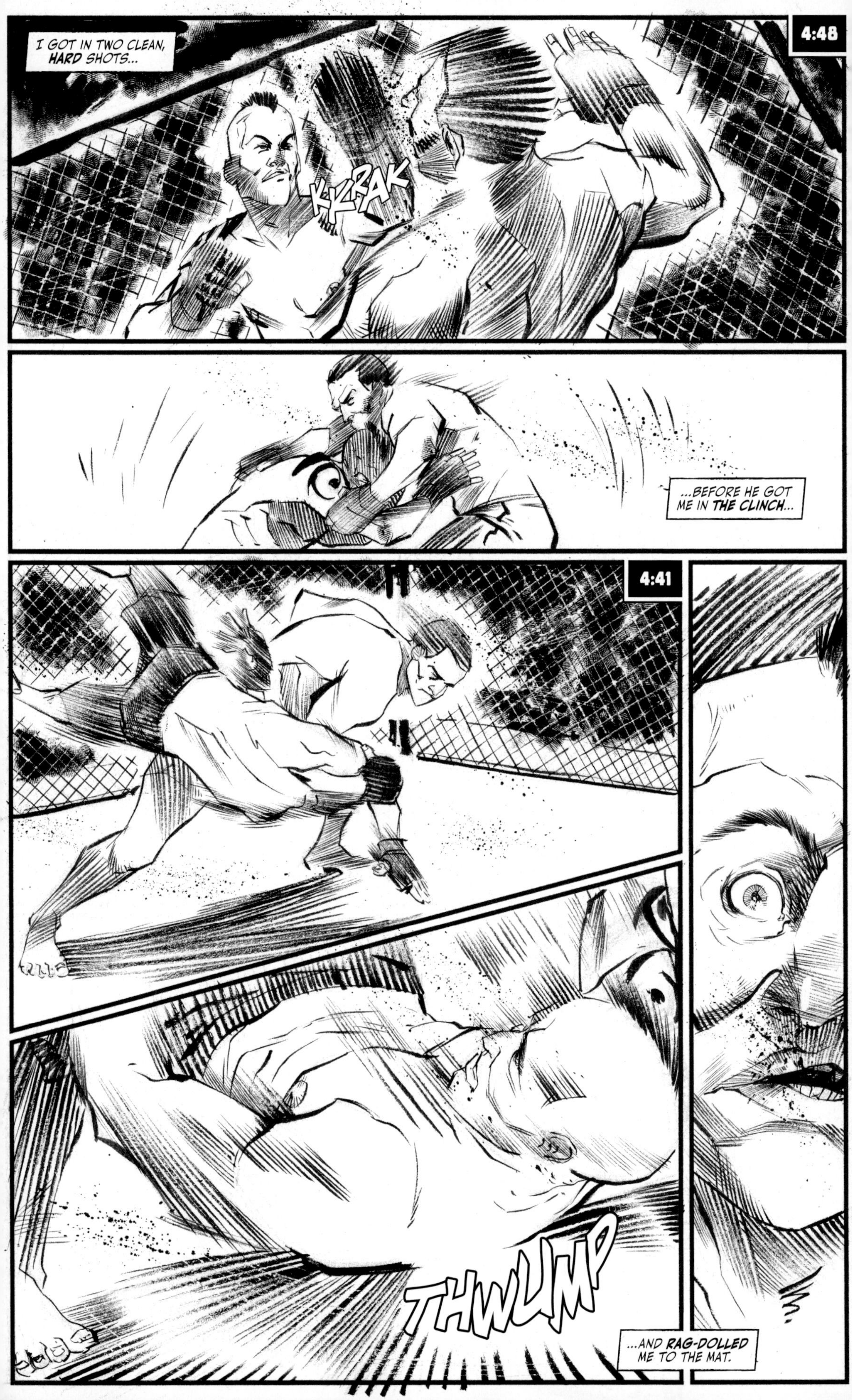
4:48
I GOT IN TWO CLEAN, HARD SHOTS...
KKRAK
...BEFORE HE GOT ME IN THE CLINCH...
4:41
THWUMP
...AND RAG-DOLLED ME TO THE MAT.

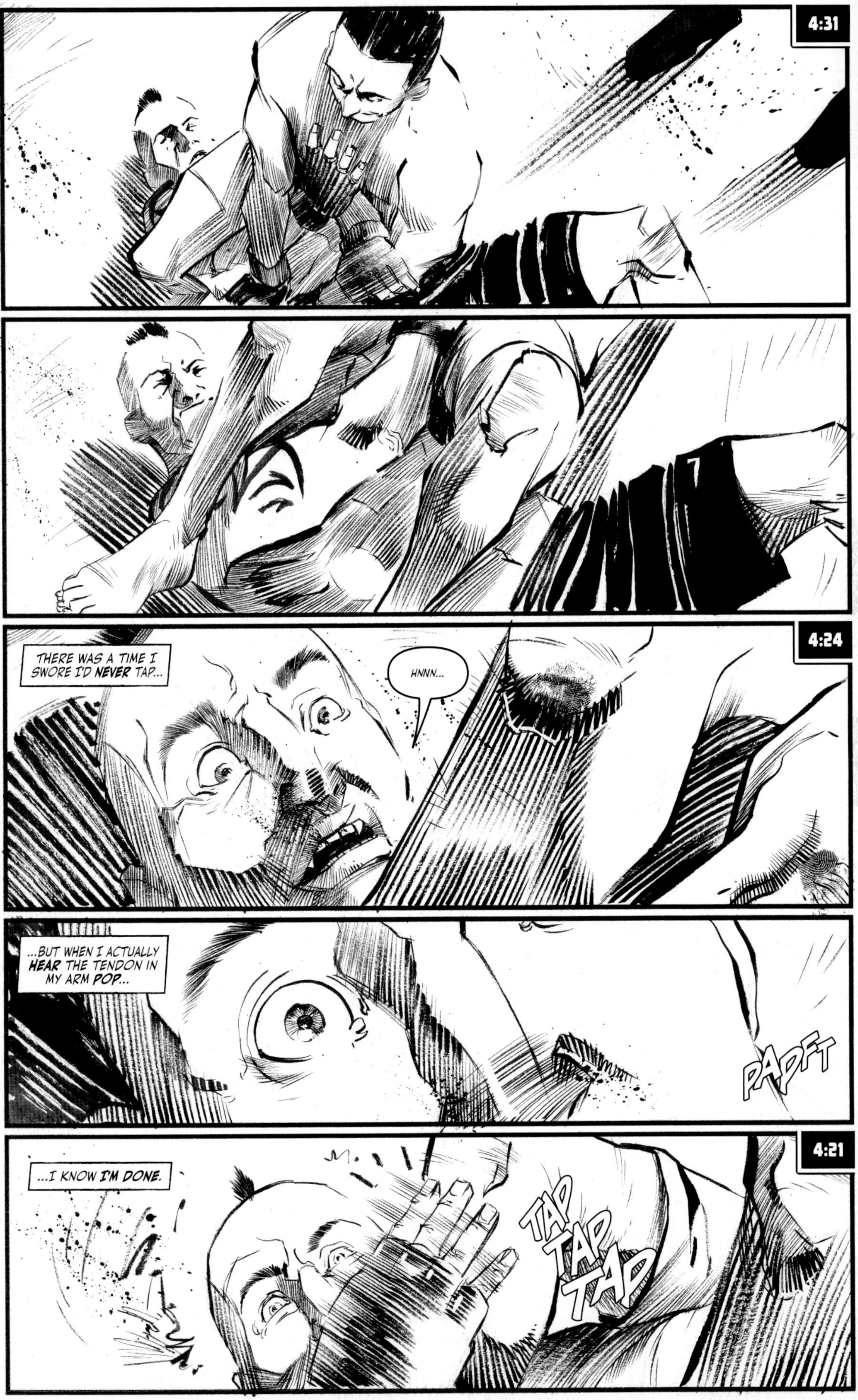
4:31
4:24
THERE WAS A TIME I SWORE I'D **NEVER** TAP...
HNNN...
...BUT WHEN I ACTUALLY **HEAR** THE TENDON IN MY ARM **POP**...
PADFT
4:21
...I KNOW **I'M DONE**.
TAP TAP TAP

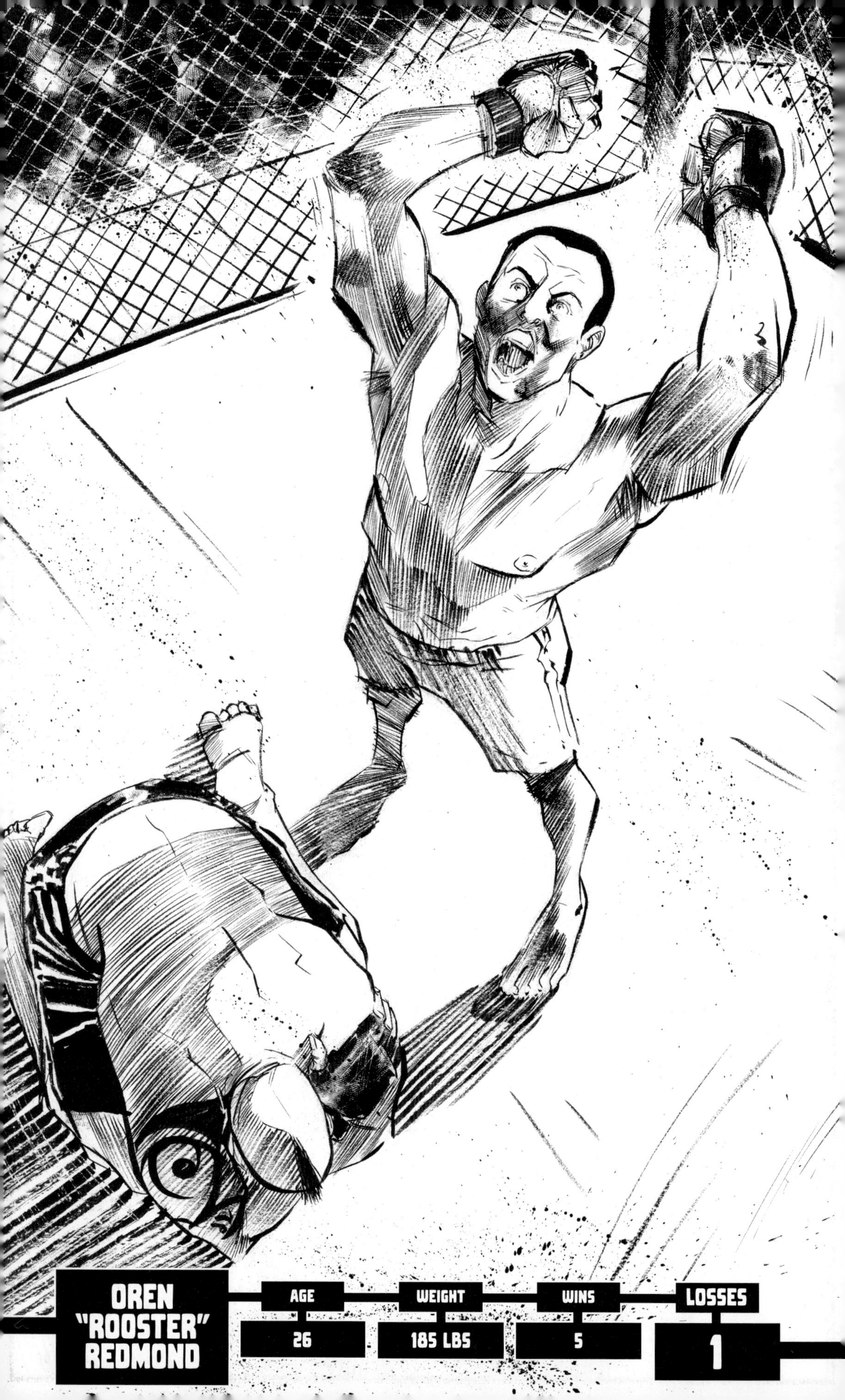
OREN
"ROOSTER"
REDMOND
AGE
26
WEIGHT
185 LBS
WINS
5
LOSSES
1

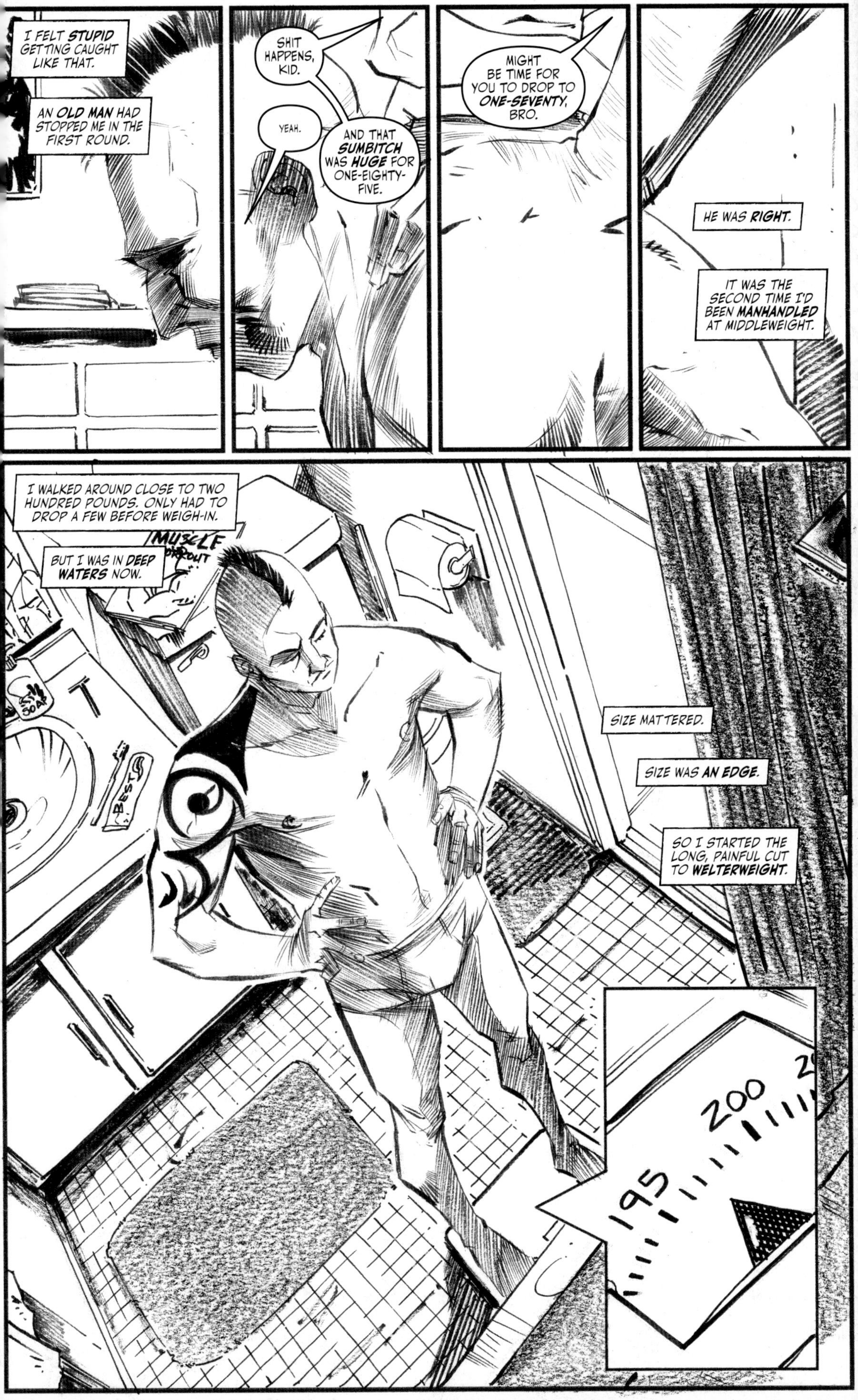

I FELT **STUPID** GETTING CAUGHT LIKE THAT.
AN **OLD MAN** HAD STOPPED ME IN THE FIRST ROUND.
SHIT HAPPENS, KID.
YEAH.
AND THAT **SUMBITCH** WAS **HUGE** FOR ONE-EIGHTY-FIVE.
MIGHT BE TIME FOR YOU TO DROP TO **ONE-SEVENTY**, BRO.
HE WAS **RIGHT**.
IT WAS THE SECOND TIME I'D BEEN **MANHANDLED** AT MIDDLEWEIGHT.
I WALKED AROUND CLOSE TO TWO HUNDRED POUNDS. ONLY HAD TO DROP A FEW BEFORE WEIGH-IN.
BUT I WAS IN **DEEP WATERS** NOW.
MUSCLE
SOAP
BEST
SIZE MATTERED.
SIZE WAS **AN EDGE**.
SO I STARTED THE LONG, PAINFUL CUT TO **WELTERWEIGHT**.
195
200

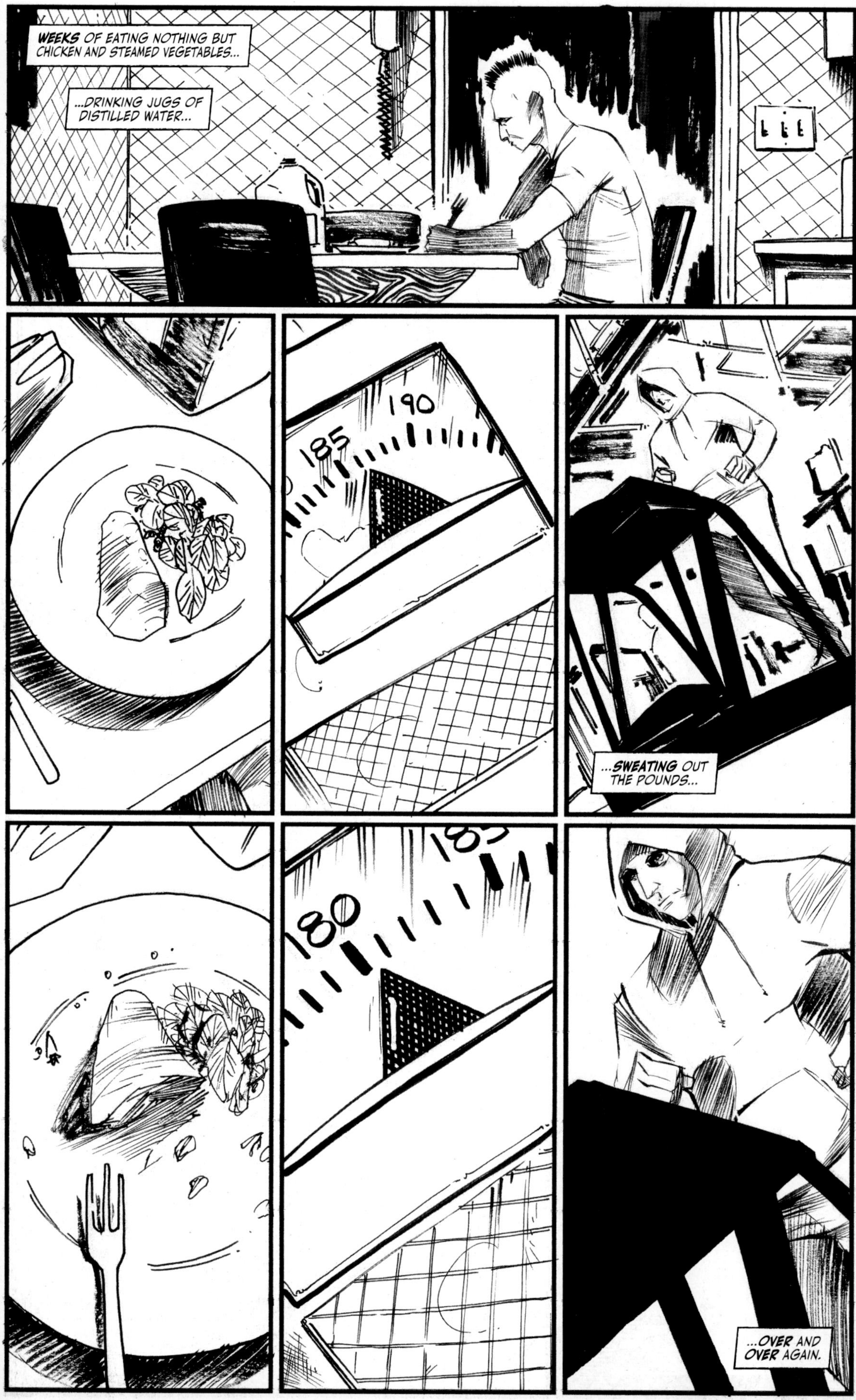
WEEKS OF EATING NOTHING BUT CHICKEN AND STEAMED VEGETABLES...
...DRINKING JUGS OF DISTILLED WATER...
190
185
...SWEATING OUT THE POUNDS...
80
...OVER AND OVER AGAIN.

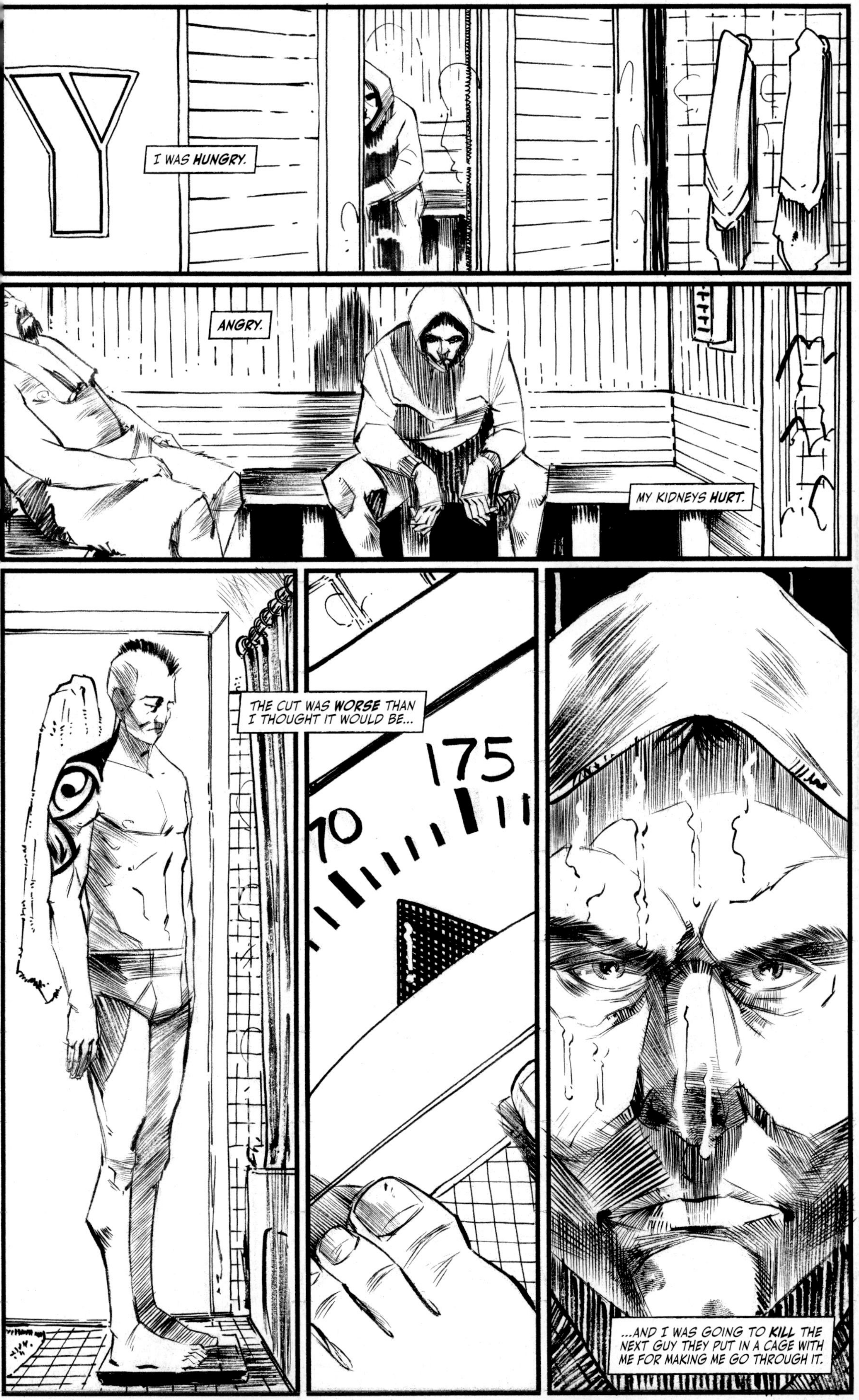
Y
I WAS HUNGRY.
ANGRY.
MY KIDNEYS HURT.
THE CUT WAS WORSE THAN I THOUGHT IT WOULD BE...
170
175
...AND I WAS GOING TO KILL THE NEXT GUY THEY PUT IN A CAGE WITH ME FOR MAKING ME GO THROUGH IT.

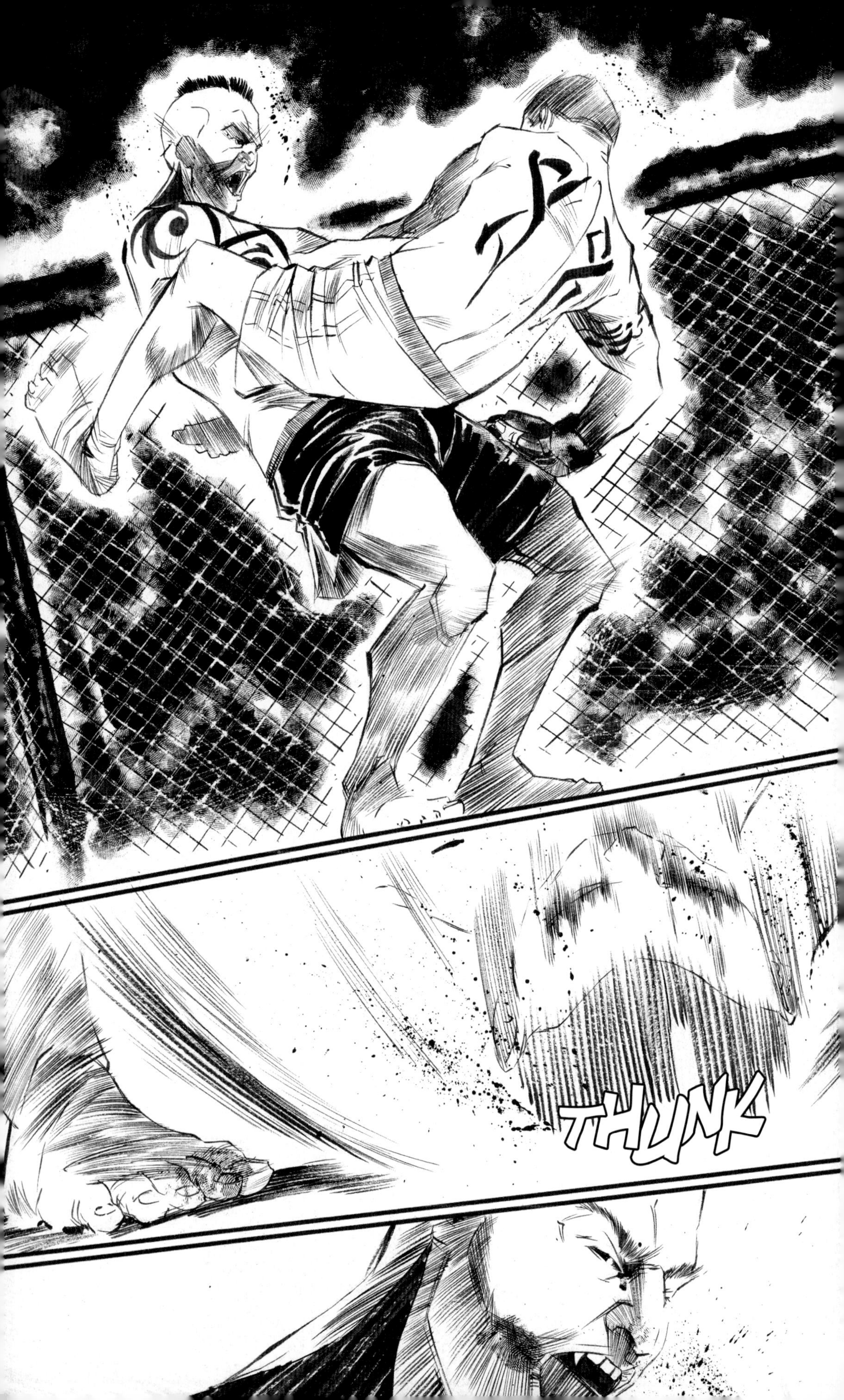
THUNK

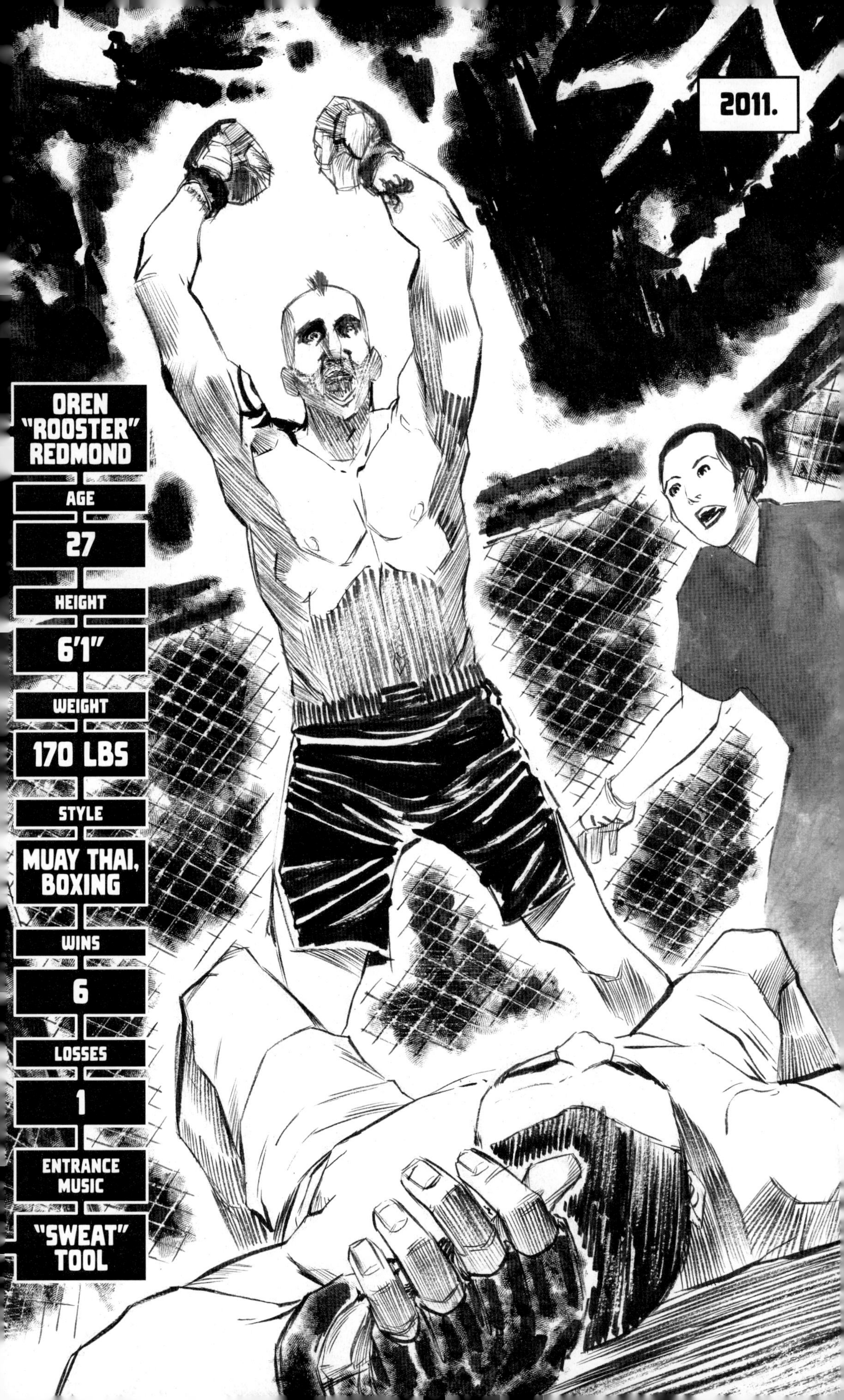

2011.
OREN "ROOSTER" REDMOND
AGE
27
HEIGHT
6'1"
WEIGHT
170 LBS
STYLE
MUAY THAI, BOXING
WINS
6
LOSSES
1
ENTRANCE MUSIC
"SWEAT" TOOL

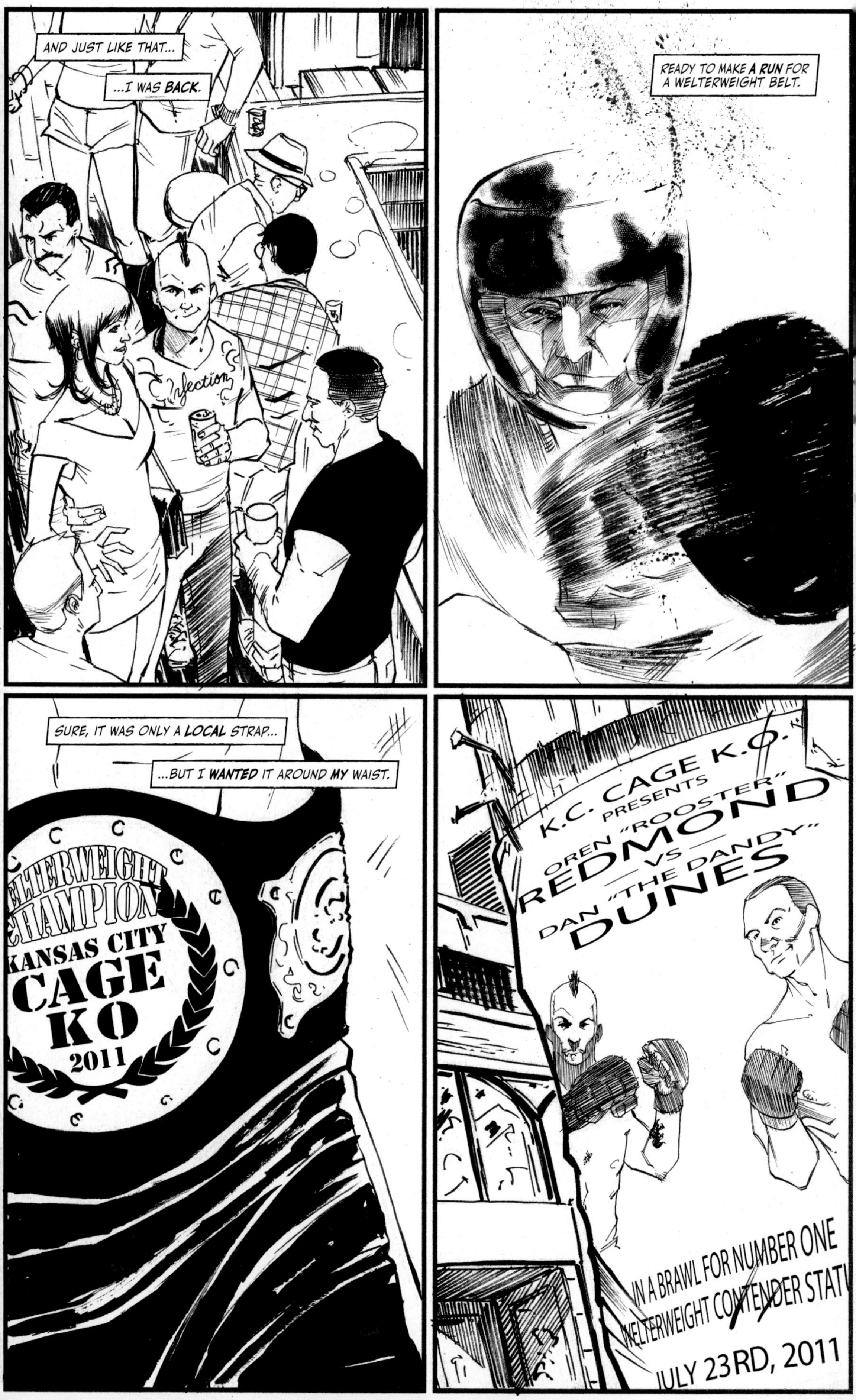
AND JUST LIKE THAT...
...I WAS **BACK**.
READY TO MAKE **A RUN** FOR A WELTERWEIGHT BELT.
SURE, IT WAS ONLY A **LOCAL** STRAP...
...BUT I **WANTED** IT AROUND **MY** WAIST.
ELTERWEIGHT CHAMPION
KANSAS CITY
CAGE
KO
2011
K.C. CAGE K.O.
PRESENTS
OREN "ROOSTER"
REDMOND
VS
DAN "THE DANDY"
DUNES
IN A BRAWL FOR NUMBER ONE
WELTERWEIGHT CONTENDER STAT
JULY 23RD, 2011

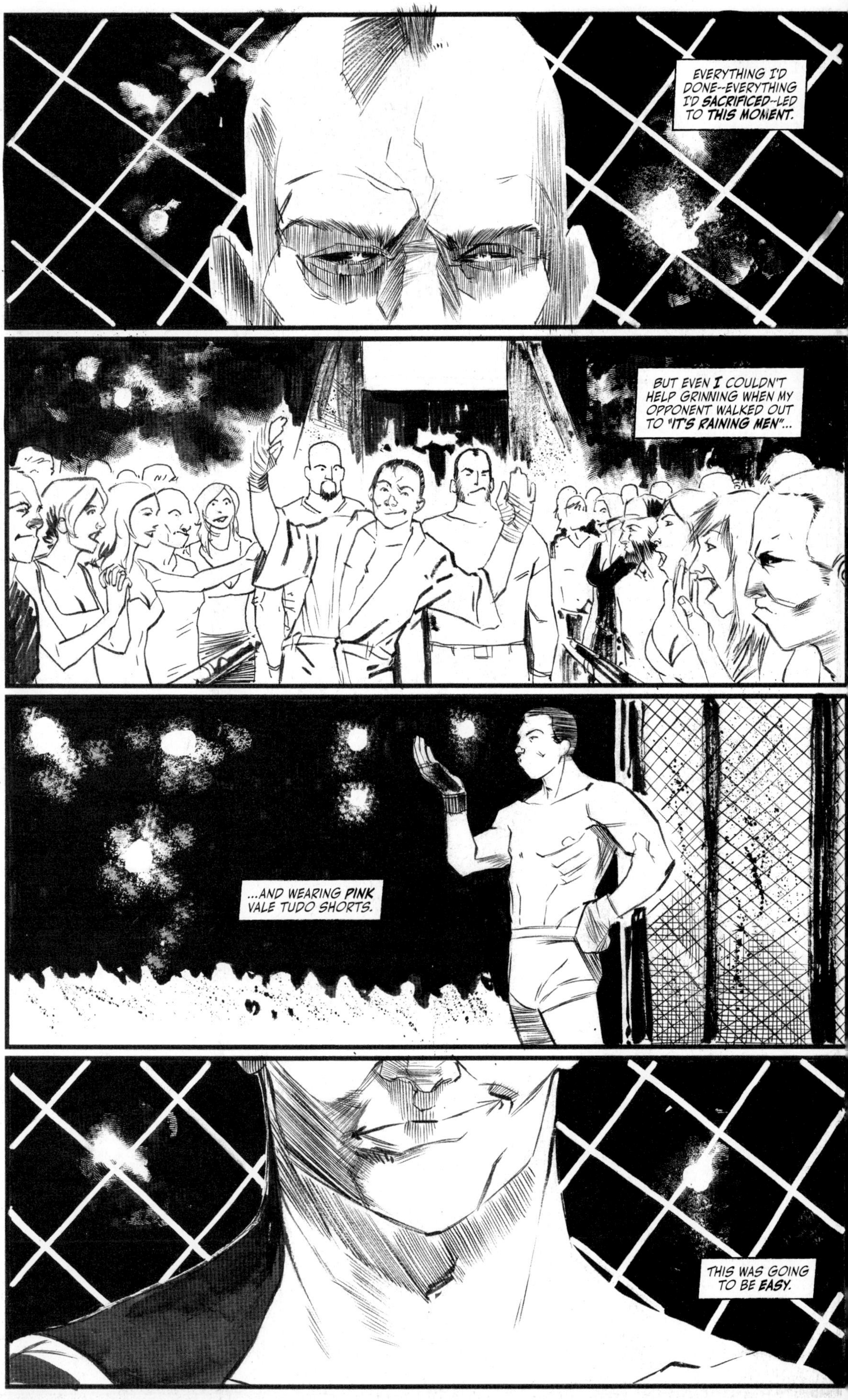
EVERYTHING I'D DONE--EVERYTHING I'D SACRIFICED--LED TO THIS MOMENT.
BUT EVEN I COULDN'T HELP GRINNING WHEN MY OPPONENT WALKED OUT TO "IT'S RAINING MEN"...
...AND WEARING PINK VALE TUDO SHORTS.
THIS WAS GOING TO BE EASY.

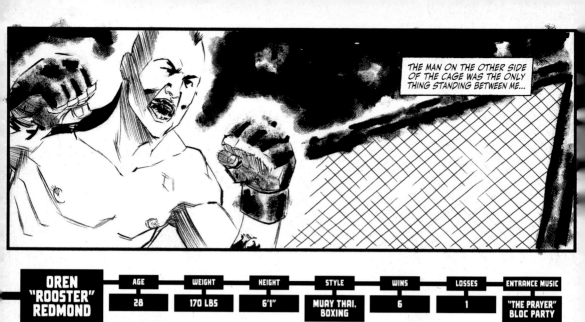

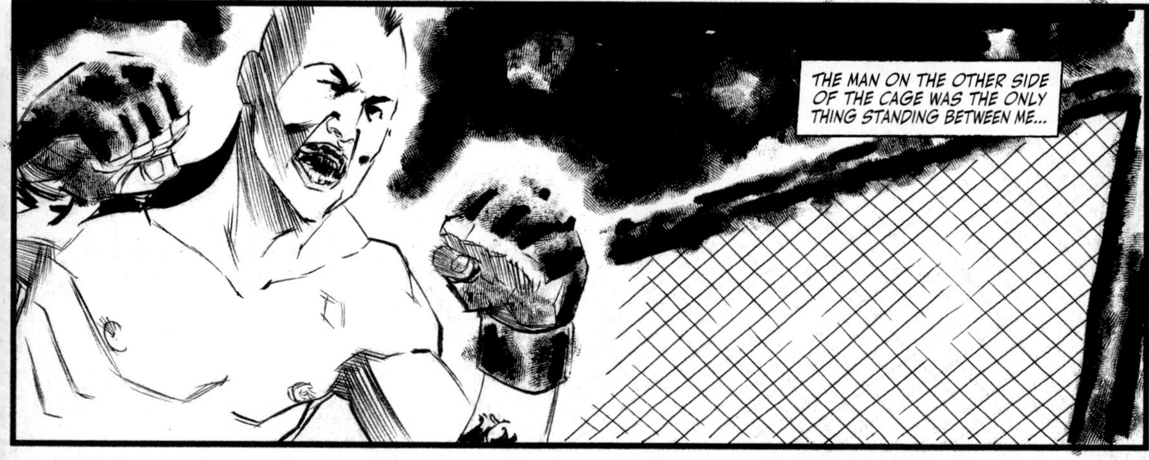
THE MAN ON THE OTHER SIDE OF THE CAGE WAS THE ONLY THING STANDING BETWEEN ME...

OREN "ROOSTER" REDMOND	
AGE	28
WEIGHT	170 LBS
HEIGHT	6'1"
STYLE	MUAY THAI, BOXING
WINS	6
LOSSES	1
ENTRANCE MUSIC	"THE PRAYER" BLOC PARTY

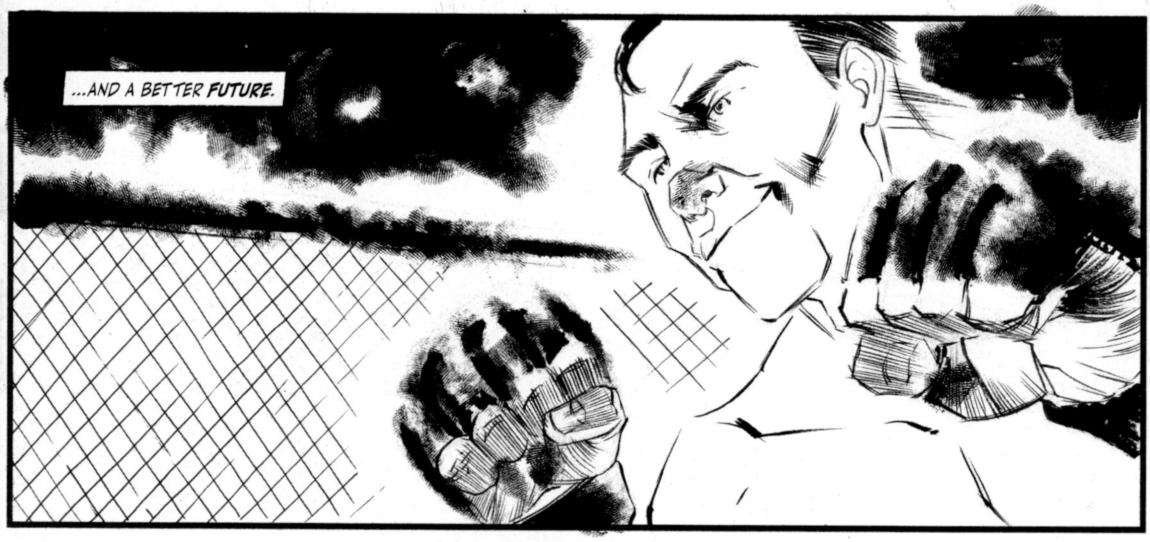
...AND A BETTER *FUTURE*.

DAN "THE DANDY" DUNES	
AGE	29
WEIGHT	170 LBS
HEIGHT	5'11"
STYLE	WRESTLING, BOXING, KICKBOXING
WINS	5
LOSSES	1
ENTRANCE MUSIC	"IT'S RAINING MEN" THE WEATHERGIRLS

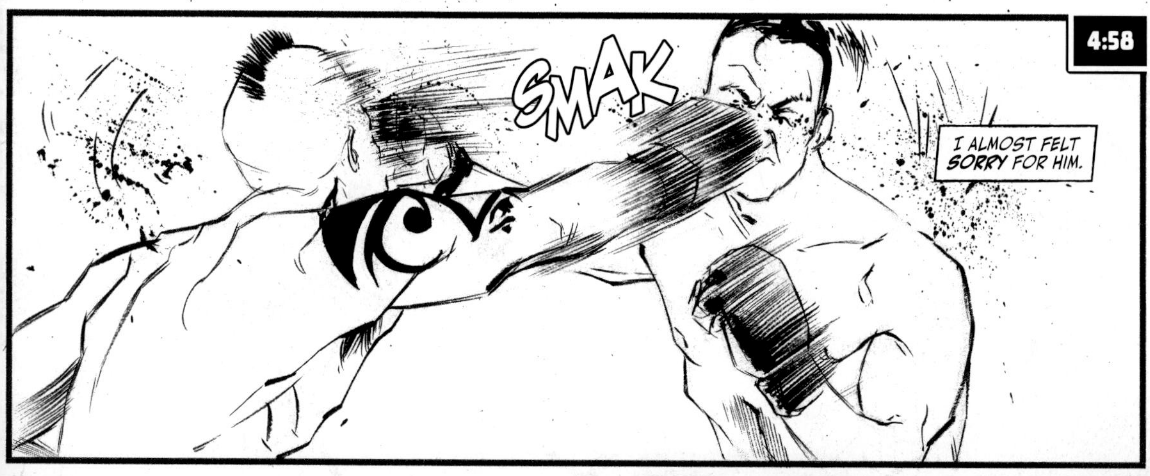
4:58
SMAK
I ALMOST FELT *SORRY* FOR HIM.

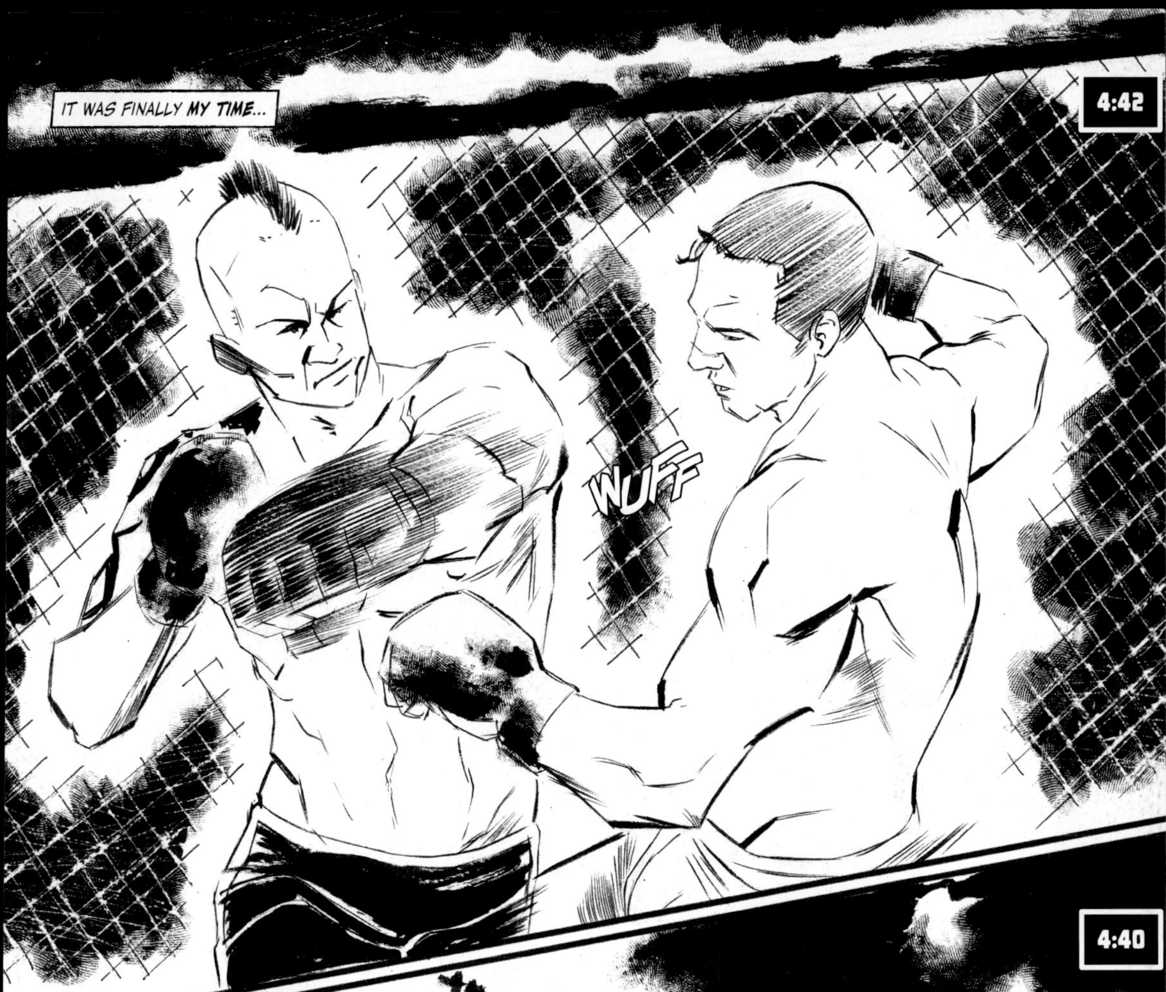
IT WAS FINALLY MY TIME...
4:42
WUFF

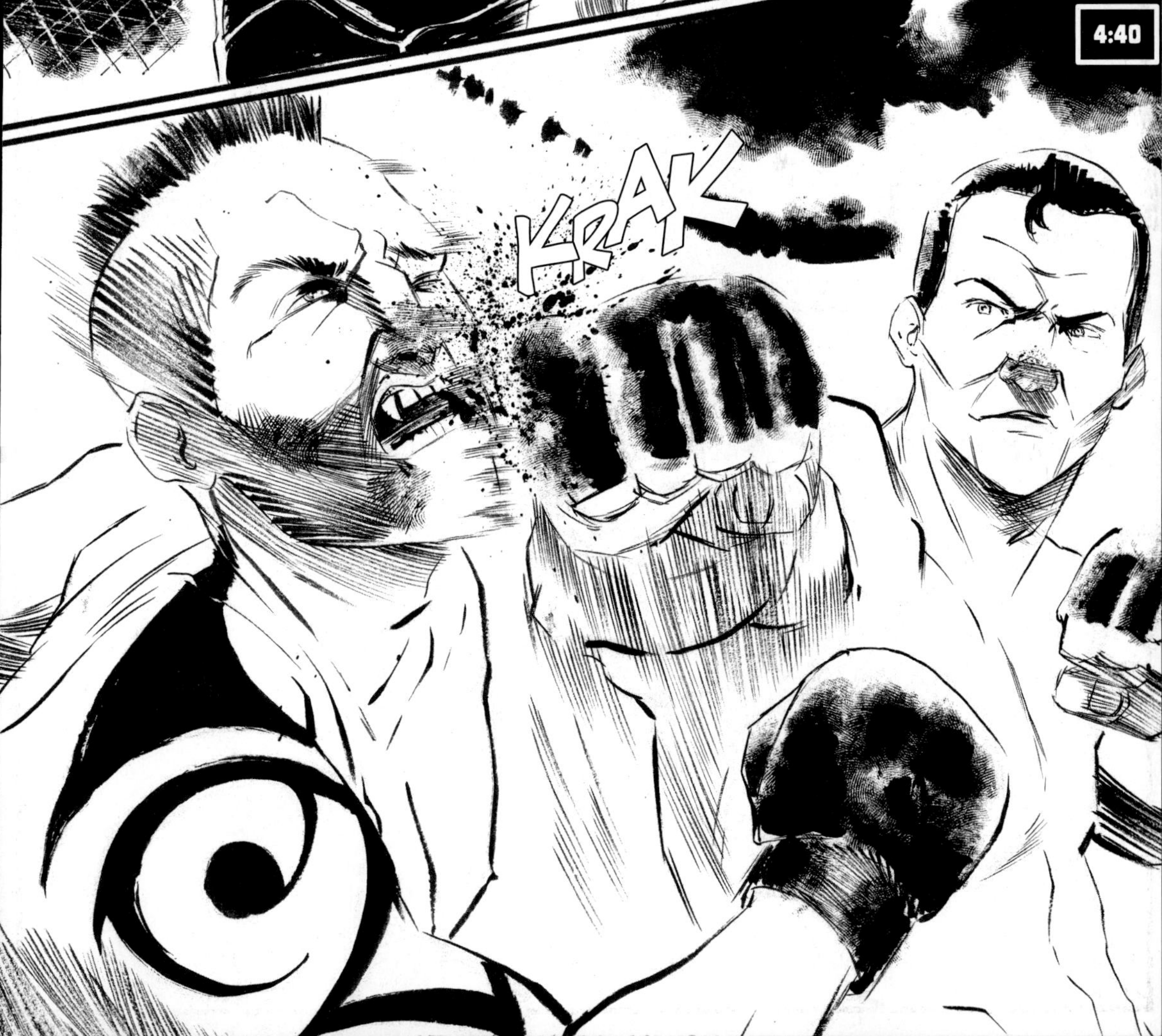
4:40
KRAK

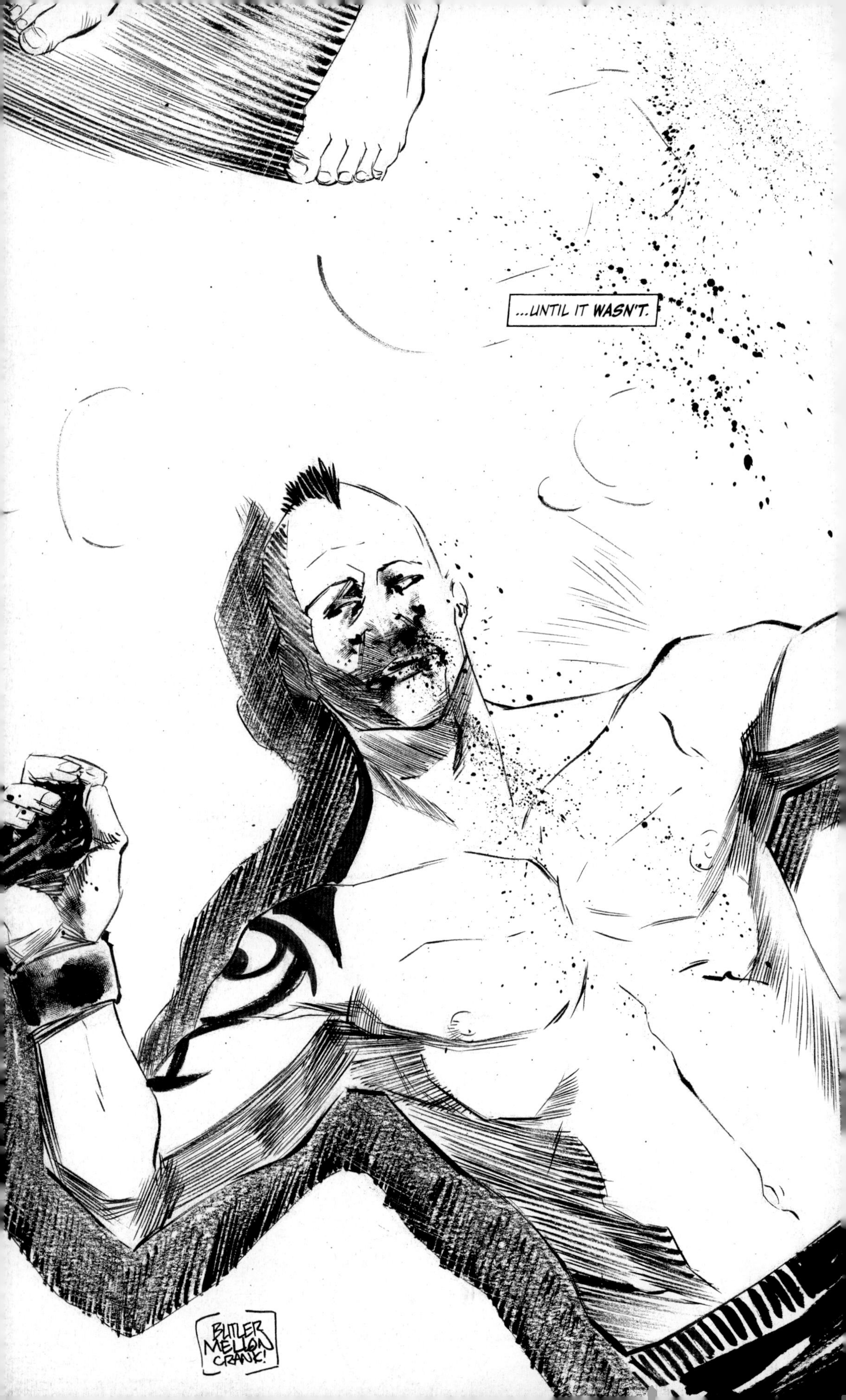
...UNTIL IT WASN'T.
BUTLER MELLON CRANK!

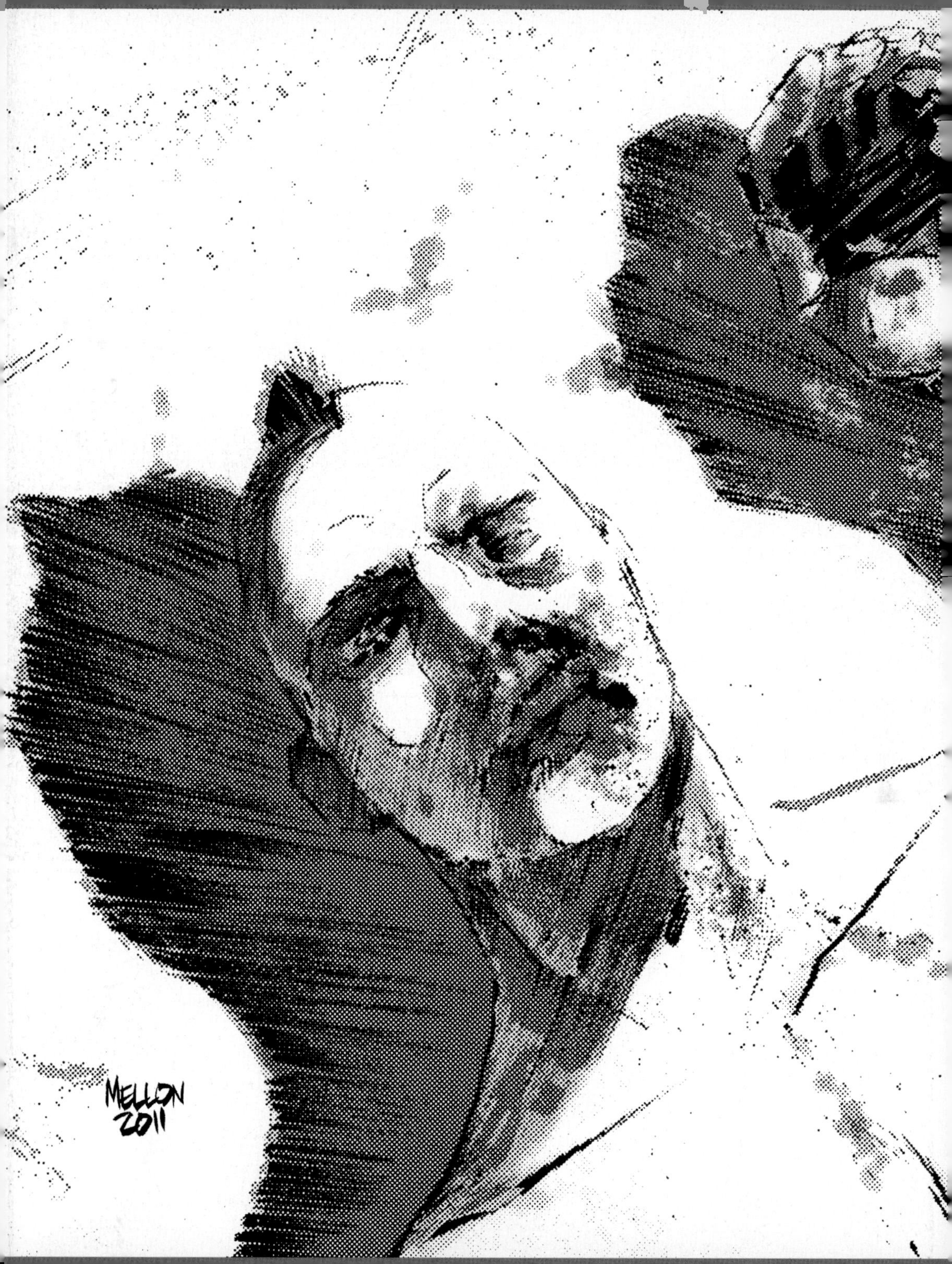
MELLON
2011

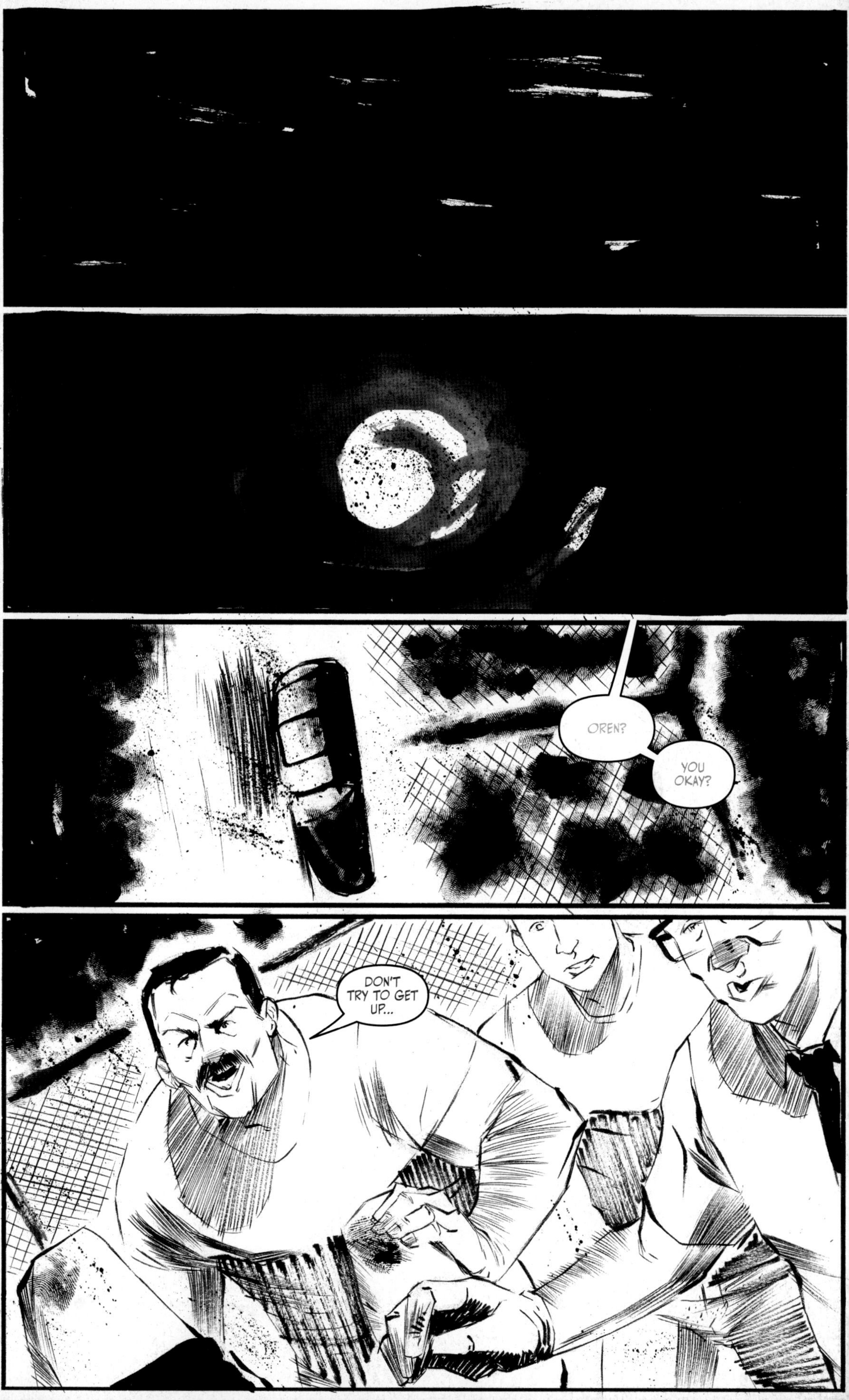
OREN?
YOU OKAY?
DON'T TRY TO GET UP...

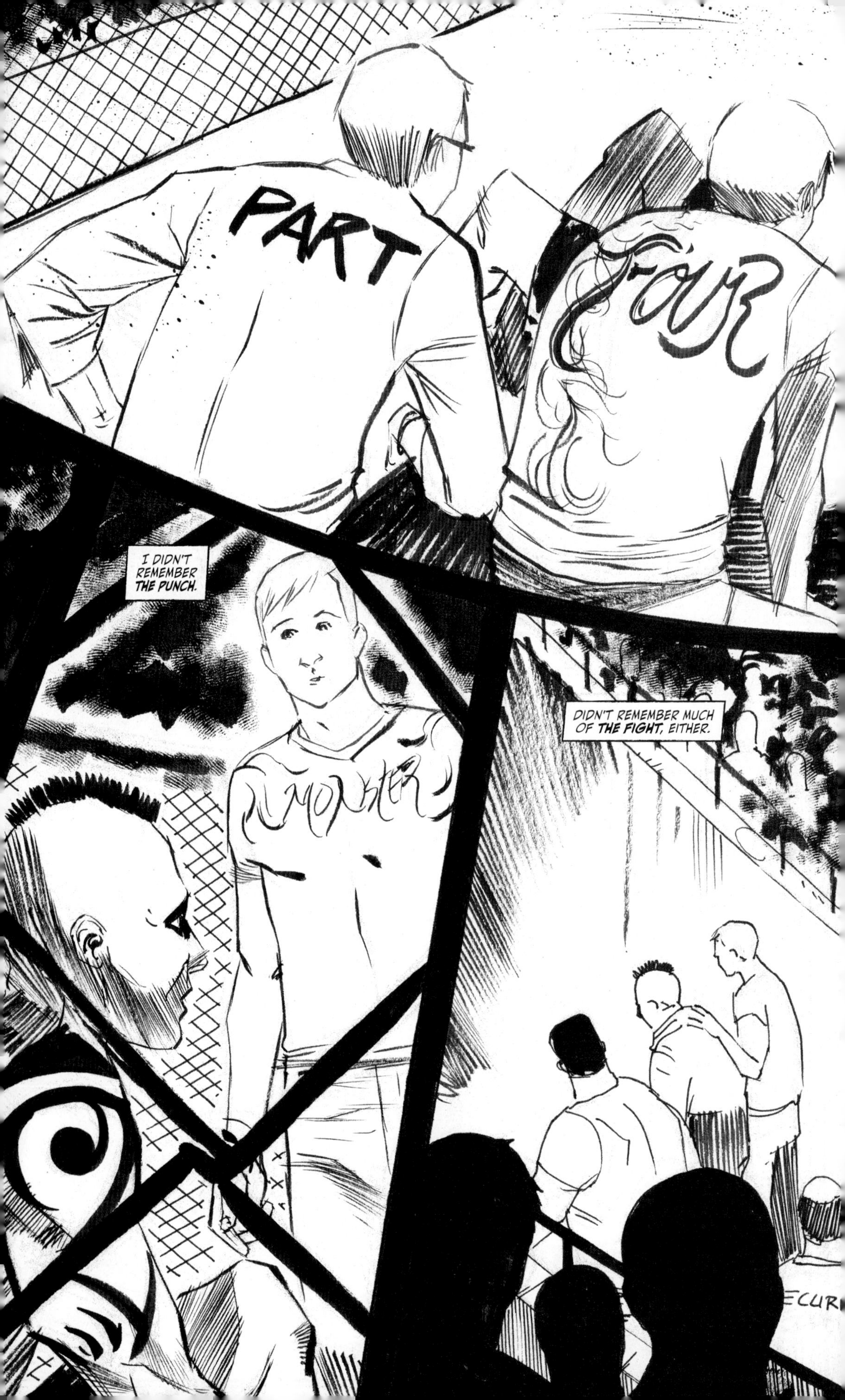
PART
FOUR
I DIDN'T REMEMBER THE PUNCH.
MONSTER
DIDN'T REMEMBER MUCH OF THE FIGHT, EITHER.

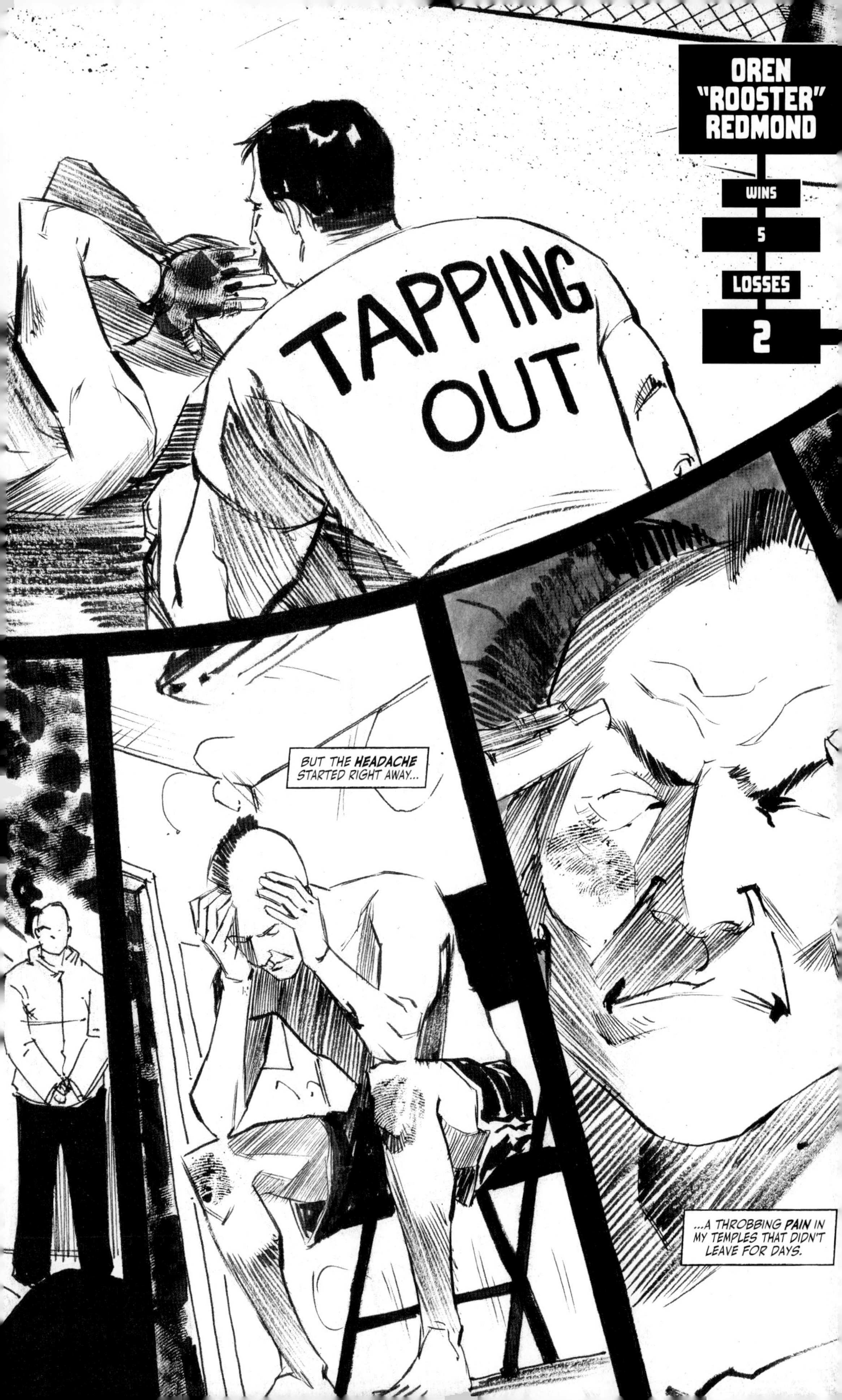

OREN "ROOSTER" REDMOND
WINS
5
LOSSES
2
TAPPING OUT
BUT THE HEADACHE STARTED RIGHT AWAY...
...A THROBBING PAIN IN MY TEMPLES THAT DIDN'T LEAVE FOR DAYS.

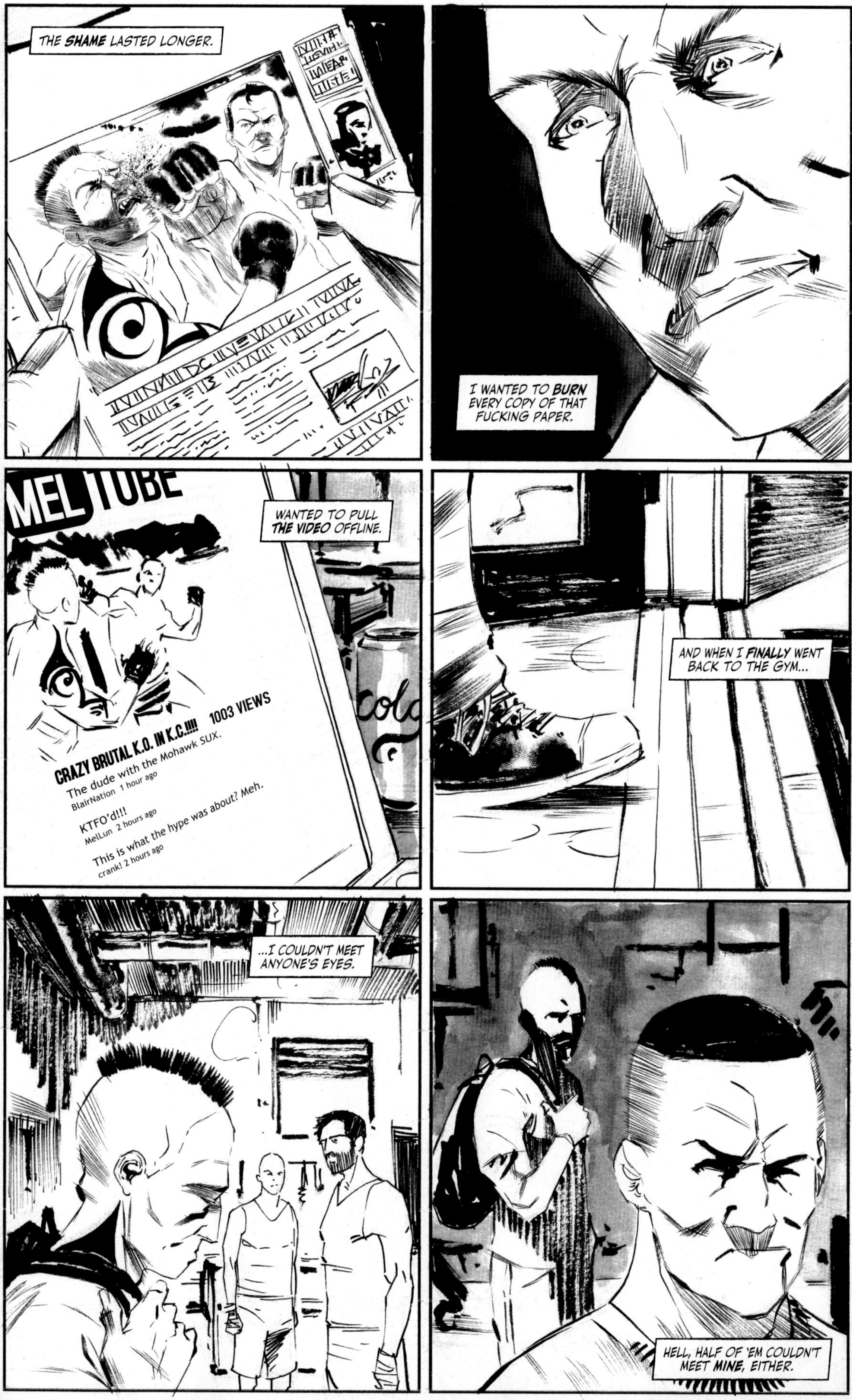
THE SHAME LASTED LONGER.
I WANTED TO BURN EVERY COPY OF THAT FUCKING PAPER.
MEL TUBE
WANTED TO PULL THE VIDEO OFFLINE.
CRAZY BRUTAL K.O. IN K.C.!!!! 1003 VIEWS
The dude with the Mohawk SUX.
BlairNation 1 hour ago
KTFO'd!!!
MelLun 2 hours ago
This is what the hype was about? Meh.
crank! 2 hours ago
AND WHEN I FINALLY WENT BACK TO THE GYM...
...I COULDN'T MEET ANYONE'S EYES.
HELL, HALF OF 'EM COULDN'T MEET MINE, EITHER.

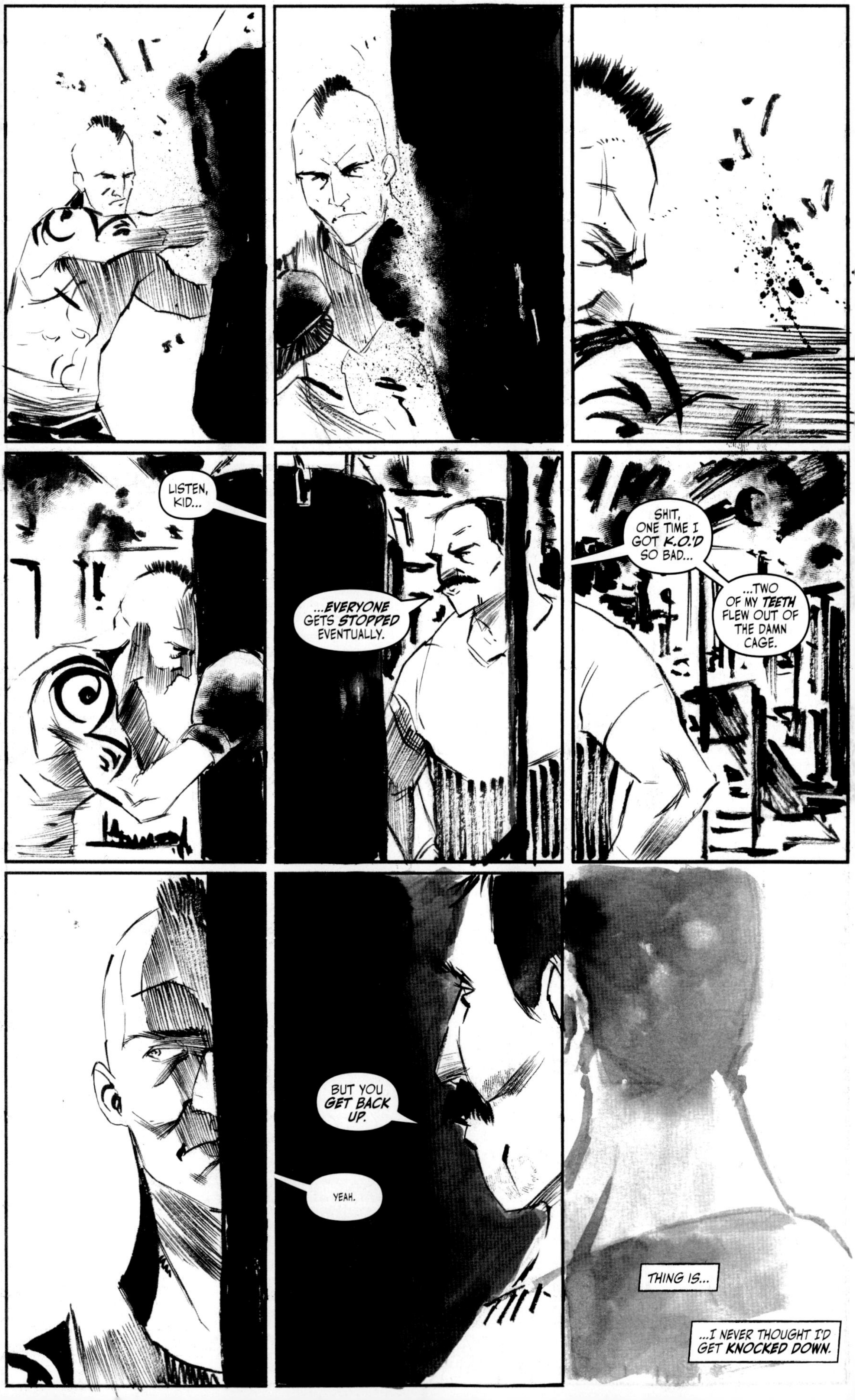
LISTEN, KID...
...EVERYONE GETS STOPPED EVENTUALLY.
SHIT, ONE TIME I GOT K.O.'D SO BAD...
...TWO OF MY TEETH FLEW OUT OF THE DAMN CAGE.
BUT YOU GET BACK UP.
YEAH.
THING IS...
...I NEVER THOUGHT I'D GET KNOCKED DOWN.

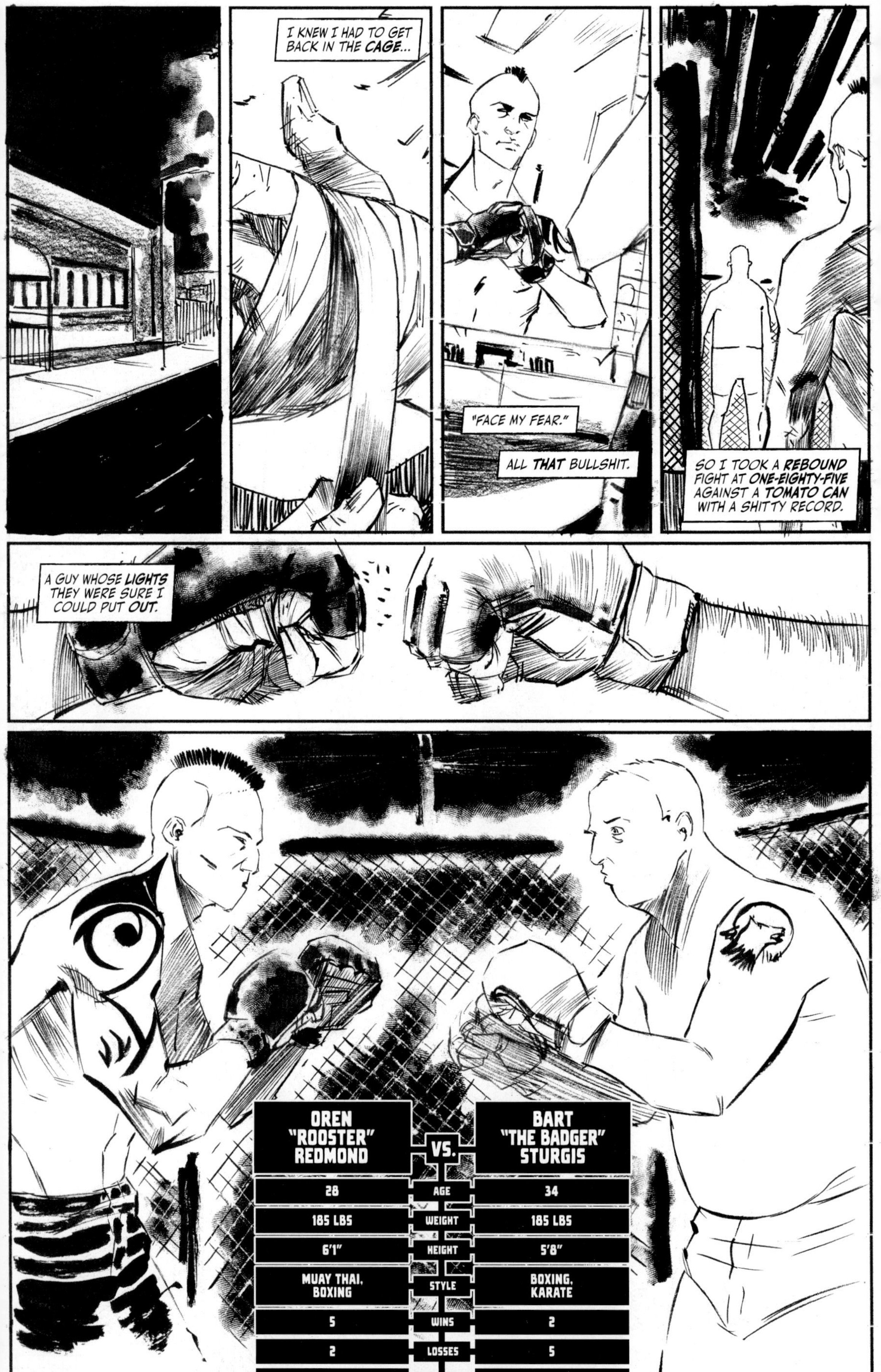
I KNEW I HAD TO GET BACK IN THE CAGE...
"FACE MY FEAR."
ALL THAT BULLSHIT.
SO I TOOK A REBOUND FIGHT AT ONE-EIGHTY-FIVE AGAINST A TOMATO CAN WITH A SHITTY RECORD.
A GUY WHOSE LIGHTS THEY WERE SURE I COULD PUT OUT.

OREN "ROOSTER" REDMOND	VS.	BART "THE BADGER" STURGIS
28	AGE	34
185 LBS	WEIGHT	185 LBS
6'1"	HEIGHT	5'8"
MUAY THAI, BOXING	STYLE	BOXING, KARATE
5	WINS	2
2	LOSSES	5
"BEAUTIFUL LASERS" LUPE FIASCO	ENTRANCE MUSIC	"I'M GONNA HANG UP MY GLOVES" CHARLIE WALKER

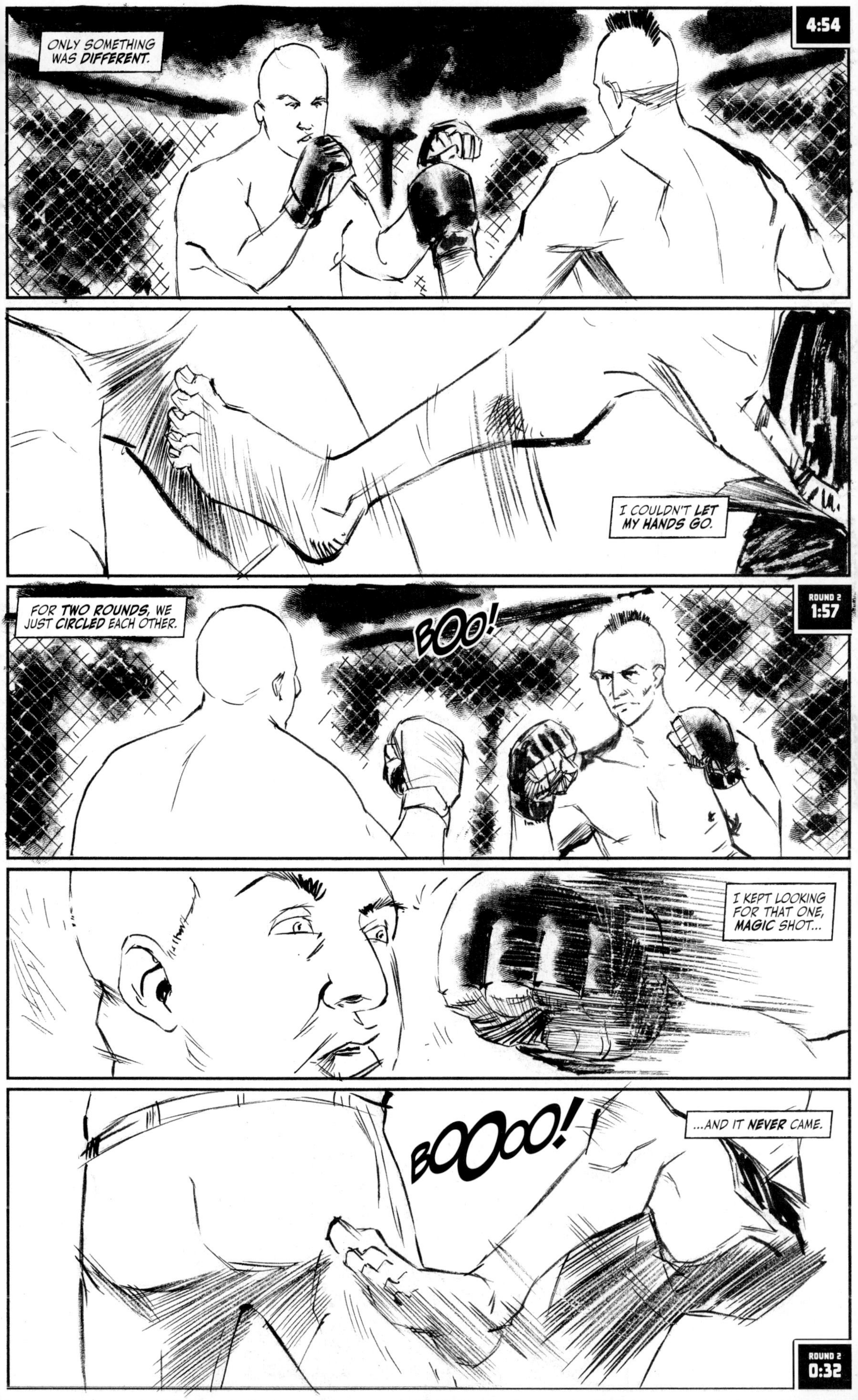

4:54
ONLY SOMETHING WAS DIFFERENT.
I COULDN'T LET MY HANDS GO.
ROUND 2 1:57
FOR TWO ROUNDS, WE JUST CIRCLED EACH OTHER.
BOO!
I KEPT LOOKING FOR THAT ONE, MAGIC SHOT...
BOOOOO!
...AND IT NEVER CAME.
ROUND 2 0:32

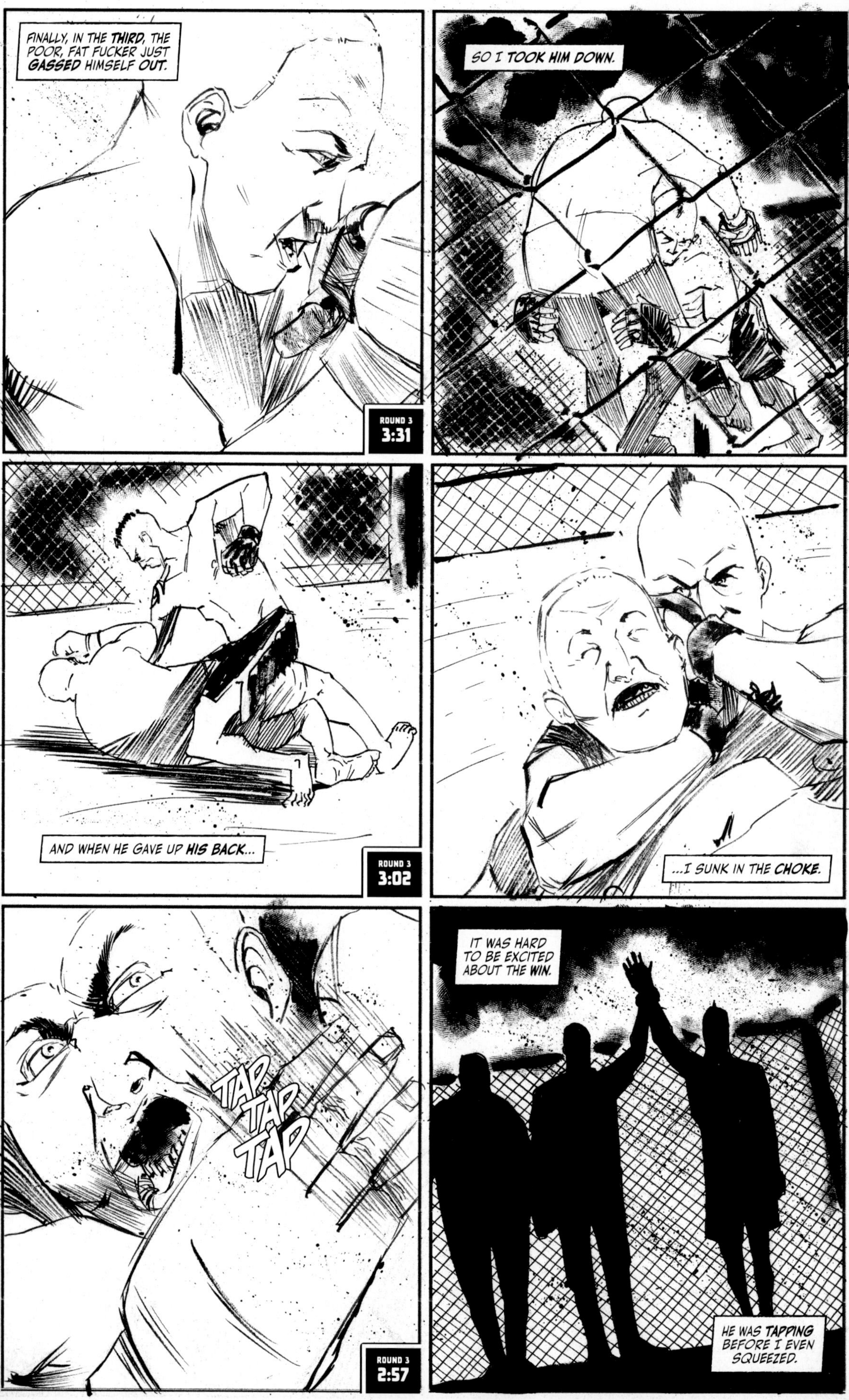
FINALLY, IN THE **THIRD**, THE POOR, FAT FUCKER JUST **GASSED** HIMSELF **OUT**.
ROUND 3
3:31
SO I **TOOK HIM DOWN**.
AND WHEN HE GAVE UP **HIS BACK**...
ROUND 3
3:02
...I SUNK IN THE **CHOKE**.
TAP
TAP
TAP
ROUND 3
2:57
IT WAS HARD TO BE EXCITED ABOUT THE **WIN**.
HE WAS **TAPPING** BEFORE I EVEN SQUEEZED.

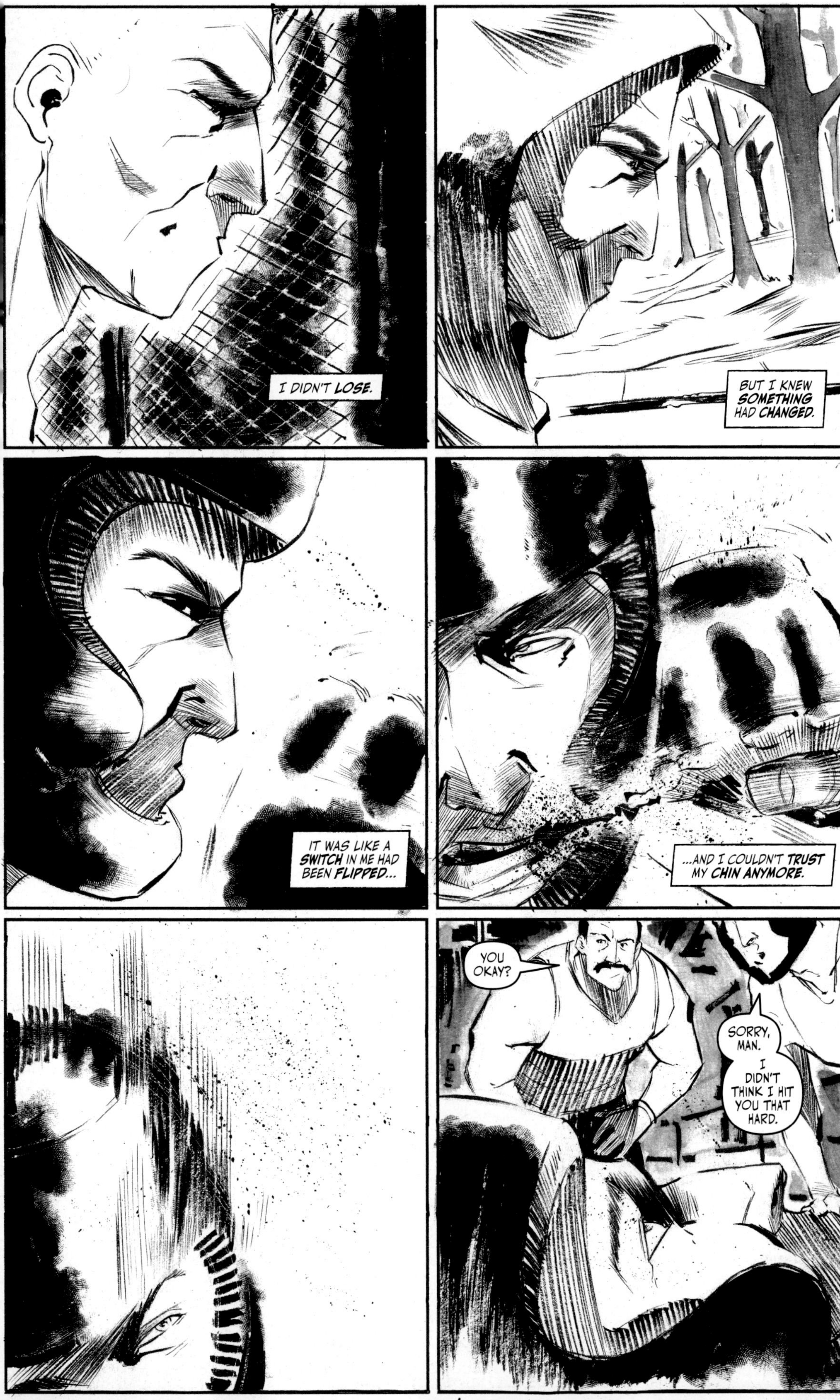
I DIDN'T LOSE.
BUT I KNEW SOMETHING HAD CHANGED.
IT WAS LIKE A SWITCH IN ME HAD BEEN FLIPPED...
...AND I COULDN'T TRUST MY CHIN ANYMORE.
YOU OKAY?
SORRY, MAN.
I DIDN'T THINK I HIT YOU THAT HARD.

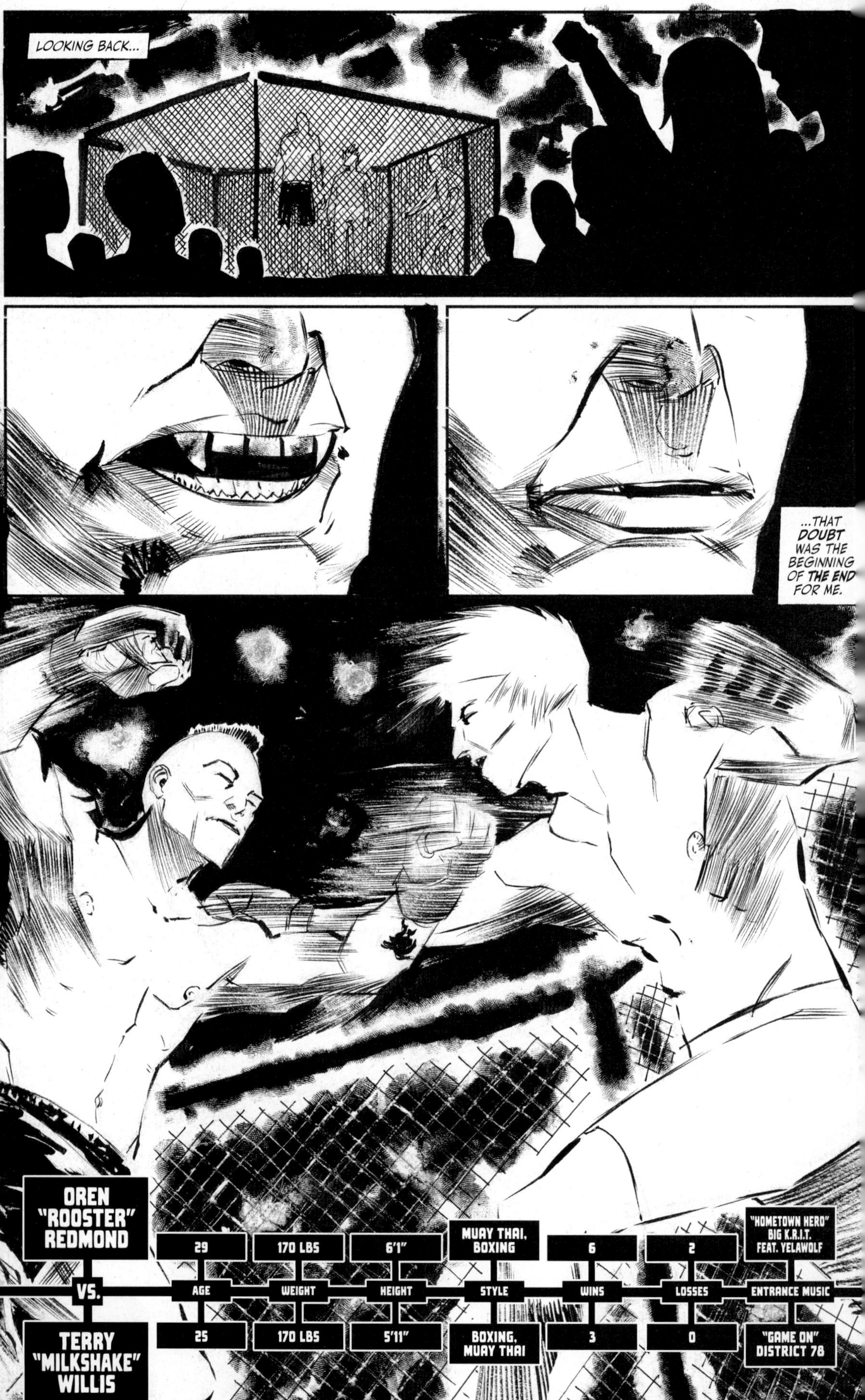
LOOKING BACK...
...THAT DOUBT WAS THE BEGINNING OF THE END FOR ME.
OREN "ROOSTER" REDMOND
VS.
TERRY "MILKSHAKE" WILLIS
AGE: 29 / 25
WEIGHT: 170 LBS / 170 LBS
HEIGHT: 6'1" / 5'11"
STYLE: MUAY THAI, BOXING / BOXING, MUAY THAI
WINS: 6 / 3
LOSSES: 2 / 0
ENTRANCE MUSIC: "HOMETOWN HERO" BIG K.R.I.T. FEAT. YELAWOLF / "GAME ON" DISTRICT 78

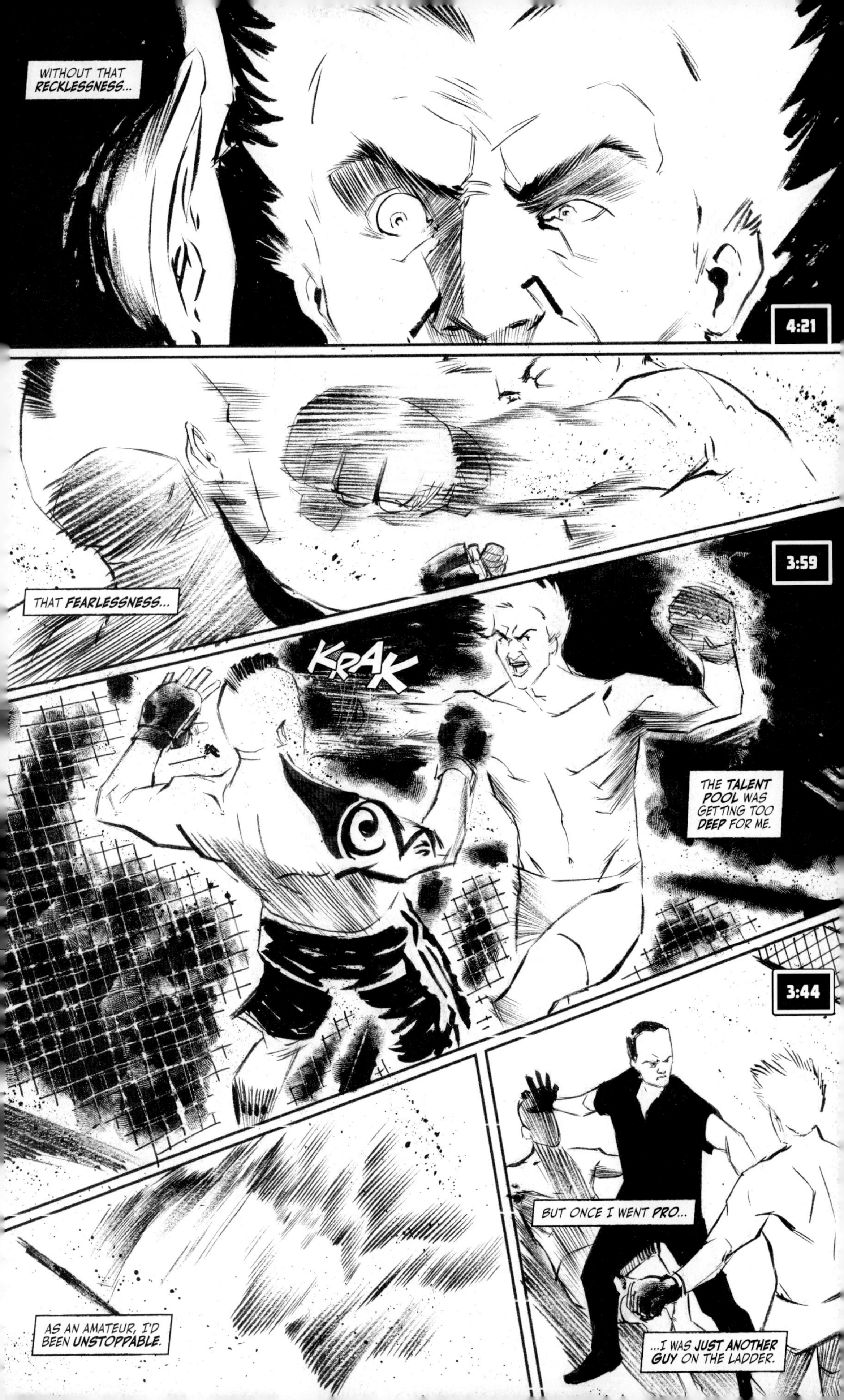

WITHOUT THAT RECKLESSNESS...
4:21
3:59
THAT FEARLESSNESS...
KRAK
THE TALENT POOL WAS GETTING TOO DEEP FOR ME.
3:44
AS AN AMATEUR, I'D BEEN UNSTOPPABLE.
BUT ONCE I WENT PRO...
...I WAS JUST ANOTHER GUY ON THE LADDER.

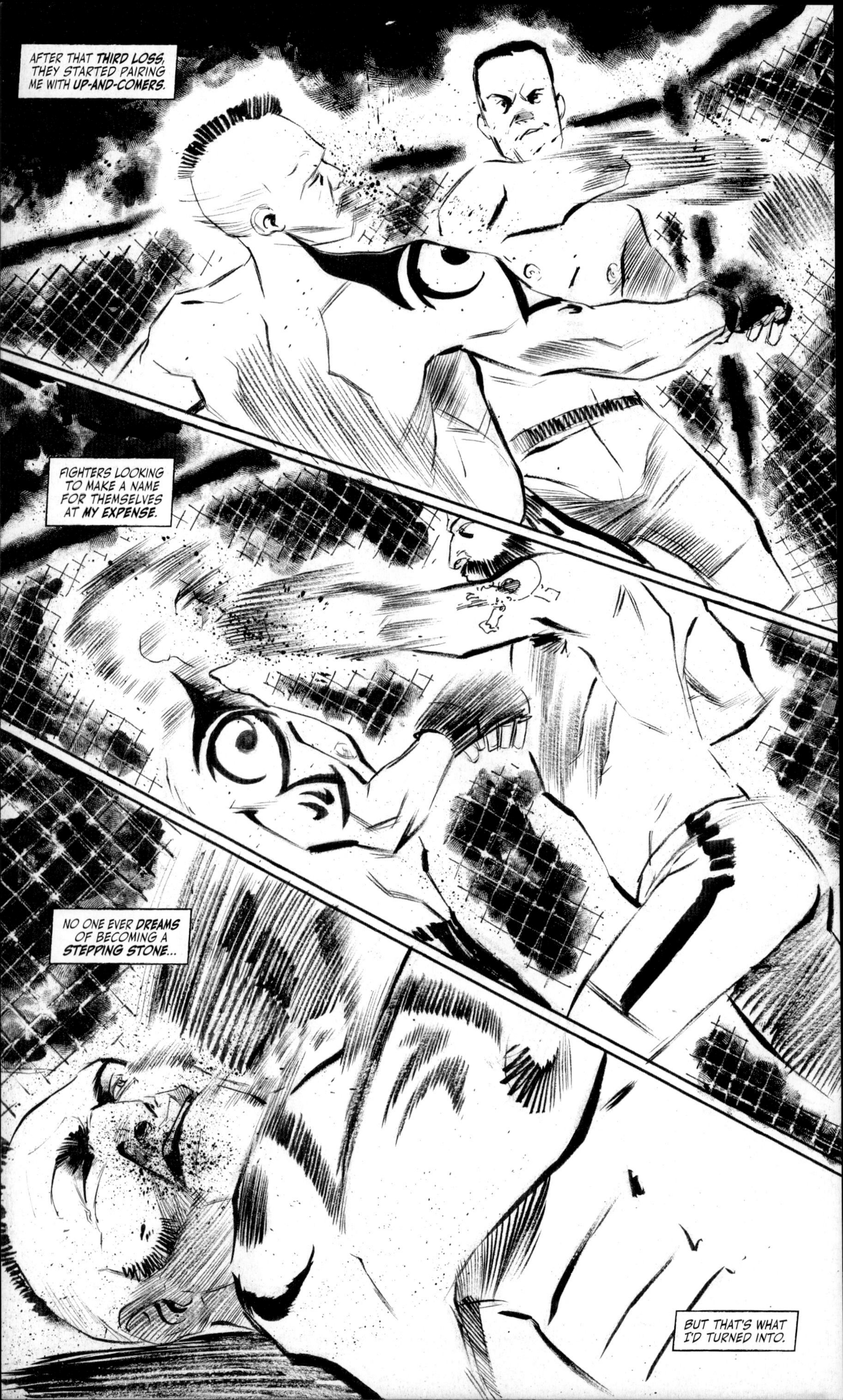
AFTER THAT **THIRD LOSS**, THEY STARTED PAIRING ME WITH **UP-AND-COMERS**.
FIGHTERS LOOKING TO MAKE A NAME FOR THEMSELVES AT **MY EXPENSE**.
NO ONE EVER **DREAMS** OF BECOMING A **STEPPING STONE**...
BUT THAT'S WHAT I'D TURNED INTO.

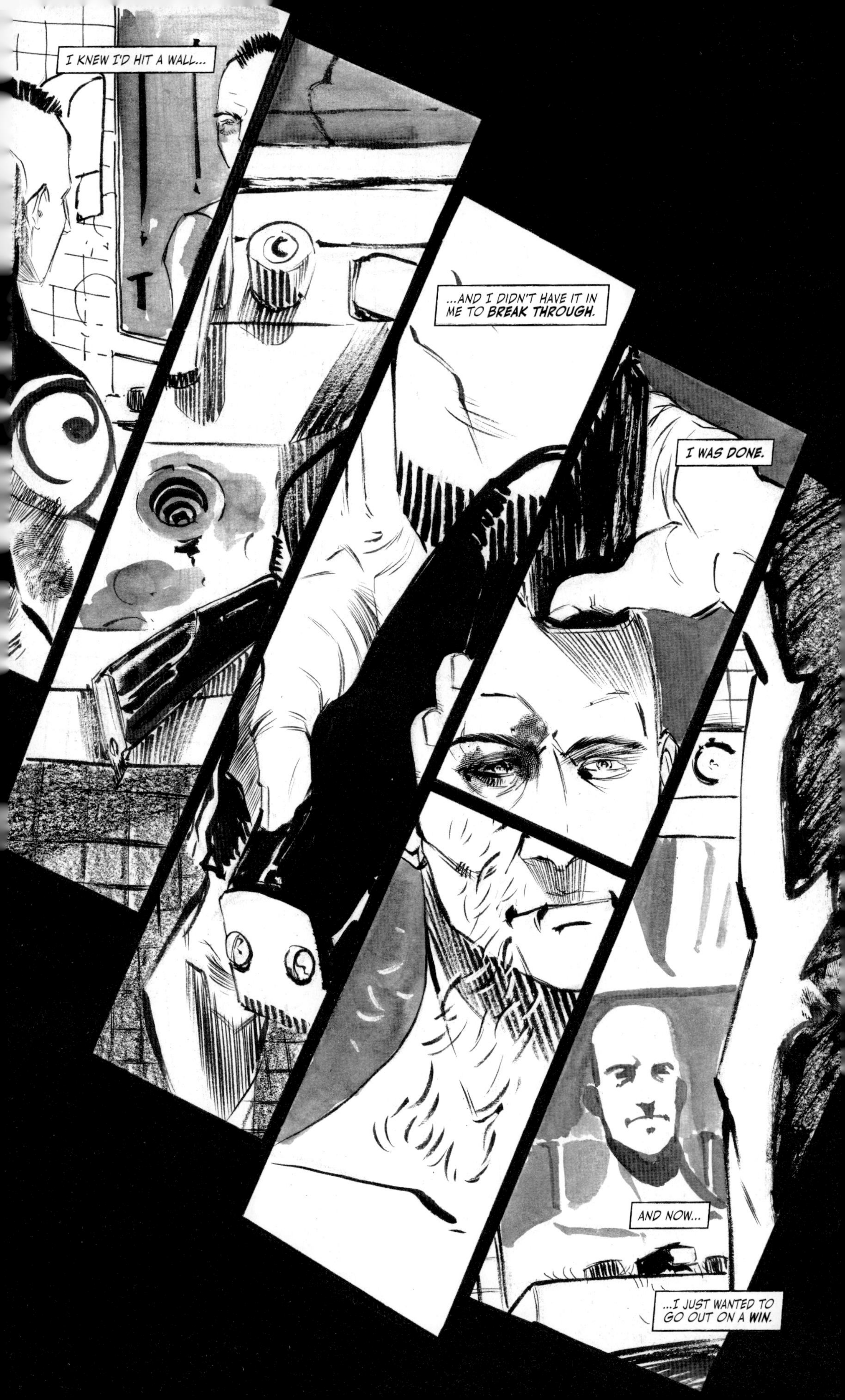
I KNEW I'D HIT A WALL...
...AND I DIDN'T HAVE IT IN ME TO BREAK THROUGH.
I WAS DONE.
AND NOW...
...I JUST WANTED TO GO OUT ON A WIN.

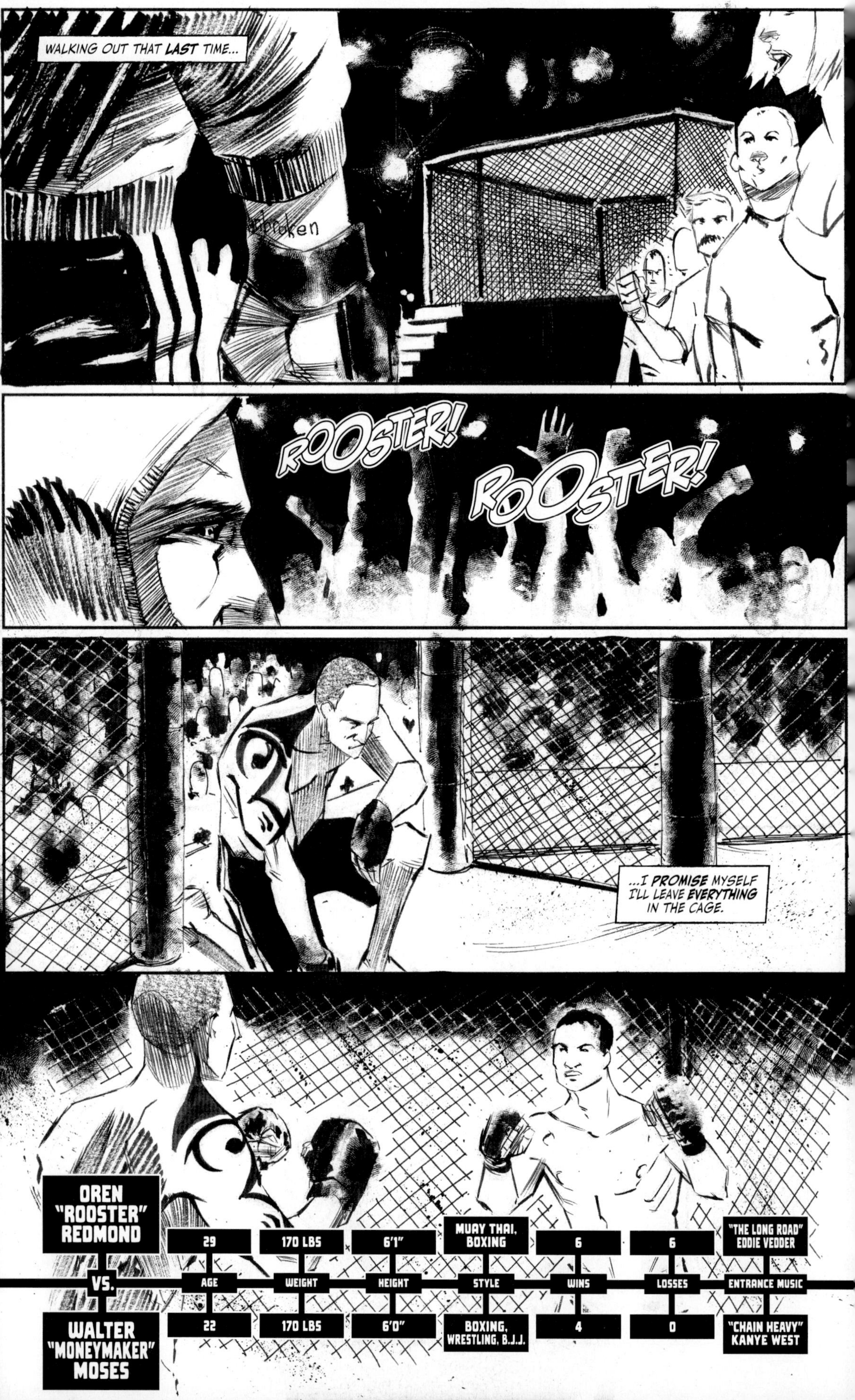

WALKING OUT THAT LAST TIME...
unbroken
ROOSTER!
ROOSTER!
...I PROMISE MYSELF I'LL LEAVE EVERYTHING IN THE CAGE.
OREN "ROOSTER" REDMOND
VS.
WALTER "MONEYMAKER" MOSES
AGE: 29 / 22
WEIGHT: 170 LBS / 170 LBS
HEIGHT: 6'1" / 6'0"
STYLE: MUAY THAI, BOXING / BOXING, WRESTLING, B.J.J.
WINS: 6 / 4
LOSSES: 6 / 0
ENTRANCE MUSIC: "THE LONG ROAD" EDDIE VEDDER / "CHAIN HEAVY" KANYE WEST

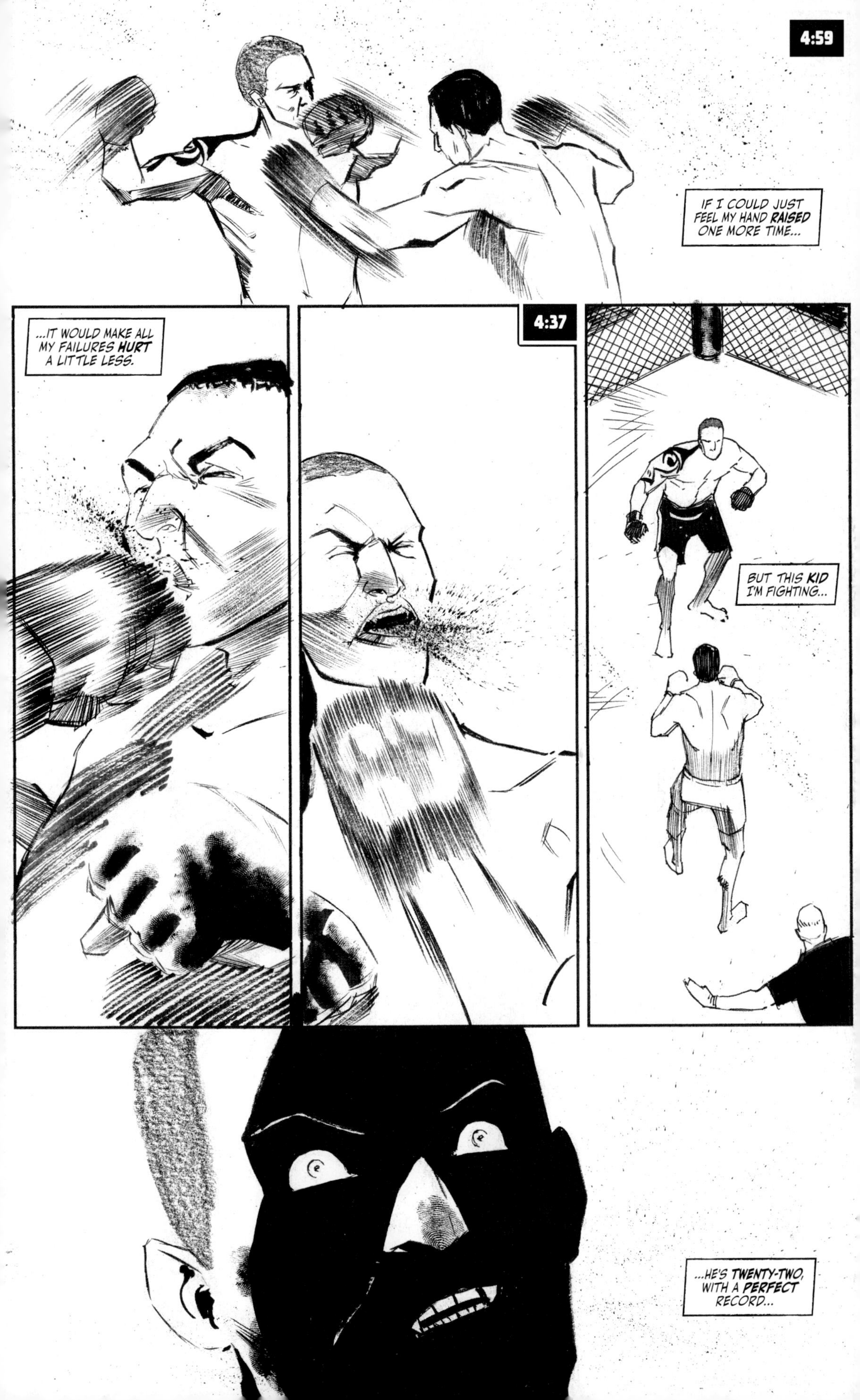
4:59
IF I COULD JUST FEEL MY HAND RAISED ONE MORE TIME...
...IT WOULD MAKE ALL MY FAILURES HURT A LITTLE LESS.
4:37
BUT THIS KID I'M FIGHTING...
...HE'S TWENTY-TWO, WITH A PERFECT RECORD...

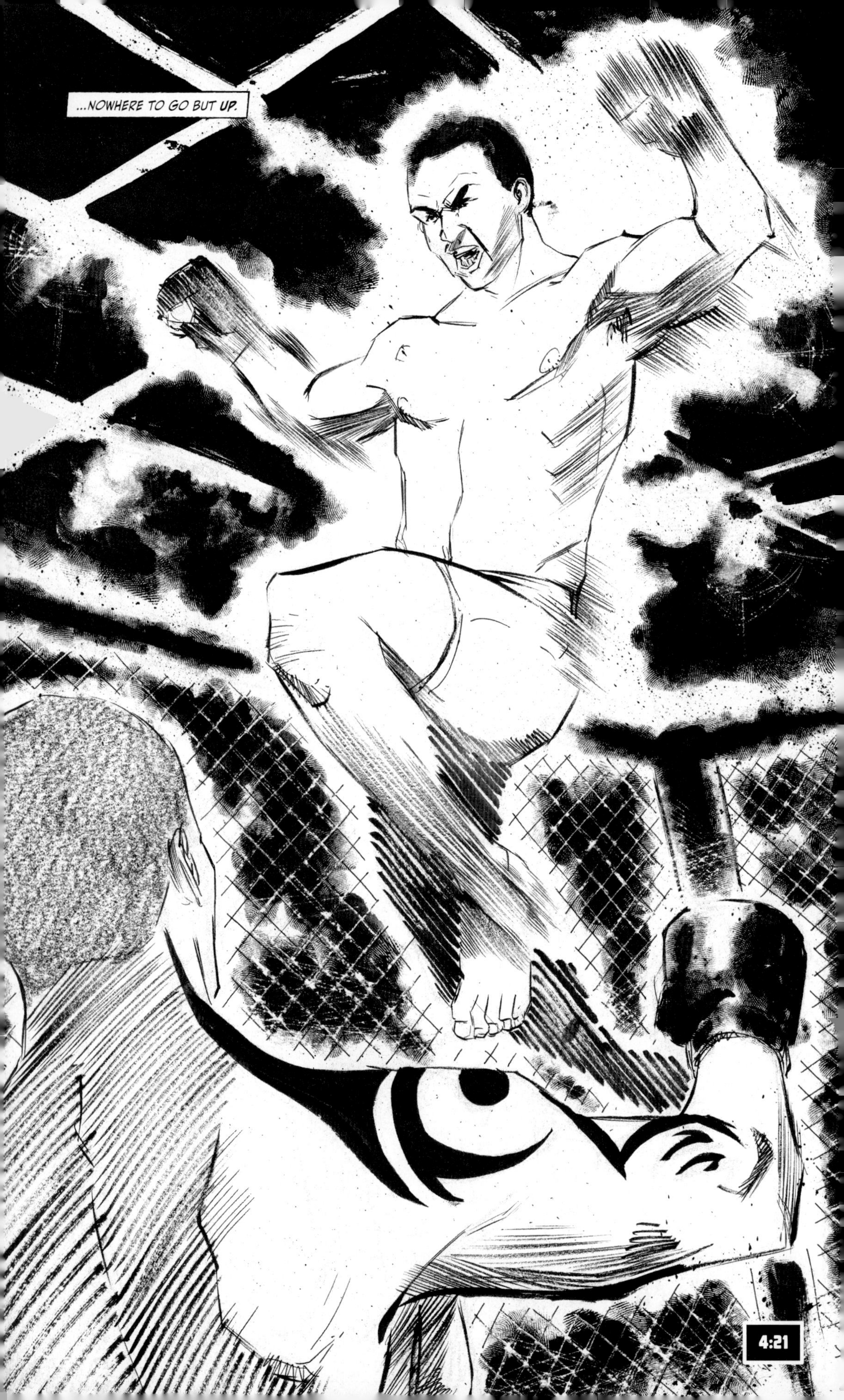
...NOWHERE TO GO BUT UP.
4:21

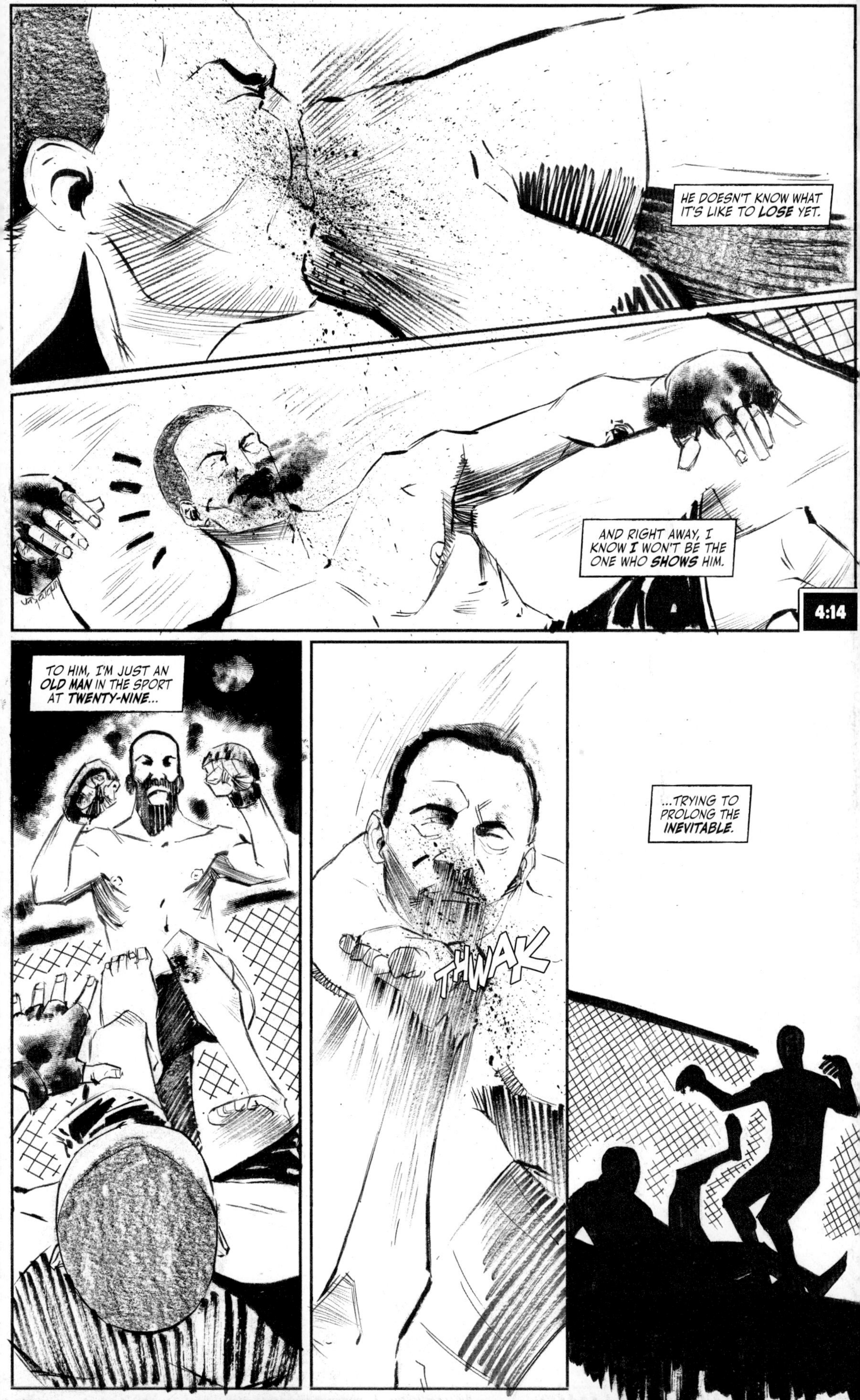

HE DOESN'T KNOW WHAT IT'S LIKE TO LOSE YET.
AND RIGHT AWAY, I KNOW I WON'T BE THE ONE WHO SHOWS HIM.
4:14
TO HIM, I'M JUST AN OLD MAN IN THE SPORT AT TWENTY-NINE...
THWAK
...TRYING TO PROLONG THE INEVITABLE.

THING IS...

...WE CAN'T ALL BE CHAMPIONS.

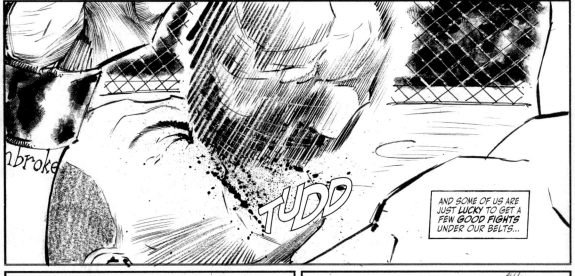

TUDD

AND SOME OF US ARE JUST LUCKY TO GET A FEW GOOD FIGHTS UNDER OUR BELTS...

...BEFORE THE GAME PASSES US BY.

KKRAK

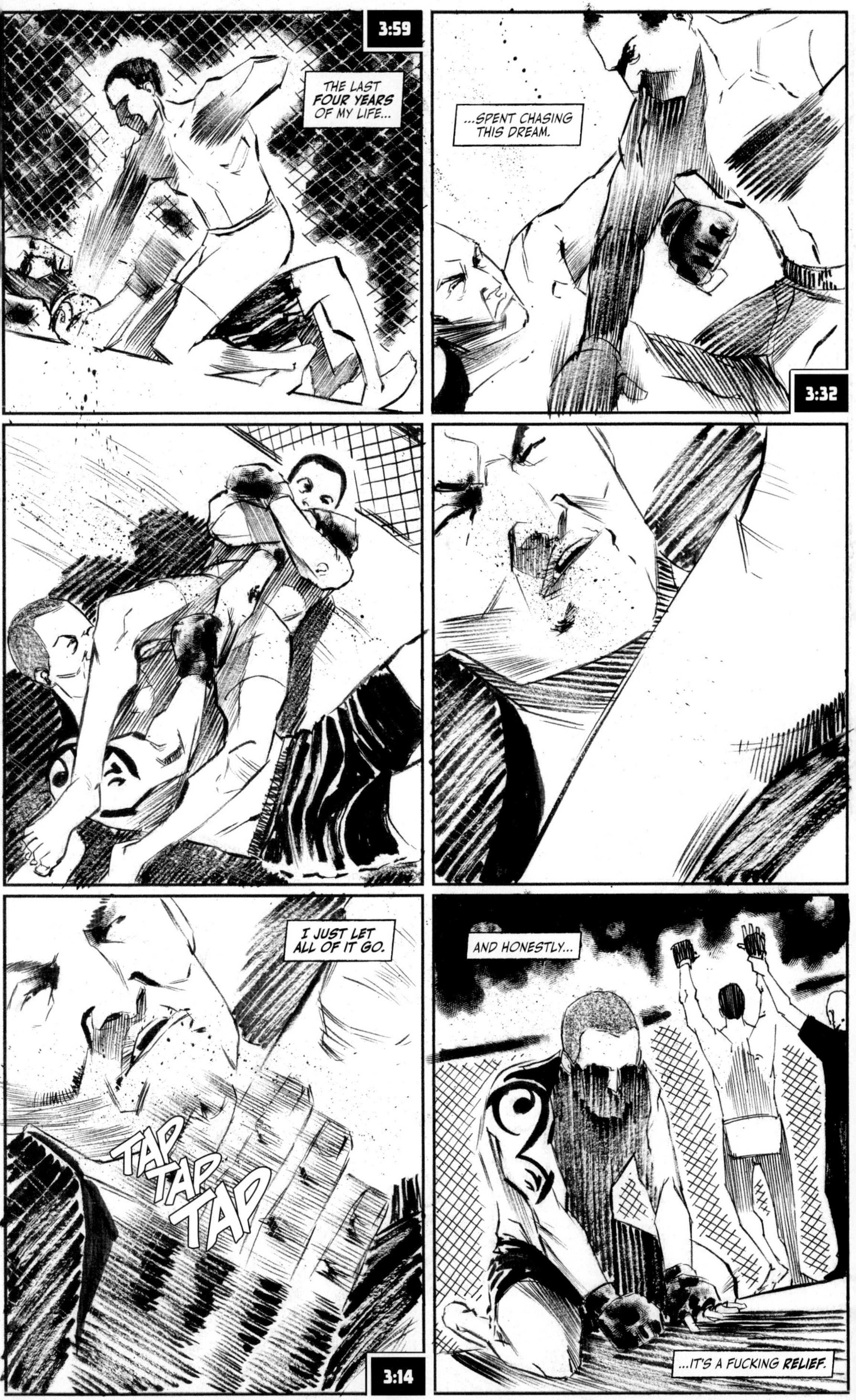
3:59
THE LAST FOUR YEARS OF MY LIFE...
...SPENT CHASING THIS DREAM.
3:32
I JUST LET ALL OF IT GO.
TAP TAP TAP
3:14
AND HONESTLY...
...IT'S A FUCKING RELIEF.

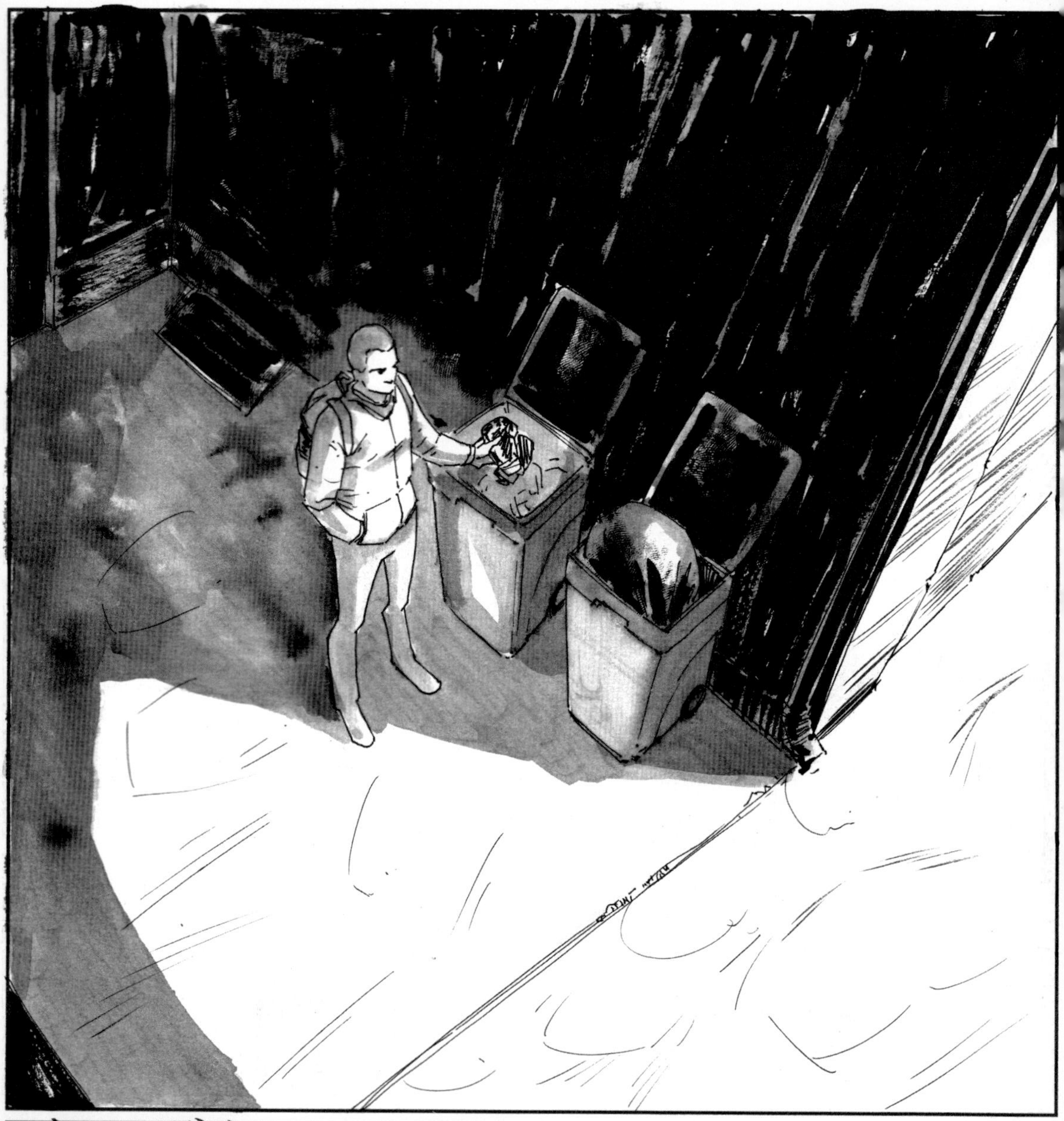

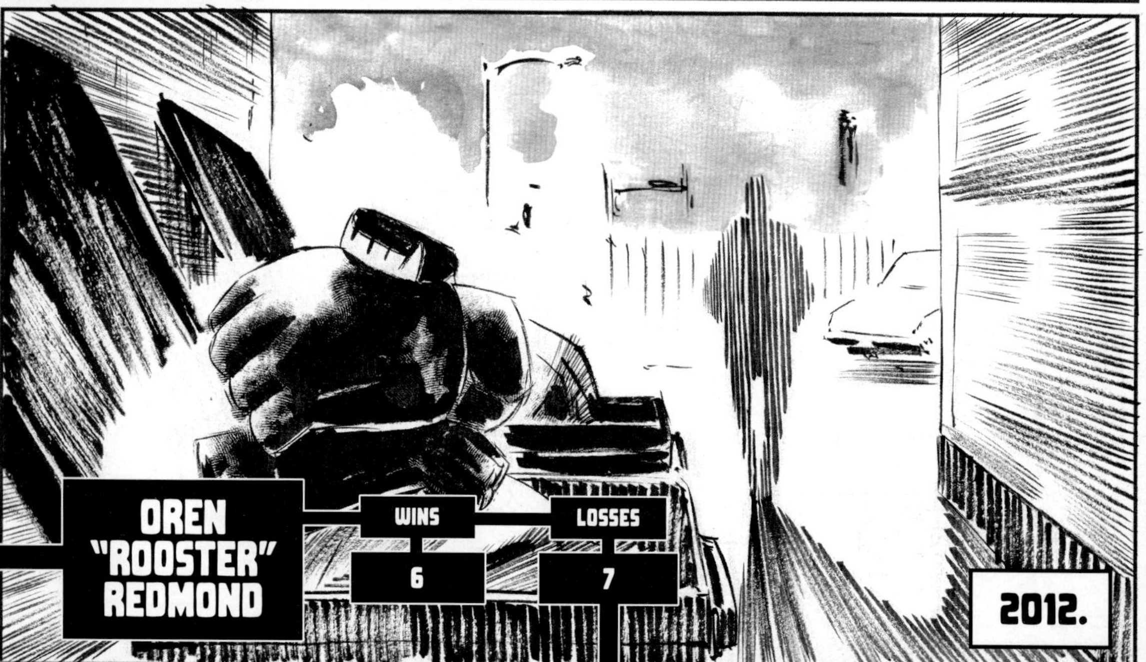

OREN "ROOSTER" REDMOND
WINS
6
LOSSES
7
2012.

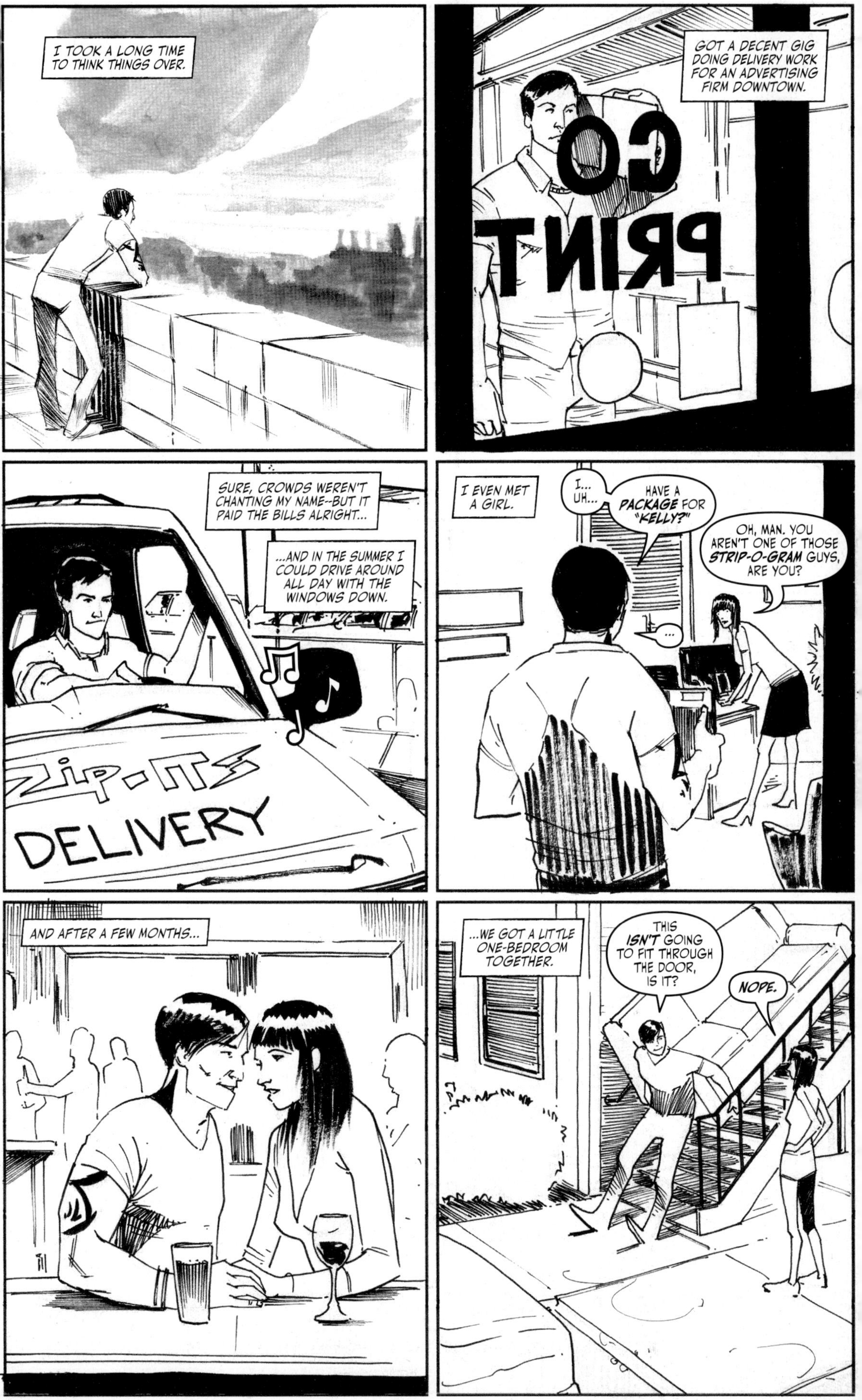
I TOOK A LONG TIME TO THINK THINGS OVER.
GOT A DECENT GIG DOING DELIVERY WORK FOR AN ADVERTISING FIRM DOWNTOWN.
GO PRINT
SURE, CROWDS WEREN'T CHANTING MY NAME--BUT IT PAID THE BILLS ALRIGHT...
...AND IN THE SUMMER I COULD DRIVE AROUND ALL DAY WITH THE WINDOWS DOWN.
Zip-It
DELIVERY
I EVEN MET A GIRL.
I... UH...
HAVE A PACKAGE FOR "KELLY?"
OH, MAN. YOU AREN'T ONE OF THOSE STRIP-O-GRAM GUYS, ARE YOU?
...
AND AFTER A FEW MONTHS...
...WE GOT A LITTLE ONE-BEDROOM TOGETHER.
THIS ISN'T GOING TO FIT THROUGH THE DOOR, IS IT?
NOPE.

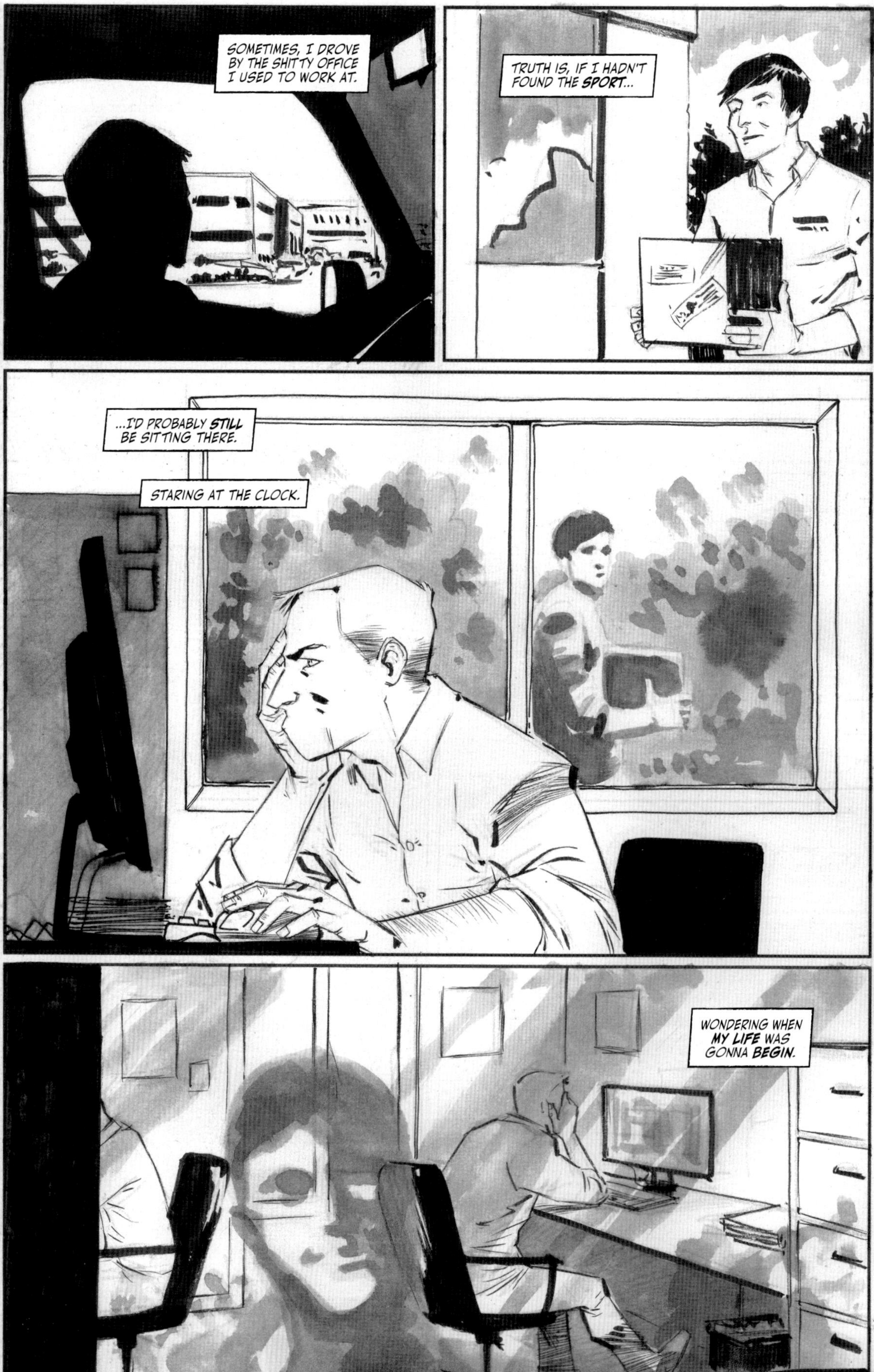
SOMETIMES, I DROVE BY THE SHITTY OFFICE I USED TO WORK AT.
TRUTH IS, IF I HADN'T FOUND THE SPORT...
...I'D PROBABLY STILL BE SITTING THERE.
STARING AT THE CLOCK.
WONDERING WHEN MY LIFE WAS GONNA BEGIN.

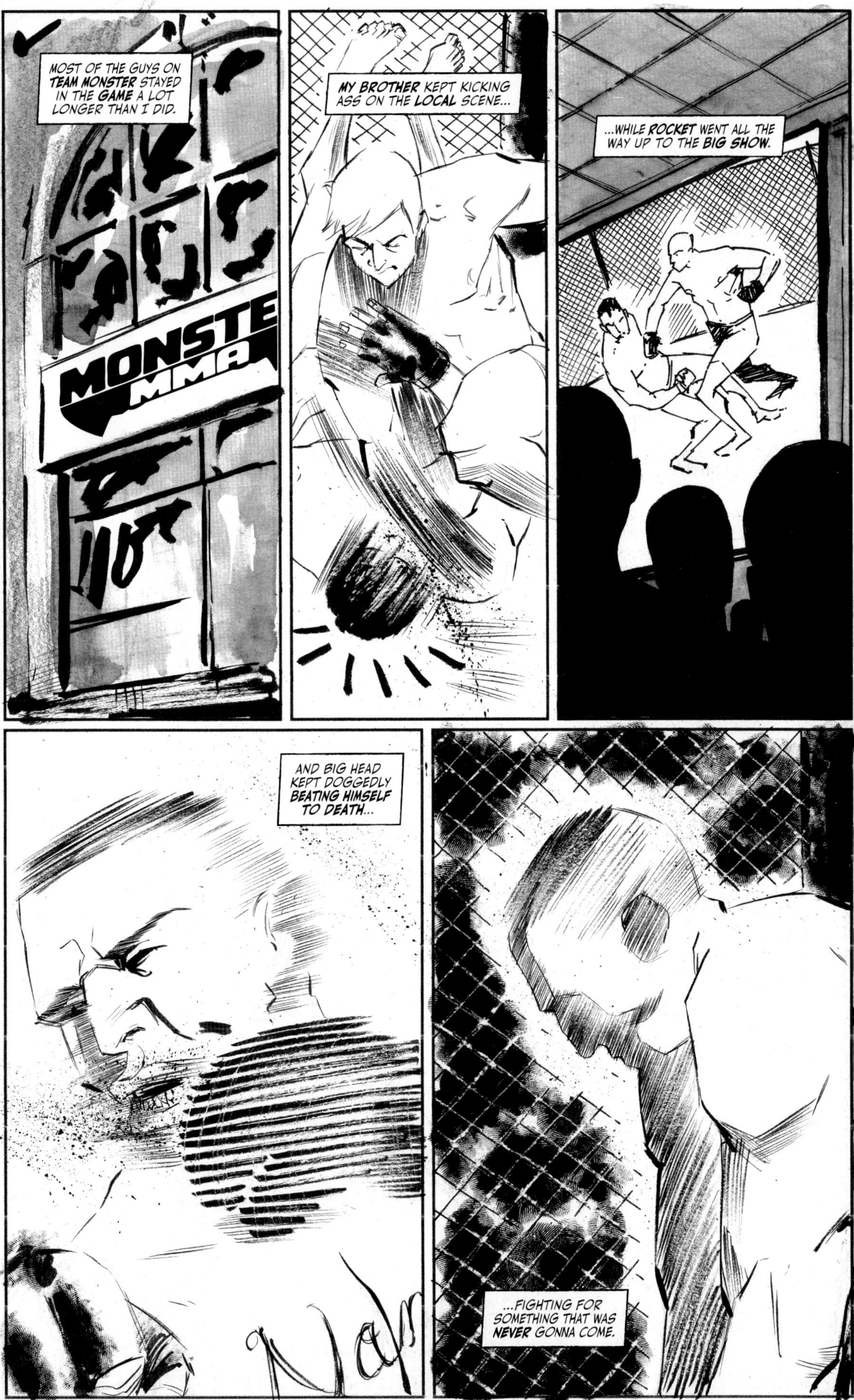
MOST OF THE GUYS ON TEAM MONSTER STAYED IN THE GAME A LOT LONGER THAN I DID.
MONSTE
MMA
MY BROTHER KEPT KICKING ASS ON THE LOCAL SCENE...
...WHILE ROCKET WENT ALL THE WAY UP TO THE BIG SHOW.
AND BIG HEAD KEPT DOGGEDLY BEATING HIMSELF TO DEATH...
...FIGHTING FOR SOMETHING THAT WAS NEVER GONNA COME.

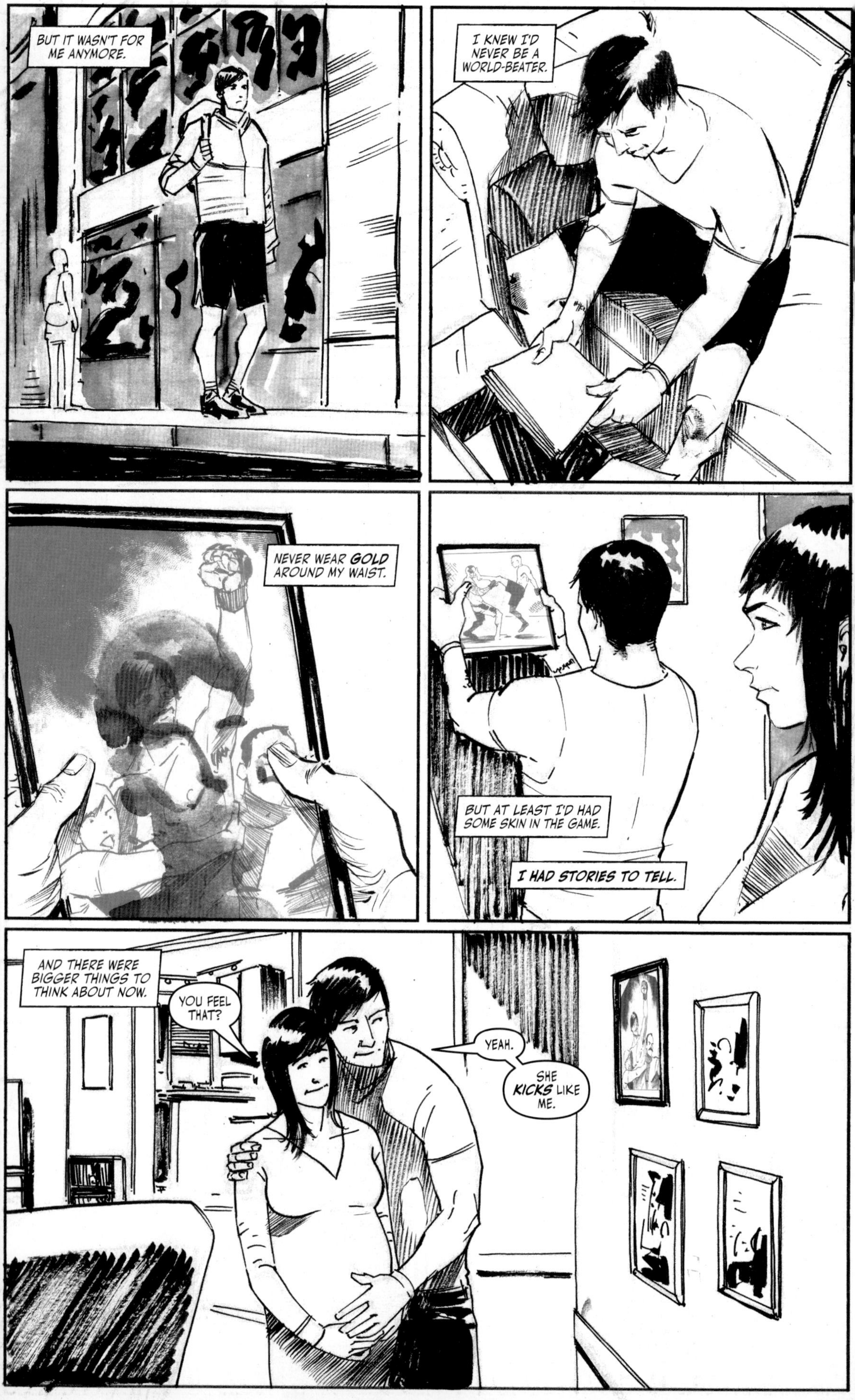
BUT IT WASN'T FOR ME ANYMORE.
I KNEW I'D NEVER BE A WORLD-BEATER.
NEVER WEAR **GOLD** AROUND MY WAIST.
BUT AT LEAST I'D HAD SOME SKIN IN THE GAME.
I HAD STORIES TO TELL.
AND THERE WERE BIGGER THINGS TO THINK ABOUT NOW.
YOU FEEL THAT?
YEAH.
SHE **KICKS** LIKE ME.

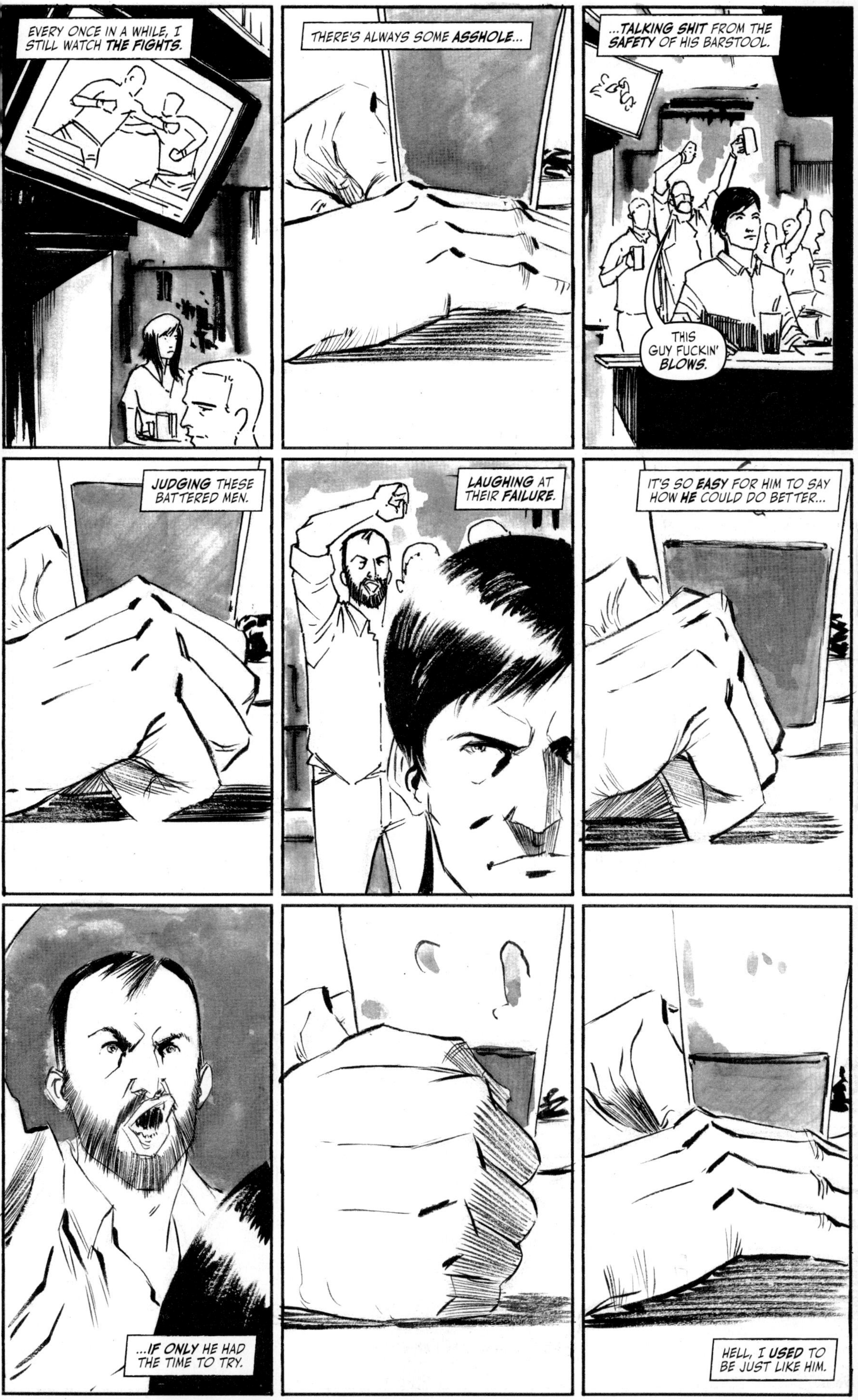

EVERY ONCE IN A WHILE, I STILL WATCH THE FIGHTS.
THERE'S ALWAYS SOME ASSHOLE...
...TALKING SHIT FROM THE SAFETY OF HIS BARSTOOL.
THIS GUY FUCKIN' BLOWS.
JUDGING THESE BATTERED MEN.
LAUGHING AT THEIR FAILURE.
IT'S SO EASY FOR HIM TO SAY HOW HE COULD DO BETTER...
...IF ONLY HE HAD THE TIME TO TRY.
HELL, I USED TO BE JUST LIKE HIM.

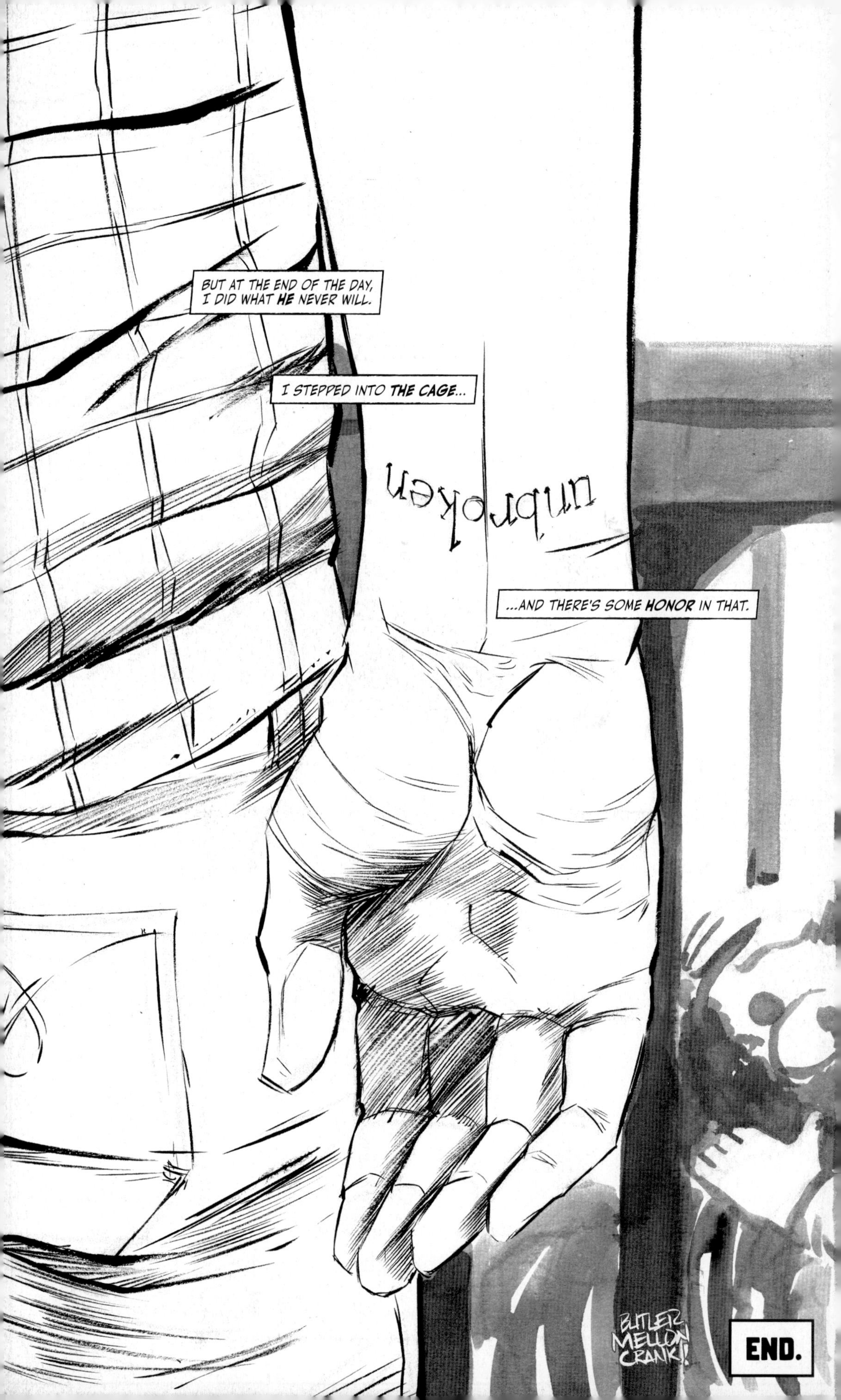
BUT AT THE END OF THE DAY, I DID WHAT HE NEVER WILL.
I STEPPED INTO THE CAGE...
unbroken
...AND THERE'S SOME HONOR IN THAT.
BUTLER MELLON CRANK!
END.

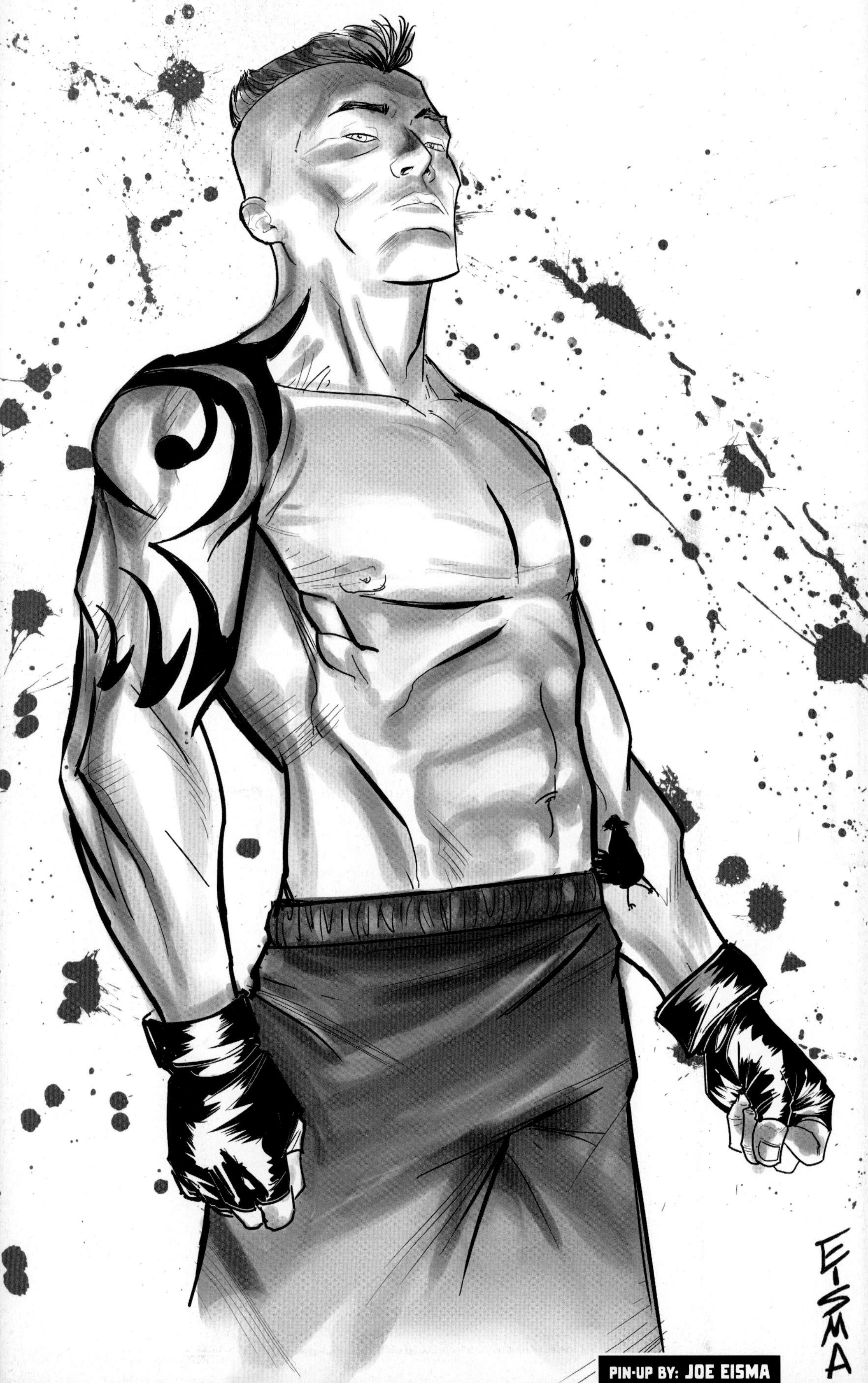
EISMA

PIN-UP BY: JOE EISMA

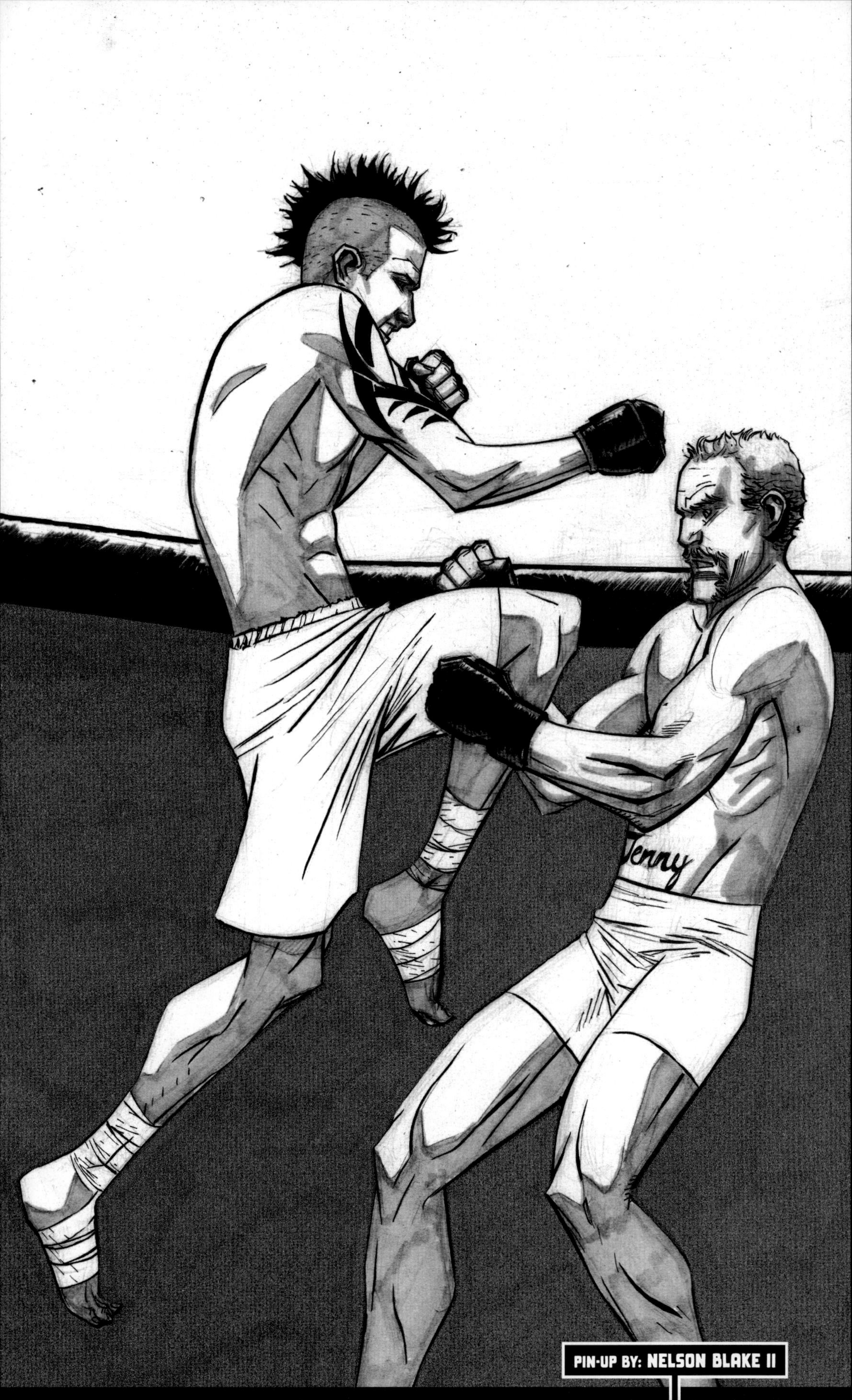
Jenny

PIN-UP BY: NELSON BLAKE II

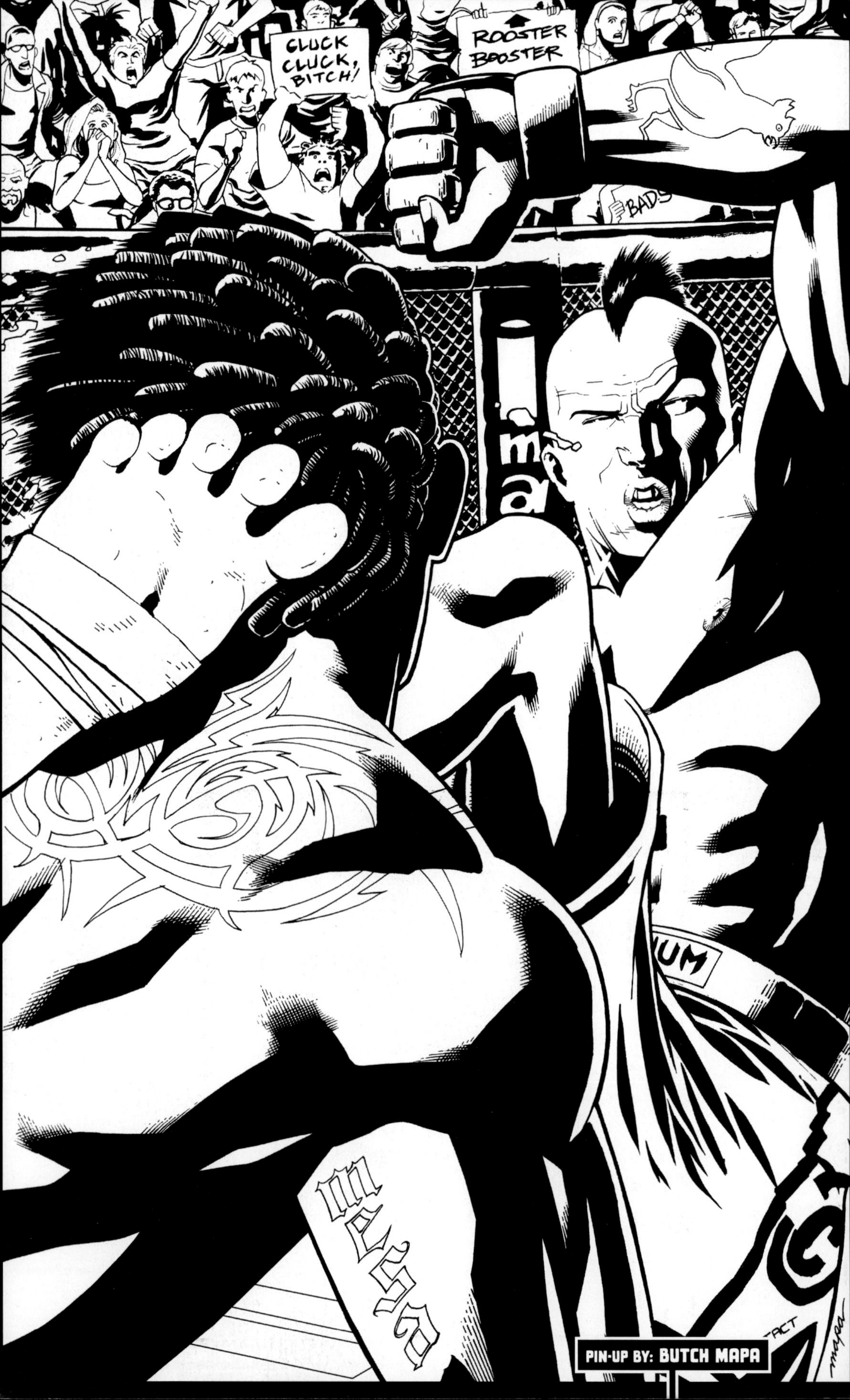
CLUCK CLUCK, BITCH!
ROOSTER BOOSTER

PIN-UP BY: BUTCH MAPA

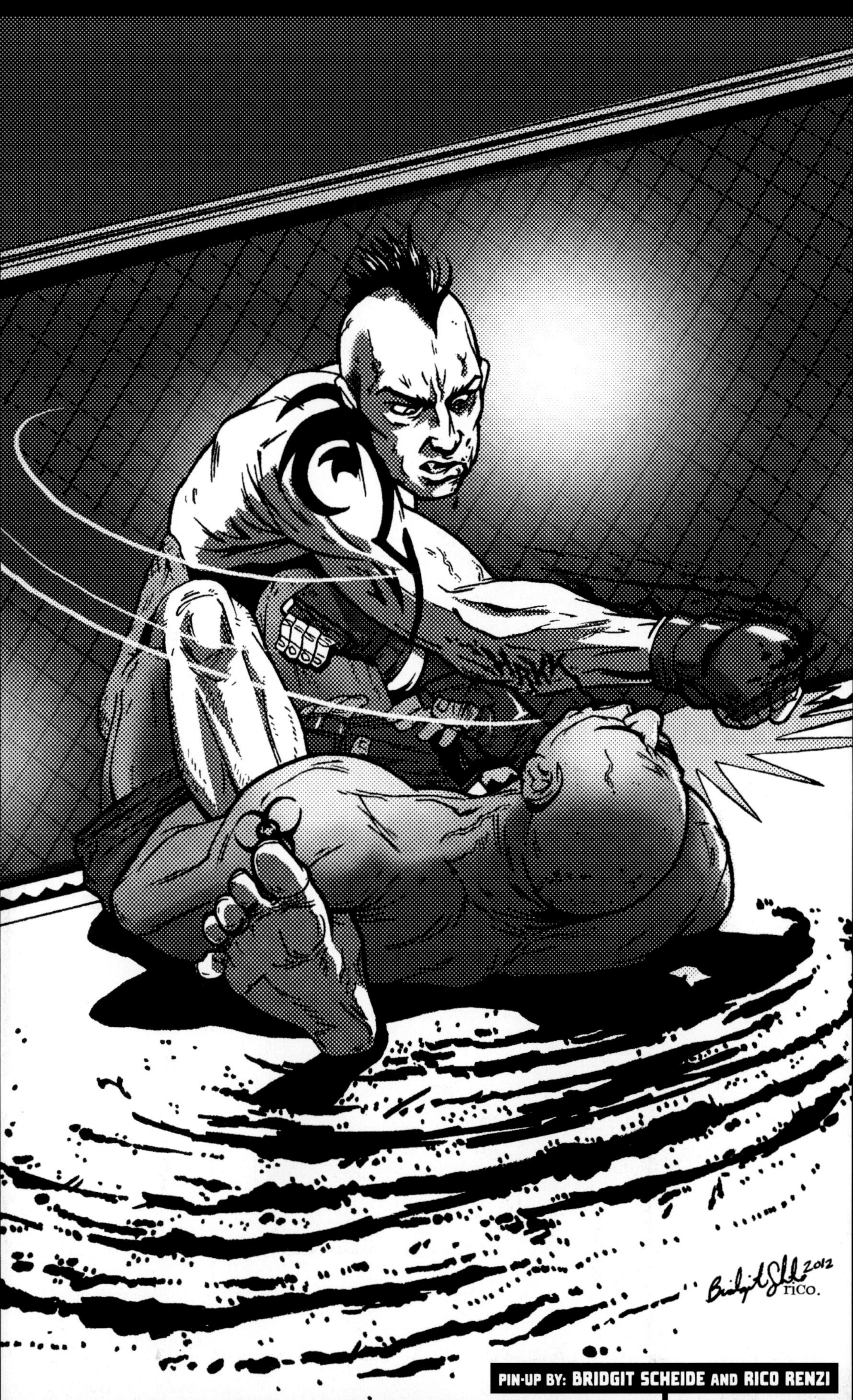

Bridgit Scheide 2012
rico.

PIN-UP BY: BRIDGIT SCHEIDE AND RICO RENZI

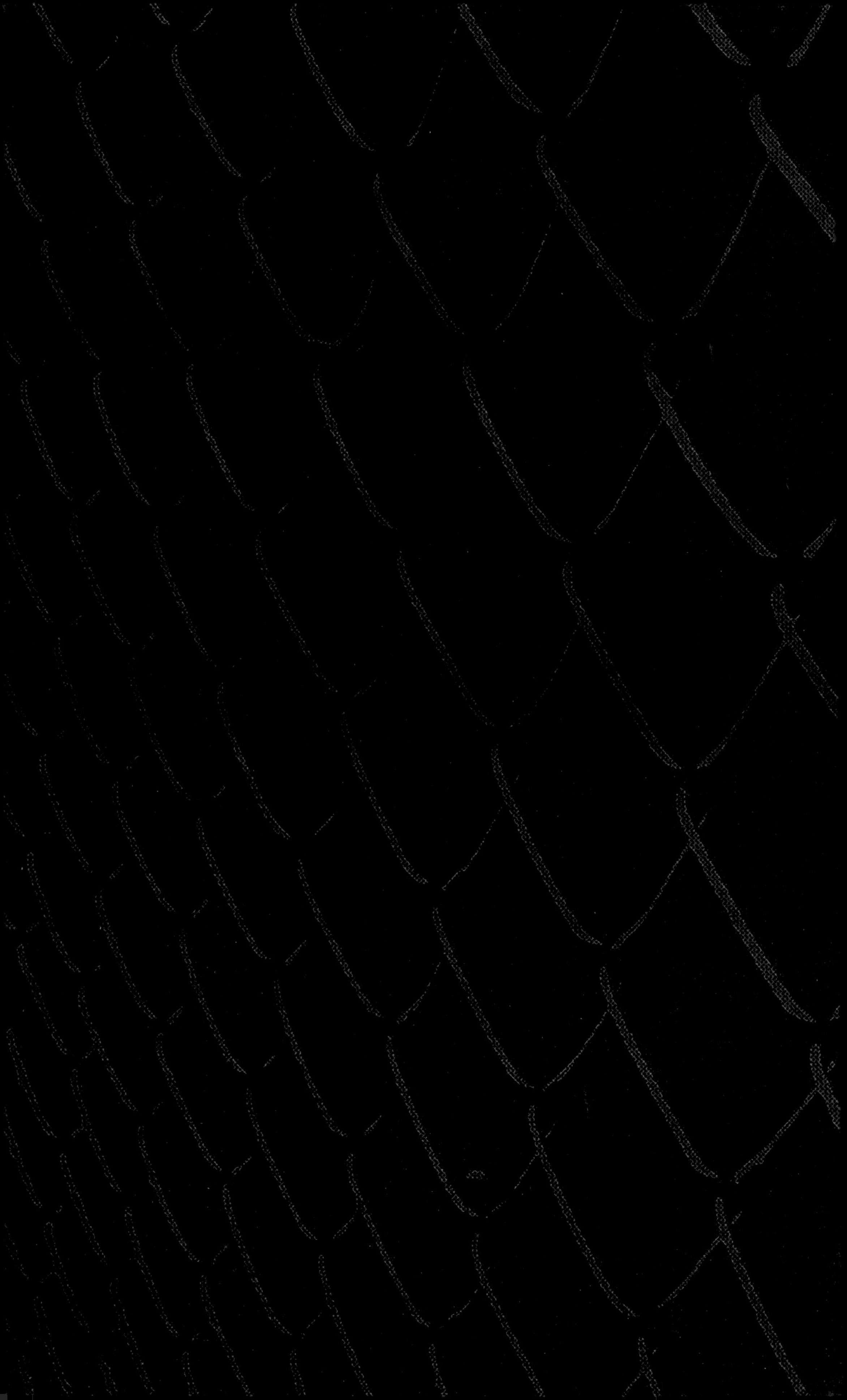

BLAIR BUTLER IS A WRITER OF COMICS, TV, AND FILM LIVING IN LOS ANGELES. SHE IS ALSO A CORRESPONDENT FOR THE TELEVISION PROGRAM "ATTACK OF THE SHOW."

SHE WOULD LIKE TO THANK TO GERRY DUGGAN, DEREK JOHNSON, JONATHAN HICKMAN, ERIC STEPHENSON, AND ALL THE FINE FOLKS AT IMAGE COMICS FOR THEIR HELP AND ADVICE. AND MOST OF ALL, THANKS TO MOM, DAD, AND ALISON FOR THEIR UNDYING SUPPORT ·· AND TO KEVIN AND CRANK FOR PUTTING UP WITH ME.

TWITTER: @THEBLAIRBUTLER

KEVIN MELLON 2002 GRADUATE OF THE KUBERT SCHOOL. CO-CREATOR / ARTIST ON "GEARHEAD" AND "LOVESTRUCK" WITH DENNIS HOPELESS.

THANKS TO BLAIR FOR LETTING ME INTO HER WORLD OF BLOOD, PUNCHING, AND VALE TUDO SHORTS. THANKS TO CRANK! FOR MAKING ME LOOK BETTER THAN I DESERVE.

TWITTER: @KMELLON · WEB: KEVINMELLON.COM

CRANK! (A.K.A. CHRIS CRANK) IS A LETTERER WHOSE RECENT WORK INCLUDES BOOKS SUCH AS "HACK/SLASH," "BATTLEPUG," "BLOODSTRIKE" AND "ITGIRL! AND THE ATOMICS."

HE'S GLAD TO HAVE WORKED WITH BLAIR AND KEVIN ON THIS BOOK AND THANKFUL TO EVERYONE WHO PICKED IT UP. YOU ROCK.

TWITTER: @CCRANK · WEB: CRANKCAST.NET